UNDERDOGS

UNDERDOGS

The Truth About Britain's White Working Class

Joel Budd

PICADOR

First published 2025 by Picador
an imprint of Pan Macmillan
The Smithson, 6 Briset Street, London EC1M 5NR
EU representative: Macmillan Publishers Ireland Limited, 1st Floor,
The Liffey Trust Centre, 117–126 Sheriff Street Upper,
Dublin 1, D01 YC43
Associated companies throughout the world
www.panmacmillan.com

ISBN 978-1-0350-1512-2

1 3 5 7 9 8 6 4 2

A CIP catalogue record for this book is available from the British Library.

Typeset in Minion Pro by Palimpsest Book Production Limited, Falkirk Stirlingshire

Printed and bound by CPI Group (UK) Ltd, Croydon, CR0 4YY

Visit **www.picador.com** to read more about all our books
and to buy them. You will also find features, author interviews and
news of any author events, and you can sign up for e-newsletters
so that you're always first to hear about our new releases.

Contents

White, British and Working Class

Percentage of adults who are white Britons and belong to National Statistics Socio-Economic Classification analytic classes five to eight, according to the 2021 census of England and Wales

0   20   30   40   50   72

No data

Preface

A few weeks before the general election in July 2024, I drove to Hartlepool to take its political temperature. Hartlepool was once an important North Sea fishing port, then it became a steel-making and shipbuilding town, and it has never quite recovered from the decline of all those industries. The streets around the town centre are among the most deprived in England. Its residents tend to feel overlooked and ignored. Teesside is isolated from the rest of England – it is neither on a high-speed railway line nor a motorway – and Hartlepool is on the edge of Teesside. But Hartlepool isn't just any struggling, post-industrial northern town. It is the town that seemed to prove an entire group of people had switched allegiance.

In 2021, the people of Hartlepool did something extraordinary. In a by-election triggered by the resignation of the town's Labour MP, they voted for a Conservative, Jill Mortimer. That snapped a long record: Hartlepool had been a Labour seat ever since the constituency was created in 1974. And the fact that Britain had a Conservative government in 2021 made the victory even more amazing. Voters usually punish incumbent governments in by-elections; it is almost unheard of for a ruling party to snatch a seat from the opposition. The Conservative triumph in Hartlepool was incredibly painful for Labour – worse, in some ways, than the disaster that had occurred in the general election two years earlier, when the party lost many of its seats in northern England, including much of the so-called 'red wall'. The losses of 2019 could be put down to voters' impatience to leave the European Union and the unpopularity of the party's then leader, Jeremy Corbyn. By 2021, Britain was out of the EU and Corbyn was gone.

Labour's new leader, Sir Keir Starmer, was so stunned by the result in Hartlepool that he considered resigning. In the end, he gave a short, uncomfortable speech, admitting that the party had lost the trust of working people, and stayed at his post. Others were blunter. It escaped few people's notice that, as well as being poor, Hartlepool is overwhelmingly white and British, although it has become a little less so in the past few years, because the government has taken advantage of its cheap houses and moved hundreds of asylum-seekers in. Paul Waugh, a journalist who is now a Labour MP, explained that the defeat revealed a fracture in Labour's base. Whereas working-class Asian people remained loyal to the party, he wrote, working-class white people had drifted away. Another MP muttered that Labour had become a bourgeois party, and had fallen under the sway of people who were too interested in statues of slave traders. The loss of Hartlepool showed that Labour had lost the white working class.

I love Teesside. It has some of Britain's friendliest, funniest people, and some of the best women's hair styles. But Teesside does not always seem to love itself. Parts of Hartlepool have become terribly neglected. Parking my car in the Dyke House neighbourhood, I noticed that the vehicle in front was more than a foot from the kerb. That turned out to be because the gutter was filled with plastic bottles and other litter. When I dropped in to see Jonathan Brash, Labour's candidate in the general election, he told me that some shop workers in Hartlepool felt sick at the thought of coming to work, because they feared they would have to deal with thieves. I wasn't sure whether to believe him until I went into a convenience store down the road from his office, looking for an apple. Almost everything in the shop was behind plastic screens to prevent people from grabbing and running. A cashier explained to me that he looks at people approaching the front door through a little window, and keeps it shut if the person seems like a drug addict. He didn't have any apples.

Mortimer had tried to please her constituents. She boasted that the government was investing in the town under its 'levelling up' schemes, which sprayed money at post-industrial places. Hartlepool is getting a new swimming pool, a new hotel in an old Wesleyan chapel and various other things. Mortimer also railed against immigrants. After a Moroccan asylum-seeker murdered a seventy-year-old Hartlepudlian in 2023, she told the House of Commons that her office was often 'besieged' by asylum-seekers. Most of them were illegal immigrants, she declared: they should be expelled from the country. Still, she seemed to know that the end was near. Her campaign was so quiet that it was almost elusive. I emailed repeatedly, asking for an interview. At last, a staff member got back to me, and we fixed a time to meet. A few hours later, her office cancelled the appointment.

Brash is now Hartlepool's MP, with a huge majority. And Labour crushed the Conservative Party in many places like Hartlepool in July 2024. It drove them out of post-industrial towns such as Stoke-on-Trent and coal-mining areas like Bolsover. It won Whitehaven and Workington on the Cumbrian coast, which had a special significance. Five years earlier, Onward, a Conservative-leaning think tank, had invented a hypothetical voter called 'Workington Man' – a middle-aged or elderly white man who had not gone to university and had voted to leave the European Union. Onward had suggested the Conservative Party could scoop up the votes of such men, and it had done precisely that. In 2024, Workington Man rudely abandoned the party. Labour also swept Glasgow, pushing out the Scottish National Party. In Wales, the Conservatives were utterly eradicated.

What on earth had happened? Part of the answer was simple. Labour had acquired a better leader and the Conservative Party had presided over a period of high inflation and worsening public services, leading to the dereliction that I saw in Hartlepool. It didn't help the Conservatives that Reform UK, a radical right-wing party, took 14 per cent of the vote nationally and won five seats. But that couldn't explain everything. Commentators and journalists like me had spent the previous few years explaining that white working-class people living in towns like Hartlepool had profoundly changed. They had become animated by cultural issues rather than social and economic ones. They had come to feel that the country was changing and leaving them behind. They resented successful, ethnically diverse cities like London, and they detested mass immigration. Then, in 2024, many places thick with white working-class residents voted for a left-wing political party led by a former lawyer from London – a man who, among his few precise promises, pledged to tear up the Conservative Party's plan to send asylum-seekers to Rwanda on his very first day in office.

Is it possible that much of what has been written and said about white working-class Britons over the past few years is flat-out wrong?

Introduction:
Discovering the white working class

Even in a tumultuous year, many days are ordinary. The thirteenth of November 1968 seemed to be one of those days. An anonymous caller told the police that a bomb had been planted in Hove, on the south coast of England; seven schools were evacuated before the warning was determined to be fake. The Queen Mother travelled to Birmingham to meet the parents of sextuplets. What they said to each other has unfortunately been lost to history – the new mother and father were so excited that they couldn't remember any of the conversation. New figures were published, showing that Britain's trade deficit had grown. And a zoo in Devon announced that it would remove a magpie from display on account of its swearing. The bird, known as Maggie, had told the manager to go away, 'in words much favoured by Lady Chatterley's gamekeeper'.

Then, in the early evening, a young Labour Party MP stood up in the House of Commons and made a bit of history. David Winnick, the member for Croydon South in London, had listened to Conservative MPs fretting about the social consequences of immigration from countries like India and Pakistan. Schools in big cities were struggling to accommodate all of the immigrants' children, the Tory MPs had complained. Anyway, they had asked, was it wise to admit thousands of immigrants when so many

Britons were unemployed? Winnick was having none of it. 'Many of those who act as the champions of the white person against immigrants,' he said, witheringly, 'have not in the past gone out of their way to defend the interests of the white working class.'

Winnick was insinuating that Conservative politicians only pose as the defenders of working-class people when it suits their purposes. Left-wingers have levelled that charge many times over the years, not always justly. But the young MP's speech in 1968 was remarkable because of the words he used. Although Winnick was not the first person to utter the words 'white working class' in the Houses of Parliament – others had previously used the term when talking about the inhabitants of South Africa and Bermuda – he seems to have been the first to describe his fellow Britons that way. He opened a sluice gate slightly. A few decades later, water would be pouring through.

Before the late 1960s, there had been little need for the concept of a British white working class. The country had a fair number of black Caribbean migrants even in the 1950s (exactly how many is unknown because the census did not ask about ethnicity), as well as many Irish people, who were sometimes thought of as not entirely white. But minority ethnic people were rarely seen outside a handful of large cities and port towns. Only in the 1960s, as more black and Asian migrants moved to northern English mill towns and the Midlands industrial belt, and politicians began to play on white people's racial anxieties, did it seem necessary to distinguish white working-class Britons from working-class people with other ethnic backgrounds. And it wasn't all that necessary. After Winnick's speech, nobody else said 'white working class' in Parliament for a decade.

Today, the notion that white working-class Britons are a distinct group of people, with special characteristics, attitudes and interests, is so firmly established that it is hard to believe the concept is only a few decades old. Politicians and pundits talk about the white working class often, either explicitly or by using phrases such as 'the traditional working class' or 'red-wall voters'. White working-class boys made it into Theresa May's very first speech as prime minister, in 2016, on account of how rarely they go to university. The increased attention is especially striking when you consider that Britain is slowly becoming more middle class and more ethnically mixed.

White working-class people are held to be politically powerful – so powerful that they have often been blamed, or praised, for turning Britain into one of the world's most nail-biting democracies. Politicians, journalists and academics agree that they are a big reason Scotland came so close to voting to secede from the United Kingdom in 2014, a big reason Britain did vote to leave the EU in 2016, and a big reason Boris Johnson ended up as prime minister in 2019 with a hefty majority, allowing him to push a Brexit deal through Parliament. Before the 2024 general election taught them otherwise, many Conservative politicians assumed that white working-class people were sturdy infantrymen for their cause. Leaked WhatsApp messages show that, during the worst of the Covid pandemic, one Tory cabinet minister referred to them as 'our voters'.

Other, more disreputable, people claim to speak for white working-class Britons. A few weeks after the election, a false rumour that three girls had been murdered by an asylum-seeker sparked rioting in many English cities. The riots themselves were appalling. Police officers and members of the public were attacked; attempts were made to burn hotels with asylum-seekers inside; a mob set up an impromptu checkpoint to check the ethnic identity of drivers. The riots also spurred justifications and excuses, which caused subtler harm by associating the entire white working class with a violent minority. Britain First, a far-right political party, insisted that the police were preventing white working-class people from expressing their concerns. Lee Anderson, an MP for the Reform UK Party, argued that the rioters were just 'British working-class lads' who had imbibed one too many drinks, as though the only thing separating a white working-class man from a violent, racist thug is a can of lager. Opinion polls soon showed that working-class people were appalled by the riots. But the damage had been done.

Britain is not alone in discovering the white working class, or in assuming that it is mostly a conservative or reactionary force. Donald Trump's political successes, especially his victory in the American presidential election of 2016, have also been attributed to his almost magical hold on their hearts. Americans and Britons speak the same language, they follow each other online, and they read each other's books. As a result, notions about white working-class people migrate easily across the Atlantic. Take 'deaths of despair', a way of summarizing the terrible toll that drugs and suicide have taken on white working-class Americans. Created by the American economist Anne Case and her (Scottish-born) husband Sir Angus Deaton, the concept has been imported to Britain. Populist politicians like Nigel Farage fly the other way, to Washington. White working-class people are also said to provide much of the fuel for Marine Le Pen's Rassemblement National in France, the Alternative für Deutschland in Germany, Georgia Meloni's Fratelli d'Italia and Geert Wilders' Partij voor de Vrijheid in the Netherlands.

Whenever and wherever they are identified, white working-class people are often said to be backward-looking and disgruntled. British ones are said to lament the loss of steady manufacturing jobs, of a culture of respect for elders, of thriving high streets and a more ethnically homogeneous society than the one Britain now has. Whatever 'woke' means, white working-class people are not it. They seem to have been left behind not just economically – as the small towns, where many of them live, quietly moulder – but also socially and culturally. In a rapidly changing country, they are said to cling to old ways and to look upon new ideas and new people with perplexity or hostility. They don't adapt, they don't innovate, they don't create new culture and they certainly don't alter their views. They are perpetually uncomfortable and out of place, like freshwater fish in a lake that is turning salty.

*

In the early 2000s, there was a burst of media and political commentary about the white working class. Several things seem to have caused it. The far-right British National Party managed to win a few local council seats in Burnley, a poor town in Lancashire, and was picking up votes in and around London. Britain was still reverberating from the racist murder of Stephen Lawrence, a black teenager, in south-east London in 1993. Brutal and sometimes funny caricatures of white working-class people were appearing on television, including Vicky Pollard, a gormless tracksuited woman created by the comedian Matt Lucas for *Little Britain*, and the dysfunctional Gallagher family in *Shameless* – a show that, like the academic ideas and the populist politicians, soon crossed the Atlantic to America.

The commentary was frequently venomous. Left-wing and right-wing journalists alike dropped insults such as 'white trash' and 'chav' into their copy. A Liberal Democrat peer wrote of being 'trapped in chav-land', after she saw a woman in a super-market explaining the plot of a soap opera while eating an enormous bun. A columnist in *The Times* attacked 'gym-slip mums who choose to get pregnant as a career option; pasty-faced, lard-gutted slappers who'll drop their knickers in the blink of an eye'. Another conservative writer advised the Tories that they should not try to win white working-class votes by banging on about immigration. They would be wiser to court ethnic-minority voters, whose 'self-reliance and belief in the family were profoundly conservative'.

Over the past ten years, people on the political right have continued to speak and write a good deal about white working-class people, but their language and arguments have changed. Especially since the Brexit referendum, they have taken to lionizing white working-class Britons as sensible truth-tellers and bulwarks against left-wing nonsense. Any problems that white working-class people might have are no longer seen as a consequence of their own moral failings, as they were in the first decade of this century. Rather, they are said to reveal the harm that liberalism has wrought.

White working-class people have come to play a crucial, though largely mute, role in a common conservative populist story about Britain. In this narrative, the country has fallen under the spell of a small group of people who went to a few elite universities and hold a narrow range of views. These people are extremely left-wing, secular and internationalist. They are keen on environmentalism, immigration and transgender rights, and are so hostile to racism that they claim to see it where it does not exist. They attempt to push their values on everyone else and brook no opposition. Occasionally, the mass of British people, who believe in sensible things like patriotism, traditional family values and tight restrictions on immigration, revolt against their progressive overlords, as they did in the Brexit vote of 2016 and the general election of 2019. The liberal elite does not give up, though. It redoubles its efforts to harangue, bully and shame ordinary people into agreeing with its point of view.

The liberal elite has damaged the country as a whole, according to this story. It has run down technical education in the mad pursuit of a majority university-educated society, and has allowed Britain's once world-leading manufacturing industries to rust. It has neglected or crushed institutions that used to bind society together, such as churches and trade unions. But the liberal elite is said to be harming white working-class people above all. The mass immigration that the elite has tolerated is crushing their wages, burdening the public services they rely on and filling their neighbourhoods with strangers. When white working-class people complain, they are called xenophobes and racists. They are barely even allowed to express their views. The ceaseless promotion of diversity and minority rights has made them feel left out and undervalued, and has deterred their children from trying hard at school. Apart from on polling days, they are mere spectators in a country that now revolves around the university educated, the sexually unorthodox and the non-white. The political scientist Matthew Goodwin wrote in 2021 of 'a sort of informal alliance between white elites, corporations and minorities against the white working class'.

This story has been told with impressive vigour and consistency in many books, articles, speeches and media interviews. It also comes in an American-accented version, represented well by J. D. Vance, who pulled off the turn from depicting white working-class people as feckless to arguing that they are victims of liberalism with amazing speed. In 2016, Vance published a memoir, *Hillbilly Elegy*, which lamented the irresponsibility of some of the people he grew up with in Appalachia – in particular, his drug-addicted mother. At the time, he regretted that many white working-class people were attracted to Donald Trump's simplistic, populist message. But within a few years Vance had joined Trump's ragged band and had dropped his earlier argument that poor white people's misery was largely self-inflicted. He soon claimed to be defending the white working class against what he calls 'the regime', a shadowy liberal elite that supposedly runs the country.

This tale is nonsense. It omits a crucial character, the elite conservative, whose power and influence is far from trivial in Britain and is enormous in America. It also gets white working-class people badly wrong. In reality, they do not all sit around resenting immigrants and metropolitan liberals, and wondering what has become of manufacturing. It might have seemed that way in Britain after the Brexit vote and Johnson's spectacular victory in the general election of 2019. But, as the election in 2024 showed, many white working-class people care more about boring things such as economic stability, inflation and the NHS. In the run-up to the election, Conservative politicians desperately tried to call their voters home by arguing that illegal immigrants threatened to destabilize British society, and warning darkly of an 'organized assault' on common sense. It did them no good.

I think that the conservative populists have got one important thing right, though. Although their analysis of modern Britain strikes me as dodgy, their focus is spot on. White working-class Britons are indeed distinctive and deserving of everyone's attention. They do live in particular places, they do think differently about some things, and they do vote differently from others. Although they share many experiences and interests with working-class people from minority ethnic groups, their bearing is unusual – as though they are part of a flotilla, but in a different boat. In a few ways, notably the performance of their children in school, the situation of white working-class Britons is especially worrying.

The left, by contrast, has mostly fallen silent on the subject. Many Labour politicians have never been comfortable talking about the white working class, at least in public (they are franker when you put your notebook away). In 2002, Tony Blair, then the prime minister, was asked why some white working-class men were drawn to far-right politics. He responded: 'I don't really break people up into those sorts of groups.' The current prime minister, Sir Keir Starmer, talks often about class, frequently pointing out that his father was a toolmaker. He does not talk about the white working class. Left-wingers often try to change the subject, pointing out, rightly, that the British working class is ethnically diverse and that working-class people from black and Asian backgrounds must cope with racism as well as class disadvantage. Some argue that it is dangerous even to speak of a white working class. To do so, they say, draws attention away from the worthy goals of eliminating discrimination against non-white people and uplifting the working class as a whole. The left appears to believe that these arguments are decisive. They are, but not in the way it thinks. It has simply decided to leave the discussion about white working-class Britons to its ideological opponents.

A good way of explaining how my view differs from those of politicians and commentators on the right and the left is to think about two questions. The first is: do you think that white British working-class people have particular problems? That is, do they face some difficulties that are distinct to them, or are larger for them than for other groups? The second question is: do you think that any problems white working-class people might have are the result of policies targeting them as a group? To put it crudely, are white working-class Britons being done down? Are other groups, particularly people with ethnic-minority backgrounds, being favoured over them?

A conservative populist would nod in response to both questions. Of course, he or she would say. White working-class people are discriminated against, their opinions are ignored or suppressed, and they are faring terribly badly as a consequence. A left-winger would answer both questions negatively. No, white working-class people do not have particular problems. They face the heavy disadvantages of their social class, but no additional ones. And no, they are not being done down. Nobody has set out to harm them as a group. Those who argue otherwise are lying. They are trying to divide the working class and yoke its white members to a right-wing political project.

To see how utterly incompatible these two positions are, and how the free-fire zone between them makes it impossible to think clearly about the problems white working-class people face, consider what happened in 2021 when Parliament tried to investigate the poor performance of white working-class boys in English schools. This is a real problem, as I explain in Chapter Two. The education committee, which had a Conservative majority, listened to various experts and produced a sixty-three-page report that said mostly sensible things. But the report also contained a section on the concept of 'white privilege'. It argued that talking about white privilege was liable to confuse poor white children, who are not all that privileged, and to sap sympathy for their plight. The report concluded that the education department should ensure that young people are not 'inadvertently being inducted into political movements'. I'm not sure what the committee meant by that, although I assume it was referring to movements like Black Lives Matter.

This was far too much for the Labour Party MPs on the committee. In an unusual move, they disowned the entire report and came up with their own conclusions. Poor white boys' bad performance in exams is simply the result of social-class disadvantage and regional inequality, they declared. It has nothing whatsoever to do with ethnicity. Indeed, the focus on white children is misguided. Black and mixed-heritage children fare worse than white children in some respects – for example, they are more likely to be excluded from school. Obsessing about white children, the Labour MPs argued, 'would systematically disadvantage other ethnic groups and increase racial educational inequalities'.

It was an awful outcome, which should shame every single MP on the committee. Parliament set out to investigate a genuine problem and ended up fighting a culture war, with both sides flinging charges of racial bias. All the careful research that has been done on ethnicity, class and education was trodden underfoot. Much nonsense was confidently spoken. Perhaps it is true that teaching children about white privilege harms them, as the committee's Conservative members claimed, but, if so, there is no evidence for it whatsoever. As for the Labour MPs' assertion that the poor performance of white working-class boys is simply a matter of poverty and place, there is good evidence that they were dead wrong. Nothing useful was learned as a result of the inquiry. The dismal educational performance of white working-class boys (and, though they were not the committee's focus, white working-class girls) continues.

My answers to the two questions I have posed are 'yes' and 'no'. Yes, I think that white working-class Britons have large problems. Some of these problems weigh particularly heavily on them. Although I agree with the left that they do not suffer because of their ethnicity (on the contrary, they tend to benefit from it), they do face distinctive difficulties that are partly a result of history and geography. Working-class white Britons tend to live in regions of the country that lack successful big cities. Within those regions, they often live far from the most dynamic, job-creating parts. Working-class minority ethnic Britons are luckier because they, their parents, or their grandparents tended to land in the places where jobs were being created, and they have stuck around.

No, I do not believe that anybody is out to get white working-class people. There is no conspiracy against them, nor is there a concerted effort to favour non-white people over them. The sneering and slights that they endure, largely from middle-class white people, are contemptible. But these slights do not point to a campaign to do them down. I find the ill-treatment of white working-class people as a group less worrying than the political exploitation of the *idea* that they are being ill-treated. They seem to have been placed at the point of a spear, which is designed to bring about a more authoritarian Britain.

This book will disappoint anybody who believes that white working-class Britons are the very hardest-done-by members of society. They have certainly been abused by some politicians and the mass media, but not as badly as some other groups (if you don't believe me, ask an immigrant from Romania or Somalia). Relative to other working-class people, they are well favoured in some ways. One of these is housing. Overall, 5 per cent of working-class white Britons in England and Wales live in households without enough bedrooms. That is bad, but others have it much worse. Among working-class black Africans the share is 33 per cent, and among working-class Bangladeshis it is 40 per cent (the fact that black Africans and Bangladeshis are younger than average and more likely to be living in families explains only some of the difference). Many neighbourhoods dominated by white working-class people are pleasant, with wide roads, ubiquitous gardens and plenty of space in which to park the car. One of the sensations that I will most remember from working on this book is the feeling of sunlight on my skin.

*

When Winnick dropped his unfamiliar term on the House of Commons in November 1968, most of his listeners could probably imagine what he was talking about. The British white working class was large and well understood, even though the name was novel. Books about the urban working class, such as Michael Young and Peter Willmott's *Family and Kinship in East London*, published in 1957, almost completely ignored immigrants and non-white people. Institutions such as council tenants' associations more or less explicitly represented the interests of white working-class people, as did certain trade unions. Some unionized workers had downed tools and marched earlier in 1968 to protest the sacking of Enoch Powell from the Conservative shadow cabinet after he argued that continued immigration from the Commonwealth could lead to rivers running with blood.

Today the concept is far more familiar, but it is no longer so clear what the term 'white working class' actually means. Even 'working class' is harder to define than it used to be, thanks partly to changes in official statistics. No institutions claim to represent the interests of white working-class Britons as a group apart from a few dire extremist outfits, which enjoy little support from anybody. Trade unions have gone from being white bastions to standard-bearers for racial justice. So anybody who writes about white working-class Britons needs to define their terms.

Although it might sound obvious, when I write 'white working class', I mean people who are white and working class. It is not code for something else. I do not use the term to mean thinly educated or bigoted. Nor do I use it to refer to a particularly desperate slice of the working class. Several times, when I told people that I was writing a book about the white working class, they gleefully directed me to the most godforsaken corners of Britain that they knew. Or, the next time I saw them, they asked how my book on the underclass was coming along. That is not what I mean.

I describe people as white Britons (or, to avoid tedious repetition in a book that is mostly about the group, do not mention their ethnicity) if they tick that box on the census, if they describe themselves that way, or if I think most people would see them as such. It is worth keeping in mind that ethnicity is not a stable, objectively verifiable characteristic like a fingerprint or an iris pattern. It is more like a judgement, a claim, or even an accent. People can and do move from one ethnic group to another during their lives. Some people switch between censuses, even though the census is prefaced with the scary warning that supplying false information may lead to a fine.

One of the ethnic categories that people in England and Wales commonly enter and leave is the white Irish group. When I use ·official statistics, I treat members of that group as distinct from white Britons. But, at several points in this book, I describe people who told me that they were born in Ireland, or are the children or grandchildren of Irish immigrants, as Britons. I am aware that the Irish in mainland Britain have a distinctive, proud, sometimes painful history. But the long history of free movement between Britain and Ireland, and the thorough blending of the British and the Irish in mainland cities, means that separating the two groups is difficult in practice. The chapter where my decision makes a big difference is the one on armed robbery. As I will show, some of Britain's most notorious armed robbers had Irish parents.

I define adults as working class if they do working-class jobs, or if the last job they did was a working-class job. The Office for National Statistics, which organizes the census, divides most adults into eight groups based on their employment and working conditions. The groups bear labels that are none too vivid: higher managerial, administrative and professional occupations; lower managerial, administrative and professional occupations; intermediate occupations; small employers and own-account workers; lower supervisory and technical occupations; semi-routine occupations; routine occupations; and people who are long-term unemployed or have never worked. Every so often, the statisticians move the boundaries slightly, moving a group of workers from one category to another. I treat groups one to four as middle class and five to eight as working class. Students do not belong to any of the eight groups.

My definition of the working class is similar to the one used by the Social Mobility Commission, a research group funded by the government. Not everyone will agree with it. The Office for National Statistics argues that its eight-part classification should not be converted into a simple two-class scheme, as I have done. Although some of the eight groups are plainly middle class (group one contains people like lawyers and architects) or working class (group six, 'semi-routine occupations', contains hospital porters and shelf stackers), some of the ones in the middle are hard to place. Meanwhile, ordinary Britons define social class in all sorts of wild and wonderful ways. Some contend that class is like a star sign, determined at the moment of your birth; others say that it is defined by your income, your accent, or whether you grew up in a council home. A few years ago, I met a Londoner who assured me, in all seriousness, that an important characteristic of working-class people is that they drive to work. Some maintain that your class is whatever you say it is.

These ways of thinking about class strike me as rich and revealing, but not so helpful. The attempt to segment society into many socio-economic groups has not caught on in practice, even though it has been around for decades and is admirably rigorous and precise. In practice, people do not refer to themselves as having an 'intermediate occupation' or a 'routine occupation'. Nor do they describe themselves as 'new affluent workers' or members of the 'precariat', to cite two of the social groups devised by Mike Savage of the London School of Economics in a clever reworking of the official socio-economic classification. They call themselves middle class or working class.

Underdogs

The popular definitions of social class can be fascinating guides to how individuals think about themselves and their family histories. If people who live middle-class lives want to identify as working class, that is fine, even commendable. But the popular definitions are hopeless if you want to understand society as a whole. If you freeze a person's class at the moment of their birth, you deny that people can change class, and describe society in a bizarrely backward-looking way: Britain's class structure is as it was when everyone was in nappies. If you rely on people's accents, or allow people to state their own class, you will end up describing people's attitudes and self-images as much as their circumstances. You will, for example, find yourself describing Lord Alan Sugar, one of Britain's richest, most powerful men, as working class. As for growing up in a council home, that is a good sign that a young person is working class but not a good sign that an old person is. I explain why in the chapter on council housing.

By my definition, 40 per cent of adults in England and Wales are working class, and 31 per cent are members of the white British working class. This is not just the underclass – which is anyway more of a slur, based on the dodgy idea that many families languish on unemployment benefits for generation after generation, than a real group of people. My definition includes people who are out of work and living on benefits, but also baristas, warehouse workers, security guards, theme-park attendants, gardeners, sewing machinists, pipe fitters, vehicle mechanics, bricklayers, chefs, childminders, home carers, shop assistants and delivery drivers. White working-class people are as widespread as they are varied. Chapter One describes three places where they are especially thick on the ground: a small town in South Wales, a suburb of Manchester and a town in Norfolk. But not all white working-class Britons live in largely white working-class places. About two million live in electoral wards where less than a quarter of the population belongs to the white British working class, as I define it. Not one of the 7,500 wards in England or Wales contains no members of the group.

In parts, this book reads less like an account of a specific group of people and more like a book about Britain. That is deliberate. The British white working class is not a mysterious tribe dwelling beyond the civilized zone, with its own peculiar dialect and folkways. It is diverse and riven with contradictions and disagreements, just like any other big group. The white working class is Britain. It is not the whole of Britain, to be sure, but it is a mightily important part. This is a book about Britain that happens to feature a large, badly misunderstood group of people.

*

Although I am white and British, I am middle class according to every conceivable definition, including all the ones I find ridiculous (I usually take the train to work). I was born to middle-class parents in a middle-class neighbourhood. I am highly educated, I do a middle-class job, and I live in a small city that is largely middle class. My life is not as gilded as my parents' lives were at my age, and my children are less privileged than I was as a child. But that sort of gentle downward mobility is itself almost a defining characteristic of the modern British middle class.

I am interested in white working-class Britons not because I want to understand myself but because I want to understand Britain. I cannot see how anybody, from any class or ethnic group, can claim knowledge of the country if they overlook three in ten of its inhabitants. And if that is not enough reason, consider that important decisions affecting everybody in Britain are taken with white working-class people primarily in mind. Politically, although of course not in any other way, a white retired steelworker who lives in Teesside matters more than a young black woman who lives in

London; I explain why in Chapter Ten. Resources tend to flow to people who matter politically. The last government's 'levelling up' policy often looked suspiciously like a scheme for funnelling money to largely white working-class parts of the country, which left less money available for spending elsewhere, such as in poor, ethnically mixed neighbourhoods. Housing policies have changed over the years in ways that make it easier to block immigrants from getting council homes, and the last Conservative government proposed to push even further in the same direction. More or less explicitly, policies like these are designed to delight white working-class people. They attempt to tap grievances, which everyone ought to understand. How do white working-class people actually feel about council estates? Why do some regard the homes therein as the property of their group?

One consequence of my outsider status is that I cannot use the most celebrated, influential book ever written about working-class Britain as a model. Richard Hoggart grew up in a poor household in Leeds. By the time he published *The Uses of Literacy* in 1957, he was an academic, so was middle class by my (and, to some extent, his) definition. But his working-class roots were essential to the story he told. Hoggart looked back at the cultural world that he had known as a child, tried to understand its workings and reflected on how it had changed. *The Uses of Literacy* is wonderful – warm and funny in places, such as in Hoggart's descriptions of pub singers, and painful in others, especially where he describes the experiences of working-class children who achieve great academic success. Along with Hoggart's later books, it continues to inspire writers from working-class backgrounds.

I am more inspired by another man, who wrote at the same time as Hoggart. Ferdynand Zweig was even more of an outsider than I am. A Polish Jew who trained as an economist, he fled to Britain during the Second World War and wrote several books about working-class life, which he researched mostly by hanging out in factories, pubs and people's homes. Zweig was attacked by academic sociologists for being insufficiently theoretical, and some of his conclusions were disproved by more careful research. But he had a good ear for people's speech, and he did not see working-class Britons as peculiar – or at least no more than he saw all Britons as peculiar. He was also dead right about one crucial thing. In contrast to Hoggart, Zweig emphasized the diversity of working-class British life. Steelworkers struck him as quite different from coal miners or builders; Yorkshiremen were unlike Devonians; women were different from men; the old were different from the young. 'The average worker does not exist,' he wrote. Amen to that, Ferdynand.

This book ranges across England, Scotland and Wales. I do not write about Northern Ireland because its politics and society are too distinctive, and I could not do it justice. I write about big cities, small towns and villages. I write about some places where lots of people are white and working class, such as the Isle of Wight and Hartlepool, and about some places where not many people are, such as Milton Keynes and Welwyn Garden City. I try to allow the diversity of people's experiences and attitudes to come through. In contrast to some people who have written about Britain's white working class, I pay especially close attention to young people and women. I often use the excellent data collected by the Office for National Statistics.

One thing my book shares with Zweig's work is that I have kept most of my interviewees anonymous. I started out by asking for everyone's names, but quickly ran into trouble. Some people declared themselves 'not bothered' about the use of their names in a book, but then, when I spoke to them a second time, insisted that they didn't want their names to appear. Others told me things that struck me as likely to cause problems for them or their children. Some of the people I interviewed for this book are themselves children, and cannot be named. So I have suppressed names and certain identifying details, although I have not disguised anybody's identity by inventing characteristics. I do, however, include the names of people who have written about themselves or enjoy some sort of public profile. In the chapter about car modification, for example, I use the names of the people who run car clubs, but not those of the petrolheads who turn up at their gatherings.

I do not believe it is possible to write a comprehensive book about white working-class Britain, and I do not try. I almost ignore some places (sorry, south-west England and the West Midlands) and I skate over some important aspects of life. I spend a whole chapter on car modification, which a small minority of white working-class people do, and another one on armed robbery, which almost nobody has ever done. I focus on those because I think they reveal things about the white British working class as a whole, and also, to be honest, because they are fun to write about.

I hope that this book changes people's minds in two ways. First, I will show that white working-class Britons are far more adaptable and forward-looking than either conservatives or liberals seem to believe. They can and do come to terms with titanic changes, such as the shift from manufacturing to services jobs and the rapidly growing ethnic diversity of the country. In practice, they rub along decently well with immigrants and ethnic-minority people, albeit without issuing the bold statements of acceptance that liberals might want to hear. One of the great unheralded changes in Britain is that many places that were once overwhelmingly white and working class are becoming ethnically mixed with hardly any trouble. Meanwhile, the British white working class has opened itself to many new members. Chapter

Six describes how, in the space of just two decades, migrants from Eastern Europe have begun to permeate it. The institutions that white working-class people have created are helping this process along.

The second thing this book shows is that we have made a serious mistake as a country by obsessing about the wrong people. Politicians, journalists and academics have spent too little time thinking about some white working-class Britons who truly need help and far too much time thinking about other white working-class Britons who do not. A young woman living in a poor coastal town who got bad marks in her GCSEs, who is now working in a shop and trying to raise a child without much help from her sickly mother or her erratically employed ex-boyfriend – the sort of woman I write about in Chapter Nine – has very severe problems. A retired miner who is in a stable marriage, who owns his house and two cars, has many fewer problems.

Yet the retired miner has plenty of opinions, which journalists, politicians and researchers have listened to diligently, and have turned into innumerable books and reports. This man probably doesn't think much of mass immigration; he is likely to believe that racial equality has gone a bit too far; he probably voted to leave the European Union in 2016. The young woman, on the other hand, does not have severe attitudes to match her severe problems. Immigration doesn't upset her much, and ethnic diversity doesn't upset her at all. She probably doesn't vote. The white working-class Britons with the problems are not the white working-class Britons with the complaints.

Politicians do not serve white working-class people well by pandering to them and assuring them that every change they find difficult can be reversed, as some on the right are wont to do. Nor do they help by pretending that white working-class people are exactly the same as other working-class people, as progressives tend to. White working-class Britons exist, they are important and distinctive, and they will continue to play a vital role in Britain for many years to come. They are also far more varied and open-minded than is generally supposed. As so often, the reality is more intriguing than the myth.

Chapter One

Heartlands, enclaves and colonies

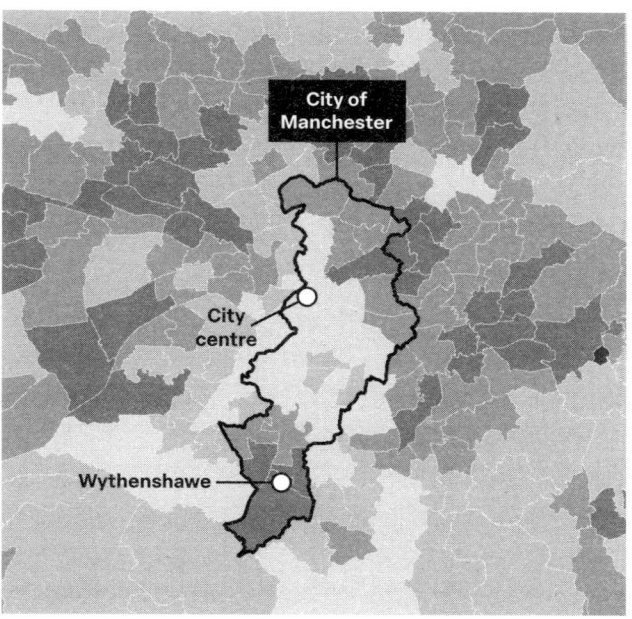

The inhabitants of Rhymney use two words often. The first, which they generally apply to their own town, is 'downhill'. 'Oh, it's gone downhill,' says one. 'Pfft, downhill,' says another, with a decisive swoop of her arm. Their small town, east of Merthyr Tydfil in South Wales, is not what it was. Some of the older residents remember when you could hardly walk along the pavement of the high street on Saturdays: the crowd of shoppers was so thick that you had to step into the road. These days, the street is quiet, with many vacant shops and hardly anywhere to get a cup of tea. What little energy it has after dark is provided by a group of loitering teenagers. And that, some of the other residents feel, is the wrong kind of energy.

Rhymney clings to a hillside towards the head of a long valley that ends in the Bannau Brycheiniog, or Brecon Beacons. The steepness of the town affects how the residents speak about it. Rhymney people talk less about north, south, east and west, as flatlanders like me do, and more about up and down. They divide their town of some 8,500 people into a top end, a middle, and a bottom end. St David's church is known as 'top church'. People come 'up' to Rhymney from Caerphilly, the administrative centre of the borough, although they don't do this often. The word 'downhill' therefore describes both decline and direction. Rhymney has gone downhill, but many places, including Cardiff, twenty miles away, are downhill from Rhymney.

Residents have different metrics for measuring the decline of their town, depending on their ages. Old people complain about shop closures. Rhymney once had two cinemas, two butchers and two post offices (or perhaps three – memories differ). It now has none of any, unless you count as a post office a short stretch of counter in a convenience store. The middle-aged lament the closure of pubs and music clubs, which once brought many people into the town from other parts of South Wales. Young people complain about the unreliable buses and a shortage of well-paying jobs. Few people of any age lament the thing that I am most struck by: the large, abandoned Nonconformist chapels, relics of a more pious era in South Wales. Then again, I didn't have to sit through the sermons.

Nobody claims that Rhymney was ever a wealthy or a salubrious town, though, for it was not. The discovery of iron ore and seams of coal in the valley led to a population boom and the utter despoiling of the landscape in the nineteenth century. 'Rhymney is perhaps the least attractive spot in a district not too remarkable for "sweetness and light", declared a guide to Monmouthshire in 1909. 'Tips, tunnels, tramroads, dumps of old brick and stone, and an indescribable litter of scrap iron abutted on the dwelling houses,' remembered Thomas Jones, who grew up in Rhymney and went on to a glittering career in the British civil service between the First and Second World Wars. At least coal was cheap, Jones wrote. Even the poorest residents could burn enough of the stuff to keep warm.

Over the decades, mines, factories and other businesses have opened and closed, and Rhymney has swung between poverty and desperate poverty. It is currently in the former state. Several firms, including medical suppliers, have been enticed to industrial estates in the town, in part because the Welsh government has paid for buildings. A road that runs along the heads of the valleys is being widened, raising hopes that Rhymney will soon be located close to an important east–west thoroughfare. Still, the town struggles. Every part of Rhymney is more deprived than Wales as a whole, which is not a high bar. One part is the eighth most deprived area out of 1,900 in the country.

A chef tells me that Rhymney increasingly seems more like a village than a town, and I can see what he means. Between 2011 and 2021, it lost a total of 306 people, or 3 per cent of its population. Young people are especially thin on the ground. Although not many teenagers from the town go to university, some do, and they tend to stay away. Rhymney has fewer children aged under ten than it has fifty-somethings or sixty-somethings. In 2018, two primary schools and one secondary school were folded into a single institution that is named after Idris Davies, a local poet. The men's choir, Rhymney Silurian, has shrunk over the years and contains a lot of white hair. At an evening rehearsal in Idris Davies School, the choir stands in silence to honour a former member who has died. Then it launches into 'Happy Birthday' for another member who is turning sixty.

In Rhymney, ethnic diversity seems like a distant phenomenon – something that occurs in Cardiff, or perhaps even further away. Of the 8,546 people in the town who put their identity on the 2021 census, 8,324 described themselves as white Britons. I happen to run into one of the few exceptions, a black woman who was born overseas. She tells me that she and her neighbours get along fine, although she sometimes receives astonished looks when she goes into shops. She is highly unlikely to be at the leading edge of a big migration into the town; Rhymney has neither the jobs nor the transport connections to entice working-age migrants of any ethnicity. It was a mostly white working-class town in the past, it is a mostly white working-class town today, and it will probably remain a mostly white working-class town for many years to come.

Its politics are similarly unchanging. Rhymney is a Labour stronghold in a corner of Britain that has been solidly Labour for a century. Dawn Bowden, the Member of the Senedd who represents Rhymney, says that residents frequently assure her they will vote Labour because their families have always done so. She isn't too keen on this: she would much prefer to hear that people will vote Labour because they like the party's policies. But perhaps she ought not to worry too much. Many people from all walks of life have better things to do than think about politics, and simply continue doing what they and their families have always done. Conservative politicians in the shire counties of England seldom complain that their constituents vote for them year after year, no matter what they do or don't do.

The second word I hear often in Rhymney is 'stranger'. It is a cohesive and friendly town, says one man who has worked various jobs, from sailor to door-to-door salesman. 'But there are a lot of strangers as well.' I hear the word again and again in one of Rhymney's community centres, where an elderly crowd gathers to chat and play music bingo. The word does not mean foreigner; it simply means somebody who is not known. I think that people in Rhymney use it so freely not because they are hostile to outsiders (they are not), but because so few people fall into the category. Nobody in the small city where I live would describe someone as a stranger, because almost everyone is. In Rhymney, strangers are still rare enough to be notable. 'The key to our way of life is our involvement in each other's affairs,' wrote a local teacher, D. T. Williams, in a book published in 1978. It still is. One retired woman tells me that she recently travelled the sixty miles to Bristol, only to receive many anxious phone calls from her neighbours in Rhymney. She had accidentally left a light on.

The few strangers who make it to Rhymney are of two types. Some are working-class retirees from far away, including England, who have been drawn to the town by cheap property and the availability of green hilltops on which to walk their dogs. They are generally approved of. Then there are younger, shorter-range migrants, who are sometimes said to be recently released prisoners, and are sometimes described as troublemakers who have been booted out of council estates further down the valley. When crime or drug abuse occurs in Rhymney, they tend to be blamed. But Carl Cuss, who grew up in the town and now represents the top end as a councillor, says this is not fair. He often meets with the police, who tell him who is causing trouble in the town. 'They're mostly local people,' he says. 'I know their names.'

If I have made Rhymney sound depressing, it is not. It is small-town insular, but also small-town friendly. Although I am a stranger, people say hello to me in the street. The place retains a pleasantly rural edge – I have seen people riding horses along the street, and some of the grass verges are kept neat by nibbling sheep. As someone who has sung in several choirs, I can say that the Silurian choir is excellent. Its members grapple manfully with songs in Welsh, a language not all of them understand, and they manage to wring a great deal of meaning out of 'The Battle Hymn of the Republic', a stomping American song born out of the civil war, by slowing it down. The hills around the town that were once scarred by mining have grown green and beautiful. And on the rare nights when it is not cloudy and threatening rain, the sky is full of stars.

*

England and Wales are divided into about 7,500 electoral wards. These vary in size, but most contain a few thousand people. The map at the beginning of the book shows the proportion of adults in every ward who are working-class white Britons according to my definition, which I explained in the Introduction. A couple of things are immediately obvious. The first is that the south-east corner of England has relatively few white working-class people. The very lowest proportion is in Southall, a mostly Asian part of west London, where they account for just 1 per cent of the population. A combination of affluence, immigration and ethnic diversity explains this. Many people in London and south-east England are middle class rather than working class, and many are not white Britons.

Northern England and the Midlands are different. Grimsby, a town on the Lincolnshire coast, contains a ward called East Marsh where 67 per cent of adults belong to the white British working class. The Valleys of South Wales, including Rhymney, are not far behind. Places like Grimsby and the Valleys are overwhelmingly white and British. As a result, economics rather than ethnicity explains why one ward has a higher or lower proportion of white working-class Britons than the next one. As you move south (or down) from Rhymney towards Cardiff, the share falls. That is mostly because there are more middle-class people near Cardiff, and not so much because there are fewer white Britons. The map at the beginning of Chapter Ten shows the pattern.

Perhaps all that is to be expected. Everybody knows that lots of people in northern England belong to the white working class. 'Red wall', a term for the cluster of constituencies including Burnley and Sedgefield that swung from Labour to the Conservative Party in the 2019 general election, is sometimes lazily used as a synonym: a 'red-wall voter' tends to be a white working-class voter. But the map contains some surprises, too. Essex, the home of gravelly towns like Basildon and the proudly downmarket TV show *The Only Way Is Essex*, has a low proportion of white working-class people – lower than much of Cornwall. The south-western county seems intensely middle-class in summer, when well-off holidaymakers arrive from other parts of Britain. It is different in January.

A second pattern that is obvious from the map is that big cities tend to contain fewer white working-class people than smaller cities and towns. The lightest shaded places are nearly all dense and urban. It sometimes seems as though the bigger and more internationally famous the city, the lower the proportion of white working-class inhabitants it contains. White working-class people are scarcer in London than in Birmingham, Liverpool or Manchester, and scarcer in those great cities than in smaller ones such as Doncaster and Middlesbrough.

The parts of England and Wales with the very highest proportions of white working-class inhabitants are often rather like Rhymney. They are small towns and villages that few Britons, let alone people outside the country, have heard of (Rhymney is known to some fans of folk music because of the 1960s Pete Seeger song 'Bells of Rhymney', which draws on a poem by Idris Davies). They often grew on the backs of industries, such as coal mining and day tripping, that have declined over the years. They are often run-down, and never glamorous. Their populations tend to be old and growing older. They are located next to places that are also largely white and working class, and they have been touched only gently by the growing ethnic diversity and internationalization of Britain as a whole. I refer to these places as white working-class *heartlands*.

Heartland areas can be insular, but they are seldom hostile or even tense. Their populations do not change much. Their character as solidly white working-class places seems impregnable, because why would other people choose to settle in them? Partly as a consequence, they have generally been spared the attentions of Britain's most loathsome political parties and demagogues. In 2022, Britain First, a far-right outfit, stood in local elections in a ward of Rhondda Cynon Taf, seventeen miles from Rhymney. The candidate did very badly indeed, coming last out of eight. Britain First later sought to explain this crushing defeat by saying that the area was 'completely unaffected by the problems of mass immigration, Islamism, multiculturalism etc etc'. Another explanation, which gives more credit to local people, is that a strong vein of opposition to racism runs through Wales.

These characteristics make heartland areas different from a second type of place that contains many white working-class people, which I call an *enclave*. Enclaves are often found on the outskirts of cities. Some of the best examples are large suburban council estates, built around the middle of the twentieth century. Whereas heartland areas tend to be located next to other predominantly white working-class areas, enclaves are hard up against diversity and change. They are next-door places, and their residents know it.

Consider Manchester, the industrial 'shock city' of the nineteenth century. The middle of the city, which used to be rather desolate in the evenings, has since the 1990s sprouted clubs, bars and tower blocks that are inhabited mostly by young, middle-class people. As the map at the beginning of this chapter shows, few white working-class people live there. Moving away from the city centre, you enter ethnically diverse working-class areas like Cheetham Hill to the north and Moss Side to the south. Then, towards the fringes of the city, the streets become largely white and working class. One of the most intensely white working-class areas in Manchester is in the far south – the giant Wythenshawe housing estate.

*

The estate is three and a half hours' drive from Rhymney, and it seems a world away. Nobody greets me in the street, or even tries to catch my eye. I am warned to avoid a particular car park, because break-ins are common. The residents of Wythenshawe are proper urbanites: harried, mouthy and funny. After a long conversation with a woman who has lived in the area for decades, her son starts teasing both of us: 'My mother is completely senile, you know. And I don't know why she's talking about Manchester. She grew up in Liverpool!'

Wythenshawe looks completely different from Rhymney, and not just because of its flatness. Although it is surrounded by green hills, the Welsh town is largely drab and grey, with homes crammed into narrow streets. By comparison, Wythenshawe's mostly red-brick, two-storey houses are generously spaced, with gardens in front and behind. Roads on the estate are luxuriously wide; trees are tall; parks are large. The schools have grassy playgrounds, which are far nicer than the asphalt rectangles that many inner-city children grow up with. The inhabitants of Wythenshawe lack a great many things, but greenery and open space are not among them.

The estate was brought into being by civic idealists. Manchester City Council started building it in the 1920s on land donated by

Ernest Simon, a liberal industrialist. Construction proceeded slowly; for many years, Wythenshawe retained wild corners where the residents could spot kingfishers and sand martins. In many ways, it resembles southern English garden cities such as Hampstead Garden Suburb, Letchworth and Welwyn Garden City. The differences are that Wythenshawe is larger than all of those places, with about 80,000 inhabitants, and much poorer. The government's Index of Deprivation for the year 2000 reported that one ward in the estate, Benchill, was the most deprived place in the whole of England. Wythenshawe is an example of deep poverty in a pleasant setting.

Whereas Rhymney has been poor for much of its history, Wythenshawe fell into it. The earliest residents of the estate were a privileged group: the cream of the working class. The council set house rents so high that poor Mancunians could not afford to live in them. Simon explained that men should just about be able to manage, so long as they could be 'content with a very small amount of pocket money' and were married to 'competent and economical' women. The inhabitants were expected to uphold high standards of decoration and decorum. The council rent man would turn up, leather money-bag over his shoulder, and chide any householder who had paid insufficiently close attention to his privet hedge. Single mothers were frowned upon, as were women who wore red nail polish. Indeed, many of the estate's female inhabitants looked rather similar, as a result of visiting the same hair salons and routinely going out in raincoats. The estate had a sniffy culture. Ann Hughes and Karen Hunt, two academics who interviewed Wythenshawe residents for the 1992 book *Workers' Worlds*, discovered that they were proudly unsociable. Women boasted that they did not drop by each other's houses to gossip or borrow tea. That was slum behaviour, not the sort of conduct expected in their smart estate.

Even by that point, though, Wythenshawe was slipping. Like council estates across Britain, it was shedding better-off residents as they bought their homes under right-to-buy rules and moved out – a process I describe in Chapter Three. Allocations policies changed, with the result that many homes on the estate were rented to desperately poor families. As Manchester was walloped by recession and deindustrialization in the 1980s, the estate became startlingly run-down. 'You'd look around, and it was not the Wythenshawe that we had been brought to,' remembers Eddie Flanagan, who grew up on the estate in the 1960s and 1970s and later returned to run the Wythenshawe Forum Trust, which looks after a library and a leisure centre.

It acquired a fearsome reputation. In 2007, three years before he became prime minister, David Cameron visited the estate as part of a campaign to show that the Conservative Party under-stood urban problems. He was taunted, albeit from a safe distance, by a white youth who could have been drafted by a law-and-order speech-writer: baggy trousers, hood pulled over head, one hand in the shape of a gun. Five years later, a sign was erected at Heald Green railway station, labelling it 'Home of Wythenshawe Town Centre'. Heald Green is close to Wythenshawe, but the proud residents of that neighbourhood were outraged. They told a reporter from the *Manchester Evening News* that the sign was 'very offensive' and that Heald Green should be viewed as utterly distinct from the council estate.

Still, people have always wanted to live in Wythenshawe. Houses on the estate are well built, especially by comparison with council homes elsewhere, and the estate is well positioned. It lies between the city centre and Manchester Airport, and is not far from Trafford, the wealthiest borough in Greater Manchester. Demand for social housing grows year by year. One local councillor tells me that more than a thousand people apply for a home when it becomes available. The local housing association has adopted a complex allocations policy that prioritizes the neediest but gives some advantage to people who have lived in Wythenshawe for a few years or have children at school there.

Among the new arrivals in Wythenshawe are black and Asian people, some of them working class and living in social housing, some of them middle-class homeowners. Between the censuses of 2011 and 2021, almost every part of the estate became substantially more ethnically diverse. The central area that includes the civic centre went from being 12 per cent non-white to 22 per cent. Bodunrin Hundeyin, a Nigeria-born entrepreneur, moved to the estate in 2004 and started selling Afro haircare products a few years later. He now runs a small shop in the civic centre. At first, he says, most of his customers were white people looking for products and advice for their mixed-heritage children. These days, he has many black customers.

On occasion, Wythenshawe's white inhabitants have lashed out against the new arrivals. In the early 2000s, some nurses from Kerala in south India settled near Wythenshawe Hospital. They and their families were greeted with violence. One man was sitting with his eighteen-month-old daughter on his knee when a rock crashed through his window. A week later, the same thing happened. A nurse complained that her car windows had been smashed and that fireworks and eggs had been aimed at her house. A Keralan girl was surrounded by youths who attempted to set her hair alight. The police responded by stepping up patrols, and attempted to counter a local rumour that the Keralites were asylum-seekers.

In 2014, the local Labour MP, Paul Goggins, died suddenly. Right-wing political parties seized their chance. The United Kingdom Independence Party saw Wythenshawe as fertile ground for its message about the dire consequences of mass immigration;

its candidate assured Chris Mason, a reporter for the BBC, that migrants were taking jobs and depressing wages, and that the Labour Party had 'betrayed the working class' by letting so many people into the country. The far-right British National Party rocked up in Wythenshawe, too. Labour trounced both parties in the election, but UKIP, which took almost one in five votes, beat the Conservative Party into third place. Every so often, a far-right group tries to rally in Wythenshawe, although lately such groups have focused on Salford, another city in Greater Manchester that is also poor and growing more ethnically diverse.

It is not difficult to find sharp views about immigrants in Wythenshawe today. Rumours swirl that lots of asylum-seekers and refugees are being housed in the area, and they are the focus of much anger and anxiety. A white hairdresser answers my bland question about how the estate has changed over the years by arguing that it has improved, but quickly adds that she keeps her children on a tight leash because of all the immigrants. She sees them not only as dangerous ('though, if I say that, people will say I'm racist'), but also as competitors with an unfair edge when it comes to social housing. 'You can't get a council property round here,' she tells me. 'The only way I could get one is if I moved to Oldham or Birmingham and went into a homeless shelter. And I can't do that, not with my children . . . But they're giving council houses to all these people who are just coming into the country. It's not right, is it?' Hers is a common gripe. 'The old "you're just rehousing people that are coming into the country",' says a local official, wearily.

People living in all sorts of situations are capable of developing racist and xenophobic opinions. But academics who have studied the subject think that places with the characteristics of Wythenshawe provide especially fertile soil. In 2017, Eric Kaufmann, a political scientist, used a large survey to show that white Britons

39

living in places that were quickly growing more ethnically mixed were more likely to support the United Kingdom Independence Party. Intriguingly, though, white Britons living in truly diverse places had little time for the party. Rapid change made people keener on UKIP, whereas diversity made them less keen. Kaufmann wondered whether places that have become ethnically mixed are hard ground for anti-immigration parties because the most anxious white people have fled, leaving calmer ones behind. But he found that was not the case: white people who move out of diverse areas seem similar to the ones who remain. It is perhaps more likely that people experience a passing shock. As a place moves rapidly from being overwhelmingly white to somewhat mixed, some white British people grow anxious and resentful. As it becomes truly mixed, they calm down again.

Some Mancunians assure me that Wythenshawe is a racist estate, but that isn't quite right. Yes, it contains people who espouse racist views. It also contains people who firmly oppose racism. In 2019, an official at a football match involving Wythenshawe Town, a non-league club, allegedly made a racist comment to a player. The club's (white) manager promptly pulled his team off the field. The manager was later fined, but he was unrepentant. And if some people in the estate speak sharply about asylum-seekers, others are immensely generous towards them. Kirsty Taylor, who runs a community centre, says that she was flooded with pushchairs and other donations when word got around that newly arrived Afghan families needed them.

The white working-class inhabitants of estates like Wythenshawe express another sentiment towards immigrants and ethnic-minority people, which is at least as powerful as resentment. It is a surprising sentiment – so much so that I heard it several times before I realized what it was. The sentiment is envy. Rightly or wrongly, white people feel that members of minority ethnic groups are more serious about education, more committed to their families, more devoted to civic action and in general more determined. A white man in Wythenshawe who has worked as a security guard tells me that many ethnic groups, including the Irish, have managed to set up cultural centres in Manchester, which help them deal with the problems they encounter. 'We don't have a door to knock on,' he says.

Britain has many places like Wythenshawe, just as it has many places like Rhymney. Quickly, sometimes very quickly, such enclaves are becoming more like the metropolises they belong to, which is to say less white and working class. Some of their inhabitants dislike this change, either because they dislike immigrants or minority ethnic people, or because they view them as competitors for resources – especially social housing – that they think should go to them. Whether they are resentful, envious or welcoming, they notice changes in the ethnic make-up of their neighbourhoods, and they sometimes think about themselves in those terms. The white inhabitants of heartlands are simply working class. In enclaves, ethnic identities sit closer to the surface. When their residents say 'we', they are more likely to mean white working class.

If Wythenshawe sounds more familiar than Rhymney, that could be because places like it have been written about more often. Michael Collins's pioneering 2004 book on the white working class, *The Likes of Us*, is about Walworth in south London – a place that has become much more ethnically mixed and is currently filling with posh flats. Another book, *The New East End*, by Geoff Dench, Kate Gavron and Michael Young, published in 2006, is about Bethnal Green, which started to become more Bangladeshi in the 1970s and later turned increasingly middle class. *The New Minority*, by Justin Gest, published in 2016, focuses on Dagenham – again an area of rapid ethnic change. *White Working-Class Voices* by Harris Beider is a 2015 book about several neighbourhoods in London and the West Midlands that are similar to the other places. All of these books describe white working-class people as a self-conscious group that feels invaded and put upon. Of course they do. They are all describing the inhabitants of the same sort of place.

*

The heartlands are extensive; the enclaves are familiar. A third kind of place, which is different from the other two and rarer, is exceptional for a different reason. It is – and readers will have to forgive the technical language – a lot of fun. Places in this group have been settled by white working-class people from somewhere else. Rather than feeling put upon and pressurized by new arrivals, these people have put the wind up those who have been around for longer. Places in this group can have a strange, throwback culture. I call them *colonies*. My favourite example is a small town in Norfolk, roughly halfway between Cambridge and Norwich in East Anglia. It is called Thetford, and it is one of the oddest and most wonderful places in Britain.

To celebrate Queen Elizabeth's coronation in 1953, the people of Thetford organized a parade. Among the entertainments was a competition for the best-decorated motor vehicle. Second prize went to a car that was covered with pots and pans – items that were, for some reason, associated with London cockneys. The *Thetford & Watton Times* reported that two people dressed in rags were positioned on top of the vehicle, which bore a sign: 'First of London's overspills'.

It was an early hint of the human wave that was about to break over the town. Just two months earlier, Thetford's leaders had revealed that they were planning to entice factories from London, together with so many factory workers that the population of their town would at least triple. At the time, the British government was keen to push industries and workers out of London and other big cities, which were seen as dangerously crowded and polluted. The same agenda gave rise to suburban 'new towns' like Basildon, Harlow and Corby. But Thetford's plan was exceptionally audacious. Working-class urbanites were usually invited to move to new towns that were one or two dozen miles from their old homes. Thetford is more than eighty miles by road from central London.

How the townsfolk must have laughed at the ragged cockneys in the parade. But they were not really in a position to look down on anyone. In the nineteenth century, Thetford had hitched its fortunes to a single company, Charles Burrell & Sons, which made steam-powered traction engines. The rise of the internal combustion engine did for Burrell's, throwing many men out of work. They could hardly fall back on farming. The soils around Thetford are poor, and in the 1920s and 1930s a pine forest had been planted on the western side of the town. At a time of rapid national population growth, Thetford was barely able to keep its numbers steady. The only way to revive the town, its leaders decided, was to take some of the workers and industries that London did not want.

Thetford's officials reckoned that, if they built thousands of new council homes with money from what was then London County Council, and provided premises for firms, Londoners would be happy to move out of the city. They were right. One of the early migrants was Thelma Paines, who moved from Elephant and Castle in south London to Thetford in 1962. When I interviewed her a few years ago, she retained something of the Londoner's contempt for provincial craftsmanship. As she remembered, her newly built house was so poorly insulated that condensation froze on the inside of the walls and she had to dress up to go to bed.

Still, the house seemed to her like paradise. With a private indoor bathroom, it was far superior to her old digs in the capital.

It was a good thing the houses were so nice, and so convenient for the factories, because the work itself was a disappointment. Jobs were easy enough to find in Thetford: in the mid-1960s, just a handful of people in the town were unemployed. And the Londoners were at first paid more than local people for doing the same work. Yet many of the men who moved from London to Thetford had to accept pay cuts. In 1971, Malcolm Moseley, a researcher, conducted hundreds of interviews in Thetford. Although the majority of the people he spoke to described their houses as very good, a mere 4 per cent said the same of men's wages. The migrants had chosen a better quality of life and had made themselves poorer.

For a while, the cockneys remained tied to London, returning frequently to visit their relatives. As they settled down in their new homes and made friends, the trips became less frequent. But they did not fully blend in to the quiet Norfolk life. After five or six decades, they still have not. Instead, the migrants boiled the working-class London culture they had brought with them until it became a concentrated broth. You can see this in their funerals, which are lavishly cockney, with horse-drawn carriages, great sprays of flowers and shiny black gravestones. You can see it in their football allegiances. Many Thetfordians shun Ipswich and Norwich City, the best local teams, in favour of London clubs like Queen's Park Rangers and West Ham. Above all, you can still hear it in their voices.

Especially in the council estates that ring the town, Thetfordians speak old-fashioned London cockney – the throaty, sandpaper accent of the actor Ray Winstone and the late singer Amy Winehouse. When saying 'Thetford', a local will begin with an F sound, as in 'fed', and will glottal-stop the middle T. A Thetford poet could rhyme 'arrow' with 'Mo Farah'. Thetfordians say 'proper' when they mean very, or really. 'Oi oi' is fine as a greeting; 'see ya later' is the standard goodbye. You do not tell people off, but have a go at them, or give them grief. People in other parts of south-east England, such as Essex, speak similarly. But there is something peculiarly old-fashioned about Thetford speech. I grew up in north London in the 1970s. No accent reminds me so strongly of my childhood as the Thetford one.

After the working-class Londoners moved to Thetford, the accent of the city they had left began to change. In the early years of this century, linguists identified a new accent that blended cockney, West Indian, African and Asian sounds and words. They called it Multicultural London English. MLE has some distinctive vowel sounds, including something wonderfully called 'extreme goose-fronting'. To make an 'oo' sound in a word like 'goose', a speaker pushes her tongue and lips forward, as though preparing to kiss someone she is not sure about. Some consonants sound different, too. Cockneys tend to drop the H at the beginning of words, rendering 'heavy' as 'evvy'. MLE speakers hit the H hard. To hear the difference, listen to an interview with Winstone or Winehouse, and then listen to an interview with an MLE speaker like John Boyega or Taz Skylar, both of them actors. MLE is spreading across England, mutating as it goes; it has even reached Thetford. But cockney dominates still.

The original inhabitants of Thetford sometimes found the cockneys hard going. Stuart Wright, a man from a Norfolk family who has served as a local councillor, remembers that some of the new arrivals dug up his grandfather's potatoes. When challenged over that, they were affronted. Spuds just grow naturally, don't they? Even some of the migrants were astonished by their fellow Londoners' lairiness. Danny Jeffrey, who moved from east London to work at Jeyes, a maker of cleaning products, eventually stopped drinking in the Londoners' pubs because of all the fights. 'You know cockneys,' he told me. 'Very full of themselves.'

Another thing arrived with the Londoners – an attitude to family and work that seemed exotic in mid-twentieth-century Norfolk. Local newspaper reporters at first assumed that only the men from London would take jobs. In April 1959, the *Thetford & Watton Times* reported that forty or so Londoners had travelled to Thetford to see their almost-finished homes and examine 'the factory in which the husbands will soon be working'. The reporters referred to the London wives as 'housewives'. They were soon surprised to discover that, in one metal-working factory, two fifths of the employees were women. Londoners of both sexes worked in Thetford, sometimes in alternate shifts so that one partner could watch the children. Occasionally it was the wives who took jobs in Thetford factories and their husbands who came along with them. That was true for Brenda Canham, latterly Thetford's mayor, whose husband was injured and unable to work when she moved from east London to work in a factory that made insulated Thermos flasks.

If they had wanted to, the Londoners who moved to Thetford could have adopted local habits. They could have switched allegiance to Norwich City Football Club. They could have settled for modest funerals. Many of the London settlers came not from the East End, home of the cockney funeral, but from north, south and west London. They moved to Norfolk and turned into East Enders. And, although the London migrants were probably stuck with their accents, their Norfolk-born children and grandchildren could have dropped the cockney. Instead, many speak it more strongly than their parents do. Their culture is an act of creation.

Frankie Dean has done more than most people to define and shape Thetford culture. He grew up in the town, as the son of migrants from north and west London, and moved to one of the first council houses built for a London migrant. When not working his day job, Dean is a rapper known as Franko Fraize. He raps about utterly ordinary things such as a check shirt that he really likes, watching *Eastenders* with a cup of tea, and the agony of supporting the England football team (his song 'Underdog' inspired the title of this book). The video for one of his songs, 'Hand me downs', shows him going out to buy a pint of milk. 'Oi oi!' is a hymn to Thetford council-estate life with all the trimmings: white trainers, Adidas threads, boxing gloves, satellite dish, kebab shop.

It is hard to rap in cockney, which is less precise and percussive than Multicultural London English. But Dean is determined to sound different from other British rappers. He wants to represent his home town, of which he is immensely proud. He feels that rapping in MLE would sound odd and inauthentic, and fears that it would appeal neither to his neighbours in Thetford nor to big-city-dwellers. He also wants to remind Londoners of the world they have lost. 'When I go to London, it's like I'm bringing their culture back to them,' he says. His cockney accent is utterly authentic, but it is also a badge and a sales pitch.

Thetfordians behave in ways that echo the culture of London when it was largely white and working class, and they do these things self-consciously, as a way of asserting their identity as exiles from a world that has disappeared. Just as Taiwanese people nurture Chinese cultural practices that are dying out on the mainland, such as traditional written characters, the people of Thetford cling to the old London. They are hyper-Londoners. For Canham, for example, a key aspect of the old East End culture was not locking your door. By the time she left London that had become impossible, but it was possible in Thetford. She describes the estate where she lives as 'a bit of the old London', especially on summer evenings, when residents assemble for impromptu games of football and toddlers stagger around in nappies. Dean loves to go out to restaurants in nearby towns and make a happy cockney racket with friends and family.

Rhymney has been a white, working-class town for longer than anybody can remember. Wythenshawe was mostly white and working class, but it is growing less so. Thetford has gone the other way. It is almost certainly more working class today than it would be if the Londoners had never arrived. Cambridge and Norwich are both successful cities with high house prices. Thetford, which is halfway between the two, would probably have become a dormitory town for middle-class commuters if the council had not cut a deal with London in the 1950s. It would have been duller, in my view.

Thetford is deeply strange, but not quite in a class by itself. White working-class people continue to nurture old customs in other parts of Britain too. I once spent a delightful morning interviewing people in Harts Holiday Park, a caravan and mobile-home site in the Isle of Sheppey, in Kent. Many of the residents turned out to be migrants from south-east London. One man, who used to build blades for wind turbines before illness forced him to stop, was tired and hung-over after staying up late the previous night drinking and singing Christmas songs. That surprised me, because it was November. But he explained that he and the other residents were obliged to return to London because people were not allowed to live in the holiday park all year round. They had got their Christmas celebrations in early. After a while, his friend, a retired building-site manager, turned up, and the man told me how they had met. After moving to the holiday park, he kept seeing someone who seemed familiar ('I'm sure I've seen that feller somewhere'). It turned out that both came from the same tiny area of south London. They had reconstructed a bit of the old capital on the windy Kent coast.

The people who colonized Thetford can sometimes be intolerant and xenophobic, especially towards the Portuguese migrants who began to arrive in the 1990s to work in packing houses and factories. In 2004, the England men's football team played Portugal in the quarter finals of the European Championship. After England lost on penalties, a Portuguese pub in the middle of Thetford was attacked by irate natives. Thetford's politics have a nativist tinge, too. The town's working-class residents had once made Thetford a Labour redoubt in a Conservative region. But the town had drifted rightward by the turn of the century, and in 2015 the United Kingdom Independence Party won more votes than any other party in two of Thetford's four wards. A year later, the electoral district that includes Thetford voted to leave the EU by two-to-one.

Still, Thetford seems to resist becoming a xenophobic, little-England sort of place. If it slid that way, it would be contravening another cockney ideal – the spirit of mongrelism. Thetfordians are brusque rather than bitter. Carla Barreto, a Portuguese woman who lived in Canada before coming to Thetford, tells me that the Londoners are broadly comfortable with diversity, and have even helped to soften up the locals. In May 2019, she was elected to the town council as an independent. Knocking on doors, she listened to people complain about the EU, then declare that she seemed all right. 'We don't get much grief these days,' confirms a Portuguese-speaking teenage boy in a Thetford school, who has acquired a flawless 1970s London accent.

The people who moved from London to Thetford retain a consciousness of themselves as transplants and outsiders, and they have passed this identity on to their children. Fully half a century after the policy of decanting working-class urbanites to new towns ended, they continue to use the word 'overspill' to describe themselves. That awareness of their own history as migrants takes the edge off any xenophobic instincts they might have. In half a dozen trips to Thetford, I have never heard anyone complain that immigrants are failing to assimilate. Perhaps that is fortunate. I would have laughed at the irony, at which point I might have discovered that the cockneys of Thetford are just as lairy as they used to be.

*

The point of this three-stop tour is not only to show that places containing many white working-class people can differ profoundly from each other, although it is always good to keep that in mind. Rhymney, Wythenshawe and Thetford might look similar to a statistician. They are all mostly white and British, they are all largely working class, and they all send few young people to university. The impression of sameness dissolves as soon as their residents start talking. That is why Ferdynand Zweig hared around Britain, dropping in on different places. It is why I am wary of people who draw sweeping conclusions about the whole country from their knowledge of a single place, however deep it may be.

I would also like to make a bolder claim: different places actually give rise to different identities. Heartland areas contain working-class people whose consciousness of themselves as white Britons surfaces rarely. A common worry in these areas is that too many people are leaving. In enclaves the concern is generally the opposite: too many people are coming. And, since the newcomers are often immigrants or members of minority ethnic groups, people in enclaves are more inclined to think of themselves as working-class white Britons. Colonies like Thetford are similar to enclaves, but their inhabitants are aware of their special status as migrants and strangers, which gives them a different outlook.

White working-class people living in different parts of Britain might differ even more than white middle-class people do. And the middle classes are varied enough. A middle-class Londoner is not the same as a middle-class Thetfordian. To the extent that the term 'metropolitan elite' means anything at all, it points to the fact that upper-middle-class people living in large metropolises differ from their equivalents in small towns and villages. They are more likely to be advertising executives or barristers than Barbour-jacketed, Hunter-booted landowners; they might be more aware of the seasons at the Metropolitan Opera in New York than of the pheasant-shooting season; they might be more left wing. But the middle-class tribes of Britain are at least aware of each other, because they tend to meet at university. Working-class people really can be strangers to each other.

In practice, the categories I have described blur into each other. Places can have some characteristics of heartlands and some characteristics of enclaves or colonies. I think this is true of Edlington, a former coal-mining town in Yorkshire, which I describe in Chapter Seven. Needless to say, even places in the same category are not identical in every way. Still, I believe it is helpful to keep the simple three-part distinction in mind. In the rest of this book, I will often describe places as belonging to one category or another. I begin in a heartland area that has a big problem.

Chapter Two

Education and its discontents

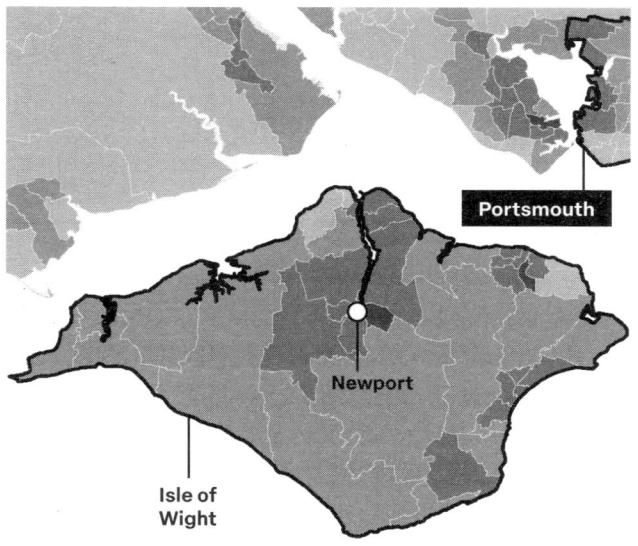

It is Facebook territory. Everyone on the Isle of Wight seems to have an account. Even teenagers rely on it: one girl, who moved to the island from south London, tells me with amazement that her new friends use it in preference to Instagram. If you run a small business on the Isle of Wight, a scathing review on the social network can be a catastrophe. A young hairdresser says that he often spends twenty minutes photographing his handi-work, making sure every hair is in place and the lighting is exactly right. Then he uploads the pictures to Facebook.

My teenage children would no sooner log into Facebook than

they would join a lawn-bowls club or wear a tweed jacket, and for the same reason. To them, Facebook is a historical relic, a website for their parents or even their grandparents. The social media that matter to them and their friends are Discord, Snapchat, TikTok and WhatsApp (they also spend an inordinate amount of time watching YouTube videos). But then, my children live in the place that people in the Isle of Wight call 'the big island' or 'the north island' – that is, mainland Britain. As islanders are well aware, their home is several years behind the rest of the country. The crab-shaped island in the English Channel, twenty-three miles by thirteen, is England with a time delay.

It wasn't always so. For a spell in the second half of the nineteenth century, the Isle of Wight was at the cutting edge. Queen Victoria and Prince Albert acquired an estate there, which attracted artists and writers. Alfred, Lord Tennyson bought a house, as did Julia Margaret Cameron, a portrait photographer who showed what could be done with the new medium. Lewis Carroll, Charles Darwin, Karl Marx and other luminaries drifted in and out. But the Isle of Wight gradually turned into a combination of bucket-and-spade holiday resort and retirement home. Although it occasionally seems posh, especially during Cowes Week, a sailing regatta with a long history, it is one of the most working-class places in southern England. Fully 95 per cent of its inhabitants are white Britons. It is a sunny heartland.

In some ways, the backwardness of the Isle of Wight is benign. Its inhabitants are relaxed and charming, in a slightly old-fashioned way. It barely suffers from the violent, exploitative 'county lines' drug-running operations that plague many towns and cities in the north island. But the island also lags behind in a much less delightful sense. Its young people fare very badly in school. Department for Education statistics show that, in 2023, just 36 per cent managed to get a grade 5 or higher in both English and maths in the GCSE exams that they took at age sixteen (a grade 5 is roughly equivalent to a C grade in the system that existed before 2020). Children in every one of London's thirty-two boroughs did better. England has 152 local education authorities. In only twelve do teenagers score worse in exams than they do on the Isle of Wight.

This failing is widely acknowledged and much discussed on the island. The local press reports on it frankly, even gleefully. When islanders talk about exam results, they use words like 'terrible' and 'disaster'. The Isle of Wight has a High Sheriff – an honorary office occupied by a new person every year. When I was researching this book, the High Sheriff was Dawn Haig-Thomas, a management consultant who had branched out into international development. I went to see her in a beautiful manor house in East Cowes, where she told me that her focus was on literacy. Children leave primary schools on the island with lower levels of basic literacy than the English average, which plainly exasperated her: 'How are we not good at literacy here? There's only one language spoken, for goodness' sake!' She was encouraging adults to go into their local schools to read with children, and doing so herself.

Islanders put forward many explanations for their teenagers' poor performance. Perhaps the smallness of the schools is to blame, they say. The island lacks a dominant city – its 140,000 inhabitants are scattered among small towns and villages – and some primary schools admit thirty or fewer pupils each year. Perhaps schools are still perturbed by the big reorganization of the island's education system which happened around 2010, when it went from three stages (primary school, middle school, high school) to two stages (primary school, secondary school). Perhaps it is too hard to persuade great teachers and school leaders to move to the island. Perhaps, perhaps, perhaps. I see the situation differently. To me, the Isle of Wight points to a bigger pattern. Places that are largely white and working class tend to get poor exam results.

*

In 2005, while trawling English education data as a newly hired journalist at *The Economist*, I noticed something. On average, white British pupils in state schools performed better in GCSE exams than children from several ethnic-minority groups. Although they did not do as well as Chinese or Indian pupils, they fared better than Afro-Caribbeans, black Africans, Bangladeshis or Pakistanis on the measure that was then regarded as most important: the proportion getting C grades or higher in English, maths and at least three other subjects. But if you looked just at children entitled to free school meals because of their parents' poverty, the picture was different. Among that deprived population, white Britons fared worse than everyone except members of the white Gypsy and Irish Traveller ethnic group.

The prevailing view was that no children were doing worse at school than those of Afro-Caribbean heritage. Trevor Phillips, who was then chairman of the Commission for Racial Equality, suggested in a television programme that drastic action ought to be taken to improve their performance, such as fining parents who failed to turn up to parents' evenings and perhaps even teaching black children separately. I wrote an article arguing that Sir Trevor (as he now is) had built his case on a false premise. Afro-Caribbean children did badly in exams, but that seemed to be because so many of them were poor, and poverty is a huge disadvantage. If you crudely controlled for poverty by focusing on children who were entitled to free school meals, they no longer looked like the biggest failures in the education system. White British children were faring worse.

My argument about Afro-Caribbean teenagers was wrong – of which more in a moment. But my observation about the dismal school performance of white British children from poor families was not. And it turned out that many people were struck by the statistics. Other journalists wrote articles similar to mine. In 2014, the House of Commons education committee published a report, 'Underachievement in Education by White Working Class Children'. Eight years later, the situation had not improved, so the committee had another crack at the same subject. Over the years, the once-obscure tables of GCSE results by ethnicity and entitlement to free school meals have become familiar. Today, when journalists and politicians argue that white working-class Britons are doing badly, they often point not to their jobs, their incomes, their health or their family lives, but to their children's educational performance.

Some people, particularly on the political left, are irked by the frequent repetition of these statistics, and quibble with them. They point out that not many white British children are entitled to free school meals – fewer than the proportion of children from many minority ethnic groups who are, because white Britons are less poor than other groups, and fewer than the proportion of children who would normally be seen as working class. About one quarter of state secondary-school pupils are entitled to free food. Roughly one third to one half of adults are working class, depending on your definition. So, if you take free school meals as your benchmark, you will miss many working-class children.

This criticism is not nearly as damning as the people who make it seem to think, however. Researchers have tried using different measures of social disadvantage, only to reach almost identical conclusions. White British children entitled to free school meals; working-class white British children: it doesn't matter. They do very badly in their GCSEs.

A 2014 paper by Steve Strand of Oxford University, 'Ethnicity, Gender, Social Class and Achievement Gaps at Age 16', shows exactly what is going on. Strand creates a single measure of social and economic disadvantage by weighing several things: whether a child is eligible for free school meals, what jobs his or her parents do and their levels of education, what kind of neighbourhood the child lives in, and whether he or she lives in a rented home. Sadly, though not at all surprisingly, children who are disadvantaged according to this yardstick do worse in their GCSEs than children from more privileged backgrounds. Equally unsurprisingly, this is true for every ethnic group. The offspring of better-off Indian parents do better than the offspring of worse-off Indian parents, and so on.

A bit more surprisingly, though, Strand shows that social advantages and disadvantages affect young people from different ethnic backgrounds in different ways. Two groups stick out. Among Afro-Caribbean children, the achievement gap between the more and the less privileged is unusually small. That is, better-off Afro-Caribbean children do surprisingly badly in their GCSEs. I was completely wrong to diminish their problems in 2005. The school performance of Afro-Caribbean children, especially boys, deserves more attention than it is getting today. It is a complex problem, which owes something to teachers' reluctance to see academic aptitude in those children and something to the speed with which black boys are labelled as troublemakers. But 'complex' should not mean 'impossible to solve'.

White British children stick out for the opposite reason. Social and economic disadvantage seems to make an enormous difference for them. Privileged white British children do just fine at school, whereas their poorer counterparts do very badly indeed. It is as though poverty is a virus that harms all children, but white Britons run an exceptionally high fever. Strand's research also reveals when the problems kick in. At the age of eleven, disadvantaged white Britons are not doing all that badly compared with similar pupils from other ethnic backgrounds. By the age of fourteen, they have started to slip back, and by the age of sixteen, they have fallen well behind. The problem of white working-class underachievement is mostly a teenage problem.

Working-class white Britons now do so badly in their GCSEs, relative to working-class teenagers from other ethnic groups, that they have dragged down the average for white Britons as a whole. The crude ethnic pattern has changed a lot since I wrote my article in 2005. In the past two decades, Bangladeshi, black African and Pakistani pupils have all overhauled white Britons. That is, a higher proportion of Bangladeshi, black African and Pakistani pupils now manage to get decent results in their GCSEs even though they are more likely to be from poor families (Chinese and Indian pupils are miles ahead of everyone else, as they were two decades ago). Of all the major ethnic groups, only black Caribbean pupils now fare worse than white Britons at school.

This is an astonishing change, and it seems even more astonishing when you look a little further back in time. In the mid-1980s, the British government asked Michael Swann, a biologist who had been made a peer, a BBC chairman and an all-round worthy, to write a report about minority ethnic pupils. Lord Swann struggled to reach firm conclusions in his report, 'Education for All', because the education statistics were so poor. But he concluded that Afro-Caribbeans were doing very badly in school, and that Asians as a whole were faring no better than white children. When he looked more closely at the second group, he saw huge variety. Whereas children from Indian backgrounds seemed to be thriving, Bangladeshi children were 'seriously underachieving'. An education official in London, where most Bangladeshis lived, suggested to Lord Swann that they had poor English skills and were surrounded by poverty and racism. It probably did not help that some children were whisked off to Bangladesh for extended periods by their parents.

The pattern that Lord Swann described seems as peculiar today as do other aspects of mid-1980s life, such as video nasties and cheese hedgehogs. London's schools have gone from being objects of pity in England to objects of envy. Children from minority ethnic backgrounds are doing much better than they were, Bangladeshi children astoundingly so. Many Bangladeshi families are poor – along with Pakistanis, they have the joint-lowest household income after housing costs of any ethnic group. But Bangladeshi teenagers started getting better GCSE results than white British teenagers in 2011, and the gap has grown wider and wider since then. As with all ethnic groups, Bangladeshi girls do even better than boys.

If GCSE results vary quite a bit by ethnic group, university campuses have become more skewed. In England, the proportion of white eighteen-year-olds from state schools who go to university is lower than for every other ethnic group – again, without adjusting for deprivation. Some universities have changed quickly in the past few years. Aston University in the West Midlands enrolled 505 white British undergraduates in 2023, fewer than it had ten years earlier. In the same period, the number of newly enrolled British Asian students jumped from 1,090 to 1,735 and the number of black British students rose from to 240 to 650.

Black and Asian students often go to less selective 'recruiting' universities, including the former polytechnics. But they are also moving into more prestigious places, including members of the elite Russell Group. The pattern is uneven across the country. Many Asian students attend nearby universities and live at home: a study for the Sutton Trust in 2018 found that this was true for 66 per cent of those from Pakistani backgrounds and 71 per cent of those from Bangladeshi backgrounds, compared with just 19 per cent of students from white backgrounds. As a result, universities in ethnically diverse parts of the country look very different from those in largely white areas. Newcastle University, a good institution in a mostly white part of England, still has an overwhelmingly white intake. The University of Leicester, a good institution in a diverse city, does not. Ten years ago, Leicester took in more than three times as many white as Asian students. Today, the two groups are about equal in number.

Britons sometimes talk about the superior academic performance of pupils from ethnic-minority backgrounds as though it is normal and expected. It really isn't. It was not the case a few decades ago. It also doesn't appear to be the case in other countries. The Organisation for Economic Co-operation and Development, a think tank based in Paris, tests a sample of fifteen-year-olds in many countries. The OECD's reports do not distinguish between ethnic groups; many European countries are more squeamish about collecting such data than Britain is, partly because they have sharper memories of fascism and fear what a government might do with such information. But the think tank does distinguish between the children of immigrants and everybody else. In many countries, immigrants' children do much worse than the children of natives in tests of maths and reading; the gaps in Germany and Sweden are especially big. In Britain, the two groups fare about the same, and immigrants' children do better after you control for poverty and language skills.

Something is happening to white British teenagers from working-class backgrounds that makes them perform badly at school and prevents them from going to university. Whatever it is, this thing happens less to working-class teenagers from other ethnic groups and to middle-class white teenagers. It happens not in the dark but in the light. Journalists have written over and over about the phenomenon of white working-class underachievement; politicians have investigated it; educationalists have quantified it. But nobody has quite managed to explain what causes it. I think you can get a pretty good idea by hopping on a ferry to the Isle of Wight.

*

One sunny morning, I sit down with a woman who I will call Jennifer. She grew up in Newport, a town of 25,000 people that is roughly in the middle of the island. Her mother works in the local hospital, her father in the building industry. Neither of them shone in the classroom, and Jennifer didn't either. 'I never got much out of school,' she says. 'The most important thing that I got were some really good friendships.' She describes scraping a few marks in her French GCSE oral exam by reciting a Kylie Minogue lyric. After leaving school, she trained as a hairdresser, but decided after a couple of years that she didn't like it. She went on to do various jobs that she describes as dull, including working in a cafe, before getting one that she enjoys.

Jennifer's son has struggled, too. He did well in primary school, but then the teenage years hit, 'and they really hit.' Now, he is 'a lad', scoring poorly in tests and frequently in trouble. Jennifer often receives phone calls from her son's school, complaining about his behaviour. She believes that the school has done badly by him, and has become biased against him. It sounds like a tense relationship. The day before we met, she received a text message informing her that her son had been sentenced to after-school detention because he had been truanting. She argues that this was unfair. Her son had not been truanting; he had been attending a funeral with her.

In Jennifer's family, educational failure passes down the generations. Her parents' poor experiences at school affected her. Her poor experience affects her son: 'If my son asks me for help with his homework, I look at it and say, "What? What the hell does that mean?"' She knows well where this leads. When a teenager does poorly in national exams, doors that he or she might have walked through are slammed shut. It happened to her: she wanted to train as a secretary, but did not achieve good enough marks. 'You can't have a career unless you have English and maths,' she says, definitively. By 'have', she means nothing more than a passing grade.

I hear stories like this over and over again on the Isle of Wight. The children of white working-class parents start school full of confidence, but they begin to fall back in their teens and end up performing badly in exams. Those who set out with bold ambitions trim them. They end up in jobs that are sometimes poorly paid, sometimes a bit better paid, but are invariably working class. The falling-off in teenagers' expectations can be abrupt and perplexing. One girl tells me that, until recently, she had wanted to be a vet. But her mother works in the hospitality industry, and her friend had decided to train as a chef. Her friend asked if she would like to join the catering course, and she said yes. Now, she plans to work in a restaurant. This is a drastic change of plan. Becoming a vet is incredibly hard – it is among the most competitive professions in Britain, and involves many years of study. I ask her, 'Were you doing well in school?' She says that she was. But, as soon as she decided to go into catering, her grades began to slide.

After the Second World War, the Isle of Wight became a slightly improbable hub for aerospace engineering. Hovercrafts were developed partly on the island. They zip to and from the mainland today, carrying passengers in a hurry, while cheapskates like me take the slow boats. In the west, a spectacular peninsula known as the Needles became a testing centre for rockets. A few engineering firms still operate on the Isle of Wight, including GKN, which makes aeroplane parts there, and Vestas, a Danish manufacturer of wind turbines. But the economy has come to rest heavily on retail, tourism, construction and care homes. 'Shops, care, hospitality – there isn't much,' says a young woman from Newport who works as a cleaner. And the lack of employment options on the island can make it hard to imagine doing anything else. The cleaner's young son has told her that he wants to be an inventor, but she thinks it highly unlikely that he will become one. Then she utters one of the most painful sentences I have ever heard: 'I was aspirational too, until I realized there isn't much to aspire to.'

Politicians and officials have sometimes assumed that the big problem with working-class children, especially white British ones, is that they do not have high aspirations. A policy paper on teaching released in 2010 was typical. 'In far too many communities,' it argued, 'there is a deeply embedded culture of low aspiration that is strongly tied to long-term unemployment.' It is also believed that low aspirations lead to poor exam results – and, therefore, that results would improve if aspirations could be raised. These convictions explain why, every year, universities invite pupils from poor neighbourhoods to their campuses and send some of their students to talk to pupils in poor areas. If only more disadvantaged teenagers hoped to go to university and had a better sense of the doors that might open for them, the thinking goes, they would do better in school.

It does nobody any harm, and it might even help a little, if pupils from poor places spend a day on a university campus. But the notions driving these outreach efforts are questionable. Most young children have high aspirations, whatever their backgrounds. A startlingly large share aspire to go to university – far higher than the proportion of jobs that require graduates. One study by Will Baker and others in 2014 found that just 2 per cent of fourteen-year-olds believed that going to university was not at all important. A working-class child from the Isle of Wight who wants to be an inventor is perfectly normal.

What children on the Isle of Wight lack is not high aspirations but high expectations. The two things are quite different. To aspire to something is to hope for it, or long for it; to expect something is to wait for it, knowing that it is coming. A child might hope to go to university, or to become an inventor, but not think that this is at all likely to happen. It seems that, in order to succeed at school, it is best to have both. Nabil Khattab, a sociologist at the University of Bristol, has shown that 36 per cent of thirteen- and fourteen-year-olds with high aspirations but low expectations went on to obtain five good GCSEs, compared with 68 per cent of those with high aspirations and high expectations.

One person with first-hand experience of this is Ros Parker, principal of the Isle of Wight College in Newport. Her college has more than 1,000 young full-time students learning things like engineering, animal care and food preparation, or doing apprenticeships. Some are brushing up their English and maths because they failed to obtain passing grades in those subjects at GCSE. Parker is a remarkable woman. She left school without any qualifications and became a single mother who sometimes wondered where the next meal was coming from. Then she returned to the classroom by taking a creative-writing course, and gradually worked her way up through the further-education system. 'Aspiration isn't the issue' with her students, she says flatly. 'Sometimes they've got low expectations of themselves, but high aspirations about what they want to do.' They dream big but anticipate little. Sometimes, sad to say, their parents expect little for them.

Before she moved to the Isle of Wight, Parker ran a college in

Southend-on-Sea, in Essex. That was a tough gig. Southend has a higher crime rate than the island – or many parts of Essex, for that matter. Parker says that it took several years, and heavy investment in security guards, before the campus came to feel truly safe. Still, she says that her students in Southend always felt connected to London and its many opportunities, which were only a short train ride away. Newport is further from a thriving city, and it feels even further away than it really is.

The Solent, which separates the Isle of Wight from the English mainland, is only about three miles wide and is crossed frequently by ferries. To young islanders, it nonetheless seems like the Atlantic Ocean. One former headteacher on the island describes the Solent as a mental as well as a physical barrier. Some children cross it only rarely: 'We took some kids for a school trip to Hastings. Some had not left the island for five years, and the last time they went was on another school trip.'

The former headteacher says it is almost as though children fall into two groups: those who are content to stay on the island and those who are committed to leaving. Young people say almost exactly the same thing. 'You get the odd one who's determined to move off the island,' says a young woman who left school at sixteen and now works in a horse-riding centre. In her secondary school, the would-be leavers stuck out: they were the ones who joined clubs and seemed keener on learning. Her current job brings her into contact with the public, and she believes she can tell the difference between long-time islanders and newcomers. The latter come across as harder-edged, more determined. She seems to envy them. Although she has found a job on the island that she enjoys, some of her friends who stuck around are doing 'not a lot'.

Because the Isle of Wight has no university, migration, education and economic opportunity are all braided together. A young person who wants to get a degree must leave, at least for a few years. And the reverse is more or less true, too. A young person who wants to remain on the island after leaving school forgoes higher education, and thereby lets slip their best chance of penetrating the middle class. Leaving or not leaving the island is a binary choice with cascading consequences, some of which are felt before a child actually grows old enough to migrate across the Solent. If you feel bound to the island, why knock yourself out revising for that French test?

The most obvious way to tie the Isle of Wight more tightly to the mainland would be to build a bridge, known locally as a 'fixed link'. That idea has fervent supporters, though not enough of them. It would bring a wider range of jobs and educational opportunities within islanders' reach, but also, it is feared, generate more traffic, more crime and more house-building. As the island's population grows older and more cautious, a fixed link seems ever less likely. All the authorities can do for now is to try to blur the distinction between the mainland and the island. It is now possible to take some university-level courses at the Isle of Wight College. Parker is talking to mainland universities about the possibility of letting islanders start their courses remotely, then slide gradually over to campus. Anything to make the big island across the Solent seem less alien.

The Isle of Wight is geographically isolated, by English or Welsh standards, although a Scottish islander might wonder what all the fuss is about. In John Wyndham's novel *The Day of the Triffids*, the hardy band of humans who manage to dodge disease and man-eating plants retreat to the island for that reason. But other parts of England and Wales feel almost as cut off. Rhymney might as well be an island, considering the distance you have to travel to reach a university or a wide range of jobs. It is sixteen miles by road from the University of South Wales campus in Pontypridd and twenty-five miles from the University of Cardiff. The East Anglian coast and the north coast of Cornwall are almost university-free zones. Not surprisingly, all have low rates of university-going. When distance is added to the many other difficulties of higher education, including cost and stressfulness, it can become too much for young people.

*

A bachelor's degree is not the only route to a rewarding job. Vocational courses and apprenticeships like the ones offered by the Isle of Wight College work just as well for some young people, or even better. Some high-level vocational qualifications boost earnings by more than the average degree does, for a few years at least. For some people, going to university turns out to be pointless, or so it occasionally seems on the Isle of Wight. 'I know people who did well at school, they did A levels, they even went to university, and now they're working in KFC,' says Jennifer, a touch smugly.

But if higher education is not the only route to a good career, it is a pretty reliable one. The average degree-holder continues to earn more than the average person without a degree, even as BAs grow as common as dandelions (it helps to attend a highly ranked university, and it helps a lot to study something that employers see as useful, such as computer science or economics). The benefits of university-going remain even when you adjust for academic aptitude. If you take two people who did equally well at school, the one who goes on to get a degree is likely to earn more. A series of dense but illuminating reports by the Institute for Fiscal Studies show that university graduates tend to see their incomes rise strongly through their thirties and even their forties, which is less true of non-graduates. And having a degree is almost the only way of landing a very high-paying job. Genuinely self-made

68

men and women, who leave school with nothing and end up rich, are rare.

Britain does higher education well. It has a wide range of institutions of different levels that specialize in different things, which attract great numbers of students from abroad every year. It does alternatives to university much less well. Politicians claim to value further education, but they seem to spend more of their time talking about universities, perhaps because their own children tend to go down that route (conservative populists, who grumble that universities are fostering a 'woke elite' and liken student unions to totalitarian dictators, are among the worst offenders). Further-education colleges are perpetually cash-strapped and struggle to hold onto instructors.

Worst of all is the meddling. Whereas sixth-form colleges and universities have mostly been left alone, the government has subjected further-education colleges to a series of discombobu-lating reforms. For years, many students took applied general qualifications, usually known as BTECs. These were useful in themselves, and they opened an alternative path to higher educa-tion, which many working-class students took. In 2018, the Social Market Foundation, a think tank, showed that 31 per cent of newly enrolled university students who were white and had working-class parents got in on the strength of BTECs rather than A levels. But, in 2021, the government announced it was scrapping BTECs and replacing them with new vocational qualifications called T levels. Two years later, unbelievably, it announced that it was abolishing T levels in favour of an entirely new qualification.

Apprenticeships have endured just as much reinvention and disruption over the years. They were common in the mid-twentieth century: in the 1960s, about one in three boys left school and became an apprentice. But they were criticized for imparting few useful skills, and, as the expectation that people would hold a job for life crumbled, they fell into desuetude. Then, in the 1990s, the government decided that apprenticeships needed to be buffed up. The state has tinkered with them ever since. England has had 'modern apprenticeships', 'national traineeships', 'foundation modern apprenticeships', 'advanced modern apprenticeships', 'advanced apprenticeships', plain old 'apprenticeships', 'intermediate apprenticeships', 'higher apprenticeships' and 'degree apprenticeships'. The current government promises new foundation apprenticeships. They still aren't as popular as they might be. Every year, three times as many young people start degree courses.

MPs and commentators sometimes argue that more young people would do vocational courses and apprenticeships if only Britons weren't so snobbish about them, and if the government weren't so determined to push people into universities. I doubt that very much. One problem with vocational qualifications and apprenticeships is that, thanks to the relentless meddling from above, their value is unclear. Everybody knows what a bachelor's degree is, whereas not everybody knows what a T level or a level-4 apprenticeship is. Another problem is that low-level apprenticeships can be pretty dismal. Many young people end up doing boring, repetitive jobs for little pay. About half of the people who begin apprenticeships do not complete them. If universities had a dropout rate anywhere near that level, it would be a national scandal.

Some apprenticeships are excellent – well designed, rigorous and highly competitive. But young people who perform badly at school are likely to find that those ones are out of reach. Nine tenths of the sixteen- to twenty-one-year-olds who start high-level apprenticeships managed to get at least five good GCSEs, including English and maths, suggesting they could have gone to university if they had wanted to. High-level apprentices are more likely to come from affluent places than from poor places. You might suppose that middle-class teenagers would all rush off to university, leaving good apprenticeships to their working-class peers, but in fact the middle classes snaffle the lot. Only a tiny proportion of young people from the poorest backgrounds make it onto the most demanding apprenticeships, which are equivalent to degree courses.

A young person in the Isle of Wight who feels that university is beyond his or her grasp is likely to feel the same way about a high-level apprenticeship. The Solent is a formidable barrier to both. One teenager studying at CECAMM, an engineering-oriented campus of the Isle of Wight College, tells me that he is trying to decide whether to pursue a career in engineering or work full-time as a barman (he is already a part-time barman on the island). Recently, he found what he calls a 'perfect' apprenticeship in mechanical engineering. But it was in Portsmouth, on the other side of the Solent, and he decided it was too far away.

Teenagers tend to see the world beyond school or college as exciting, yet filled with uncertainty and danger. Seeking safety, they are drawn to paths previously trodden by their parents. 'If Dad's a bricklayer, that's what the boys will do. If Mum's a teaching assistant, that's what the girls will do,' says a veteran leader of secondary schools in north-west England. If they do not follow their parents, young people may be influenced by aunts, uncles, cousins and friends. Or they simply try to do the jobs that they see around them. This is just as true for middle-class children as it is for working-class children. It was estimated a few years ago that a doctor's child is twenty-four times more likely to become a doctor than a child chosen at random. That is not a happy thought if you're about to have a complicated operation and need the best possible surgeon.

Sammy Wright, a head teacher in Sunderland who writes

insightfully about schools, sees this magnet-like phenomenon all the time. Sunderland used to be dominated by heavy industry, but its economy has changed. It now has as many jobs in health and social work as in manufacturing, and Wright's pupils are often drawn to those – as he puts it, 'You do what you see.' Even his most able pupils do not necessarily think about going to university. It is not that they are against it on principle; rather, they do not see the point. They know lots of people who seem to be living perfectly good lives, earning decent amounts of money, surrounded by friends and family, who did not go to university.

'We have ended up with a transactional model of education – if you do X, you will get Y,' Wright says. From a purely high-minded perspective, this is a great shame. Britain once had many institutions, such as the miners' libraries of South Wales, which were built on the conviction that working-class people hungered for learning for its own sake. And there is a practical problem, too. The transactional model does not impress people who see many examples of contented living among those who did not do X. 'Once you turn it into a transaction,' Wright says, 'you're inviting them to say no.'

If a working-class life in Sunderland strikes some teenagers as perfectly acceptable, a working-class life on the Isle of Wight probably seems even better. The weather is gorgeous. There are usually jobs to be had, especially in summer, when tourists arrive and the music festival kicks off. Your neighbours are likely to be congenial. The meanest streets in the entire island can be found in the Pan housing estate, east of Newport city centre, and they are not all that mean. Pan is poor; the local food bank, run out of Downside Community Centre, does a roaring trade. But serious crime is uncommon, the houses are decent, the streets are well kept, the air is clear and the views are fine.

It is easy to lament the compounding effects of low achievement and low expectations in white working-class areas. People do poorly at school, then send their children to the very same school, with much the same result. But a child who grows up in a place where her parents grew up has some advantages, too. She might well have a large network of friends and relatives. When a job comes up locally, she is likely to hear about it. For white working-class teenagers in the Isle of Wight, and in many other parts of Britain, higher education and middle-class jobs seem remote, in both senses of the word. They're jobs that they don't understand and jobs that are far away. But work of some kind is generally available, as are friends, family members and more-or-less affordable homes. The young woman who works in the riding centre has a simple explanation for why many of her classmates have stayed in the Isle of Wight. 'It's easy,' she says. 'They have family everywhere.'

In the sociological jargon, white working-class islanders have little bridging social capital (the kind of personal connections that help people get ahead in life) but plenty of bonding social capital (the kind of local connections that help them get by). Jennifer is a good example. Although a social scientist would call her disadvantaged, she is very far from being powerless. She is shrewd, charming, eloquent, and highly respected by those who know her. Handily, she also knows people in the building trade. It is because of her that her son has been able to secure weekend work on a building site. While working there, he has met various tradesmen, who have explained to him what they do. Recently, he decided that he wants to become a plumber. With his family's help and contacts, he seems quite likely to manage that.

*

To teenagers from ethnic-minority backgrounds, almost everything looks different. They are much more likely to live in cities, so they are close to universities and varied job markets. Half of all black Britons in England and Wales live in London. So do half of all Bangladeshis, although they are no longer crammed into a few districts of the old East End, as they were when Lord Swann wrote his gloomy report. Young people in the capital may well be poorer than their counterparts in the Isle of Wight, but higher education seems like a smaller step. Pupils in inner-city districts can easily be taken to visit companies, university campuses and museums. I see them often when I work in the British Library in central London, walking in sweet, well-drilled crocodiles.

Many black and Asian Britons are either immigrants or the children of immigrants. One third of black Caribbeans, about half of Bangladeshis, Indians and Pakistanis, and two thirds of black Africans were born outside the United Kingdom (the great majority of mixed-heritage people are British-born). That fact shapes their working lives and their attitudes to education. Immigrants often lack contacts, recognized qualifications and fluency in English, so they are forced to take a step or two down the occupational ladder – think of the taxi driver with a master's degree. They may be middle class in their heads, even as they do working-class jobs. And they will be damned if they allow their children to follow in their footsteps. Many Pakistanis drive taxis; many Bangladeshis work in restaurants. Such jobs have unsociable hours, low status and frequently pay little. Their homes are often cramped, and likely to be costly to boot. How can immigrants ensure that their children will have better lives than they do? The answer is obvious.

The stereotype of immigrants and ethnic-minority parents pushing their children to succeed in school is broadly accurate, although some are pushier than others. A report for the government's business department in 2015 found that two thirds of disadvantaged white parents expected their children to stay in education beyond the age of sixteen, compared with at least nine tenths of disadvantaged parents of Indian, Pakistani, Bangladeshi, black Caribbean and black African heritage. Research on what is known as the 'London advantage' – the mysterious fact that poor London children do so much better in exams than poor children in other parts of England – finds that it is caused almost entirely by ambitious pupils and parents from ethnic-minority backgrounds. Sometimes adults try to convince children that the advancement of an entire community depends on their academic success. I was once invited to an event put on by Somali immigrants in Leicester to celebrate their children's performance in exams. It was both inspiring and embarrassing. I was the only man not wearing a suit (in my defence, I had come straight from a boxing club), so I felt out of place and disrespectful. I slipped out as quickly as I could.

The wonderful thing about education, from the point of view of an ethnic-minority immigrant or an immigrant's child, is that it is blind. Racial prejudice may (and in fact does) exist in the classroom, but not in the examination hall. GCSE examiners do not know that a paper about Lady Macbeth was written by the daughter of a Pakistani immigrant in the East End of London. The government has mused about stripping names from university applications. And educational success helps immigrants and their children to overcome serious disadvantages. Minority ethnic adults definitely suffer discrimination in the job market: this is clear not only because they have worse jobs and lower wages than they should, given their qualifications, but also because researchers have created fictional job applicants with identical characteristics, and found that those with Asian- or African-sounding names are less likely to be invited for interviews. By doing well in exams, black and Asian Britons are attempting to compensate for racial bias.

Minority ethnic Britons often approach higher education differently from white Britons. They tend to live at home and commute to campus. They are drawn to courses that seem likely to lead directly to jobs, such as business, law or pharmacology, and are unlikely to study the creative arts. They strain to get a place somewhere, even at a recruiting university. They go even if their grades are barely adequate: black and Asian teenagers are more likely to start degrees than white Britons with identical grades. After they graduate, they often struggle to find jobs that make good use of their qualifications. Jack Britton, Lorraine Dearden and Ben Waltmann of the Institute of Fiscal Studies have shown that Bangladeshi, Pakistani, black Caribbean and black African men with degrees earn less than white Britons with degrees. Remarkably, and depressingly, a thirty-year-old Pakistani man who has gone to university earns only as much as a thirty-year-old white British man who has not gone.

For black and Asian Britons, a degree is generally a superb investment all the same. Although Pakistani men who go to university tend to earn rather little at first, Pakistani men who do not go to university earn such a pittance that the difference between having a degree and not is enormous. University boosts women's earnings even more than it boosts men's earnings. The researchers estimate that seven in ten white British men will see positive financial returns from higher education over the course of their lives, accounting for the years of full-time earnings lost while at university and the cost of repaying student loans. More than nine in ten Bangladeshi, Indian and Pakistani women can expect to see positive returns. The exact percentages will change over time as the student-loan system changes, but the gap between groups is likely to remain. For minority ethnic young people, especially women, doing an unglamorous degree such as computing or pharmacology at an unglamorous institution will probably remain an incredibly good use of money and time.

Given these facts, the big differences in GCSE performance

between white Britons and others begin to seem a little more understandable. Working-class black and Asian Britons, especially girls, simply must do well in school if they are to avoid lives of penury. They can see a route to a richer life that involves a spell in university, and they tend to take that route. Working-class white Britons, especially boys, need not do so well in order to achieve a decent standard of living. They can probably see a more attractive path than the one their friends and family are on, but it seems rather hazy and distant, and its rewards are uncertain.

If white British teenagers from working-class families do not always strive to obtain the grades necessary to go to university, it does not mean they are stupid or lazy. They have enough sense to see how the British job market works. They weigh their few options, and they make their decision. If they end up as plumbers or cleaners in the Isle of Wight, surrounded by family and friends, that is not such a tragedy.

I think it a pity, though. Low academic achievement is bad in itself, and it looks worse when you zoom out from individuals to consider families. Britons tend to talk about young people's performance at school, and their movement through the education system and the job market, as though they have neither ancestors nor descendants. A child is born deprived or not, succeeds at school or does not, starts an apprenticeship or a degree or not, and gets a well-paid job or not. But Britain is not a collection of individuals living separate lives. People are born into families; they breathe in ideas about learning and work from their earliest days, and their own children will learn from them. A small step up in education or training is an important achievement not only for the person who makes the step, but also because it allows their children to start on a slightly higher rung. It is probably too much to expect a truly deprived child to go to a top university and land a highly competitive job, although it is wonderful when this happens, and I believe that everything should be done to make such a heroic leap easier. It is not too much to expect that their child or their grandchild will manage it. That is what is not happening on the Isle of Wight.

Chapter Three

Council estate of mind

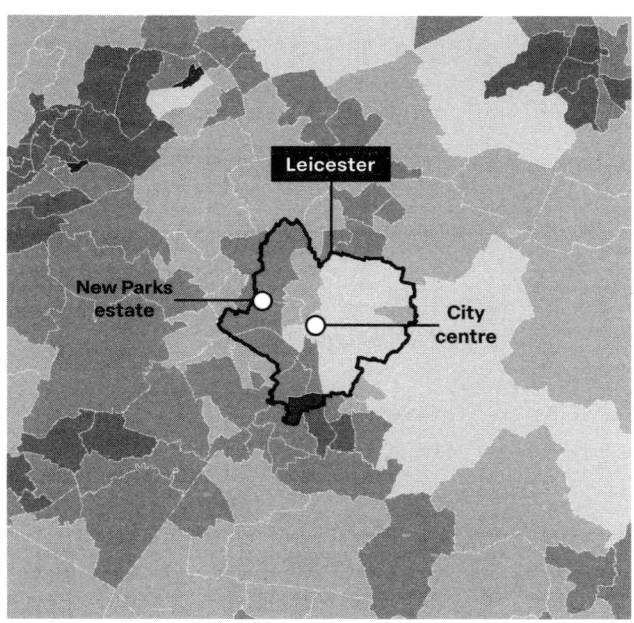

It is generally a bad sign when a criminologist shows an interest in the street where you live. But, by 1992, the inhabitants of the New Parks council estate in Leicester were probably not too surprised by the attention. In November and December of that year, questionnaires were pushed through the letterboxes of 1,750 homes in the estate, asking people about their experiences of burglary and other crimes. A second batch was delivered a year later. The two researchers behind the study, Roger Matthews and Julie Trickey of the University of Leicester, wanted to know whether burglars could be deterred by using techniques that had worked in other places, such as setting up Neighbourhood Watch groups and handing out superior door locks. They reached uncertain but rather disappointing conclusions, and their study has been largely forgotten. It does not reveal much about how to tackle burglary. But it does reveal a lot about New Parks. By accident, the researchers took a snapshot of a large suburban English council estate at its low ebb.

Half of the people in New Parks who received questionnaires filled them in. Their answers show that they were struggling. More than a fifth of the respondents turned out to be unemployed, and about the same share were single parents. Few were involved with local institutions such as the tenants' association, and many had become anxious and suspicious of their neighbours. Two fifths described themselves as very afraid of the teenagers who gathered on street corners. As one woman put it: 'Gangs of youths loiter late at night outside the Co-op on Aikman Avenue. This has been going on for years. The language they shout at you is really obscene.' Lots of people said they felt unsafe on that road, which was (and still is) the main shopping street in New Parks. Sadly, a quarter said they felt unsafe everywhere on the estate.

New Parks looks like any number of large English council estates built in the mid-twentieth century. Apart from a few blocks of flats near Aikman Avenue and some bungalows, homes are two storeys high. Most of the houses are arranged in blocks of two to four, on gently curving streets and cul-de-sacs, with gardens in front and behind. The estate sprawls languidly over a landscape that was once farmland. New Parks is divided into sections by boulevards, which are astonishingly wide. I struggle to think of how to describe the estate, until a local teenager sorts me out. 'It looks like America,' she says. And it does. New Parks is a typical English suburban council estate with just a hint of Levittown.

A burglar would immediately spot the problem with New Parks.

Council estate of mind

With so many semi-detached homes surrounded by gardens, most properties have several potential access points. Lots of the residents who responded to the criminologists' questionnaire said that their houses had been robbed, often more than once. The inhabitants of one street, Pool Road, reported fifteen burglaries in the previous year. That was almost certainly an undercount, since not every household received a questionnaire.

Victims of crime often believe that the offender must have come from outside the area – the idea that a predator lives nearby may be too terrible to contemplate. Not so the residents of New Parks in 1992. Half of them guessed that the people who had burgled their homes lived on the estate; startlingly, a quarter believed they knew who the offenders were. Those people turned out to be correct, as far as Matthews and Trickey could ascertain. With the help of the police, the researchers tracked down some burglars and interviewed them in a young offenders' institution and in two estate pubs, the Rocket and the Good Neighbours. All turned out to be drug users, and they were indeed local men. Very local, in fact. The report quoted one of them: 'I only break into houses near where I live, 'cos I haven't got a car so I have to carry everything home.'

The burglars usually crept into residents' back gardens, then used screwdrivers or similar tools to prise open ground-floor windows. They found it easy. One said that the window frames were so poorly constructed that they disintegrated under the slightest pressure. Doors were irrelevant, locks were irrelevant and, as a result, any attempt to reduce burglary by handing out better door locks was doomed to failure. Burglary fell slightly in New Parks in 1993. But Matthews and Trickey thought that was because some prolific offenders had been locked up, not because the scheme was working.

It was a disheartening result, and the picture of New Parks that has been preserved in the study is even more disheartening. A housing estate with more than 10,000 mostly working-class inhabitants was being preyed on by its own people. Crime, antisocial behaviour and fear were widespread. Neither the residents nor the authorities seemed to know how to restore order. The sorry state of New Parks in 1992 represented a terrible decline from the early days of the estate. If you had told the original inhabitants that their neighbourhood would come to such a pass less than half a century after the first key was handed to the first resident, they would not have believed you.

*

Council housing is not as ubiquitous as it used to be. In 1981, 32 per cent of English households occupied homes rented from the local council. Today, only 16 per cent live in 'social rented housing', a term that covers a variety of situations, including council housing, homes built by councils that were later transferred to non-profit housing associations, and privately built homes that have been acquired by social landlords. Many properties built by councils have been bought by their inhabitants or by investors. As a result, estates contain a mixture of tenures. One morning, I get into conversation with a group of women in New Parks who are watching their children play. All complain bitterly about the difficulty of obtaining a house on the estate. After a while, I realize that they are talking about renting homes from private landlords.

The 2021 census of England and Wales shows that just over a quarter of white working-class Britons live in social rented housing. That is not a huge share; more live in homes that they own outright, without a mortgage. Council estates (known in Scotland as 'schemes') are important to white working-class people all the same. Many, like the mothers I met in New Parks, rent privately or buy homes in the estates. And estates shape people's lives and identities more powerfully than mere neighbourhoods do. Judith Wray, a retired Methodist deacon who runs a charming drop-in social club in New Parks, has worked in estates all over England. She loves the way they provide a sense of identity: 'a sense of, this is where we are, this is who we are'. When older white working-class people summarize their lives, they sometimes end up ticking off a list of estates. A woman who has turned up to one of Wray's gatherings describes her childhood to me by saying: 'I was born in Braunstone. I went to Braunstone Frith when it was all new. My mother couldn't settle there, so she took me back to Braunstone. I went to New Parks at the age of fifteen.' She feels no need to explain to me, an outsider, where those three council estates are. Nor does she say where on the estates she lived, even though some of them are enormous. She does not say, 'I lived near the ring road' or 'I lived on the southern edge of Braunstone.' She mentions the estates as though they are self-contained entities. It is as though she is saying: 'I was born in Germany, then I moved to France, then Britain.'

Some people love living in New Parks. They praise its quietness, talk about the number of people they know there, and swear that they cannot imagine living anywhere else. Others hate the place – but they cannot imagine leaving, either. In the early 1990s, Matthews and Trickey found that hardly anybody was planning to push off, despite the crime and chaos around them. One white working-class woman in her thirties, who has lived in New Parks all her life, offers a brutal assessment of the estate today: 'It's a shithole . . . I've got to stay local to home, because you're not safe anywhere. Your items are not safe in your garden . . . No one hardly goes out now because they're too scared. You don't know if you're going to get robbed, stabbed, kidnapped . . . I'd love my kids to play out, I'd love my kids to go and explore, but they're not safe. But I'm not saying it's all bad. You do feel a part of here, you feel at home here. I couldn't ever come out of New Parks.'

I have omitted parts of our conversation, which was periodically interrupted by a hungry child. She nonetheless moves from 'it's a shithole' to 'I couldn't ever come out of New Parks' in just a few minutes. Her assertions about the level of crime (which are greatly exaggerated) sit alongside a commitment, or at least a resignation, to the estate. She feels despondent about it but can barely contemplate leaving, much as a person might despair about the state of Britain but not have any plans to emigrate.

Council estates are important in another, touchier way. They have long been lightning rods for working-class white Britons' feelings about how they are treated relative to immigrants and members of ethnic-minority groups. In 1969, the Institute of Race Relations released the results from a survey of three English towns (Bradford, Wolverhampton and Nottingham) and two London boroughs (Ealing and Lambeth). It turned out that 43 per cent of white people in those places believed that councils should not rent homes to non-white immigrants. Even more remarkably, 20 per cent persisted in this view even when they were told to imagine that the immigrants had spent a lot of time on a housing waiting list. The main reason they gave was that council homes should be reserved for 'our own people'. Jack Dash, a communist and trade unionist active in the 1960s, believed that more working-class people were drawn to far-right organizations because they were upset about council housing than because they thought immigrants were stealing their jobs. 'It wasn't on unemployment,' he said. 'Most of the fascist popularity came from housing.'

Today, many fewer people would argue that homes should be reserved entirely for natives. But those white working-class people who are inclined to believe that immigrants threaten their interests tend to put council houses at or near the top of their list of grievances. 'They're taking the houses' is still a more common complaint than 'they're taking the jobs', 'they're taking benefits' or 'they're taking school places'. Politicians and journalists have frequently indulged this view. 'We should look at policies where the legitimate sense of entitlement felt by the indigenous family overrides the legitimate need demonstrated by the new migrants', argued the Labour MP Margaret Hodge in 2007. The last government occasionally let it be known that it was working to give British citizens a higher priority in social housing, although it never got around to doing anything. Conservatives have pointed to the large proportion of Somali-born people living in social housing as though this fact is outrageous on its face.

Immigrants and minority ethnic Britons are not in fact privileged when it comes to public housing. If anything, the reverse is true. Whereas some immigrant groups, like Somalis, are much more likely than average to live in social housing, others, like Romanians, are much less likely to. Overall, foreign-born people occupy about as many social rented properties as you would expect, given their numbers. The Migration Observatory, a research group attached to Oxford University, estimates that 16 per cent of British-born people (of every ethnicity) live in social housing, compared with 17 per cent of people born overseas. A far more important difference between those groups is that foreign-born people are more than twice as likely to rent privately as British-born people, and are more likely to live in overcrowded homes. When minority ethnic people end up in social housing, they tend to inhabit the least desirable properties. A large housing survey conducted by the government finds that 25 per cent are dissatisfied with their homes, compared with 17 per cent of white social tenants. The fact that minority ethnic people are more likely to live in London, where many homes are cramped, explains only a small part of the difference.

The New Parks estate is not as homogeneous as it used to be. In 1992, a mere 4 per cent of the residents who responded to the criminologists' survey were not white. Today, the proportion of white residents in the estate ranges from half to more than four fifths, depending on the neighbourhood. Yet, like many suburban council estates, New Parks is much whiter than the city it belongs to. The 2021 census showed that 41 per cent of Leicester's inhabitants are white, whereas 43 per cent are Asian. New Parks is part of a belt of largely white, working-class estates around the western edge of the city. It is a good example of an enclave, as described in Chapter One – a place that was once overwhelmingly white and working class but is becoming less so. The residents of New Parks have noticed that change, and many others besides.

*

In 1949, Stanley Gale, a civil engineer, wrote what he hoped would be the definitive guide to building a council estate in Britain. The first part of his opus, *Modern Housing Estates*, covers practical details such as sewers and street lights. The second part describes a few pioneering estates, including New Parks. The estate was still being built, he explained, but when completed it would provide 3,000 homes for 10,000 people. Gale believed that it would become a model for other estate planners. New Parks would contain schools, shops, an open-air swimming pool, a boating lake and a cinema. It would have wide boulevards. In its residential roads, the estate would feature: 'alterations in design of front fences; communal gardens; expert tree planting; variation in size of plots catering for the garden enthusiast and his opposite; variation in street design; variation in housing types; intermixture of classes, etc.' A perfect little world.

The last item on Gale's list, 'intermixture of classes', shows that the people who created the New Parks estate were au fait with the planning orthodoxy of their day. Introducing a housing bill to the House of Commons in 1945, the health minister Aneurin Bevan argued that the practice of building neighbourhoods only for working-class or middle-class people was 'a wholly evil thing' that led to 'castrated communities'. Britain's council estates ought to resemble old-fashioned villages, 'where the doctor, the grocer, the butcher and the farm labourer all lived on the same street', he said a few years later. In practice, councils did not usually go in for precise social engineering. But they did try to ensure that their lovely new estates would not be dominated by the poor. Rents were high in post-war estates like New Parks – higher than in the inner-city slums where many of the tenants came from – and the cost of living was higher still. New Parks was built without an industrial zone, so residents had to drive or take buses to factory jobs in central Leicester. The estate promised a decent, respectable life, not a cheap one.

Just in case high rents did not keep out the riff-raff, local councils often did it explicitly. In Newcastle, housing officers visited the homes of people who applied for council properties and graded them according to criteria such as 'appearance of occupants' and 'condition of furniture'. The grades ranged from A plus to C minus. As a rule, families that scored lower than B were not offered homes on new estates but were shoved into older ones. Housing officers were a self-assured bunch: one, in Bristol, declared that he could judge people as soon as they opened the door to him. And the housing officers' snobbery rubbed off on the people who passed their social tests and were granted access to the new estates. James Tucker, a journalist who became a prolific crime novelist, toured estates listening to residents as research for a book that was published in 1966. He found so many examples of pride and haughtiness that he concluded it must be an inherent feature of council estates. He met people who were haughty about the residents of other estates, and people who were haughty about residents in their own estate. If a couple of researchers were to turn up at opposite ends of a council estate and start asking residents where the bad part was, Tucker wrote, it is likely that, at some point, two people would be standing on their doorsteps pointing in each other's direction, 'like a pair of distant duellists'. Tucker called his book *Honourable Estates*.

The oldest residents of Leicester's council estates can just about remember that sniffy era. One retired factory worker recalls being allocated a two-bedroom house in Braunstone Frith, an estate south of New Parks, by a housing officer whom she describes as 'a regal lady'. Not only did the housing officer interrogate her and her husband before agreeing to rent a home to them, she helped them move in, and told the couple which items to put in which cupboard. But I do not have to rely on old people's hazy memories to find out about New Parks in its earliest days, because the tenants wrote about it. For a few years, they produced a quarterly newsletter, the *New Parks Voice*, which described what they were up to. Amazingly, the first few issues of this obscure publication have been preserved in the archives of the British Library in London. They capture a prelapsarian world – an estate before the fall.

The first two issues of the *Voice*, published in 1948, open with missives from local politicians. May Goodwin, a councillor, enjoined 'all tenants to keep the Estate a good example of what bright, happy homes should be'. The local MP, Barnett Janner, hoped that a 'big family' spirit would develop: 'I am convinced that your Estate will become – in a short space of time – a glowing example of progress.' The residents seem to have shared their idealism. Within a year, they had organized a sports day, including a tug of war and a wheelbarrow race. They held a whist drive to raise money for that event and for a children's fancy-dress parade.

A silver cup was offered for the best garden on the estate. A women's group organized talks on subjects both practical and intellectual: 'jamming and bottling, child management and teaching methods, Council house rents and post-war Germany'. A year later, New Parks seems to have sent a delegate to a Soviet-friendly peace conference in Paris. It was soon putting on dances and plays, starting with *Blithe Spirit* by Noël Coward. Because the estate had not yet acquired a community centre or a church, the residents met in homes or a local canteen. The canteen had no electric lights, so people with cars pointed them at the building and switched the headlamps on.

They were an assertive group, conscious of their rights. Shortly after moving in, the tenants wrote to Janner, complaining about the shortage of schools in New Parks. They also lamented the lack of a doctor – a big problem given the huge number of babies being born. They complained about the council's slowness in providing wooden gates for their back gardens, and refused to be fobbed off with the excuse that timber was in short supply nationwide. Most of all, they griped about the lack of buses. The estate was 'the Cinderella of the transport service', they argued. In 1949, the residents managed to collect 1,100 signatures on a petition and sent it to the transport minister in London. 'Our homes may be palaces inside', the *Voice* declared, but the council needed to invest properly in local services.

Even in those bright early days, there were a few reports of disreputable and antisocial behaviour. One anonymous tenant complained that certain householders had edged their front gardens with fruit boxes, tubing and bedsteads. Others chucked their rubbish onto a green. The bus company complained that children threw stones into the path of vehicles and vandalized bus stops. Still, the residents felt they were well on top of the situation. In 1949, the tenants' association invited Mr Fogg, a probation officer and lecturer on juvenile delinquency, to talk to them. 'It was gratifying to learn from him that our Estate does not even begin to look like having a black mark in regard to this serious problem,' noted the *Voice* proudly.

Over the next few decades, the estate ticked along. Schools and churches were eventually built and buses were provided. Residents drank in the local pubs, danced in the social club, went swimming in the pool and travelled to work in textile factories and engineering firms. Children grew up and had children of their own. The tenants' association became less active, as such bodies generally do when they have dealt with the teething troubles of a new neighbourhood. But if New Parks was no longer a model community, it was a thoroughly ordinary, even boring one. Beginning in the early 1970s, the terraced streets of central Leicester were transformed by the arrival of Asians fleeing from east Africa, especially Idi Amin's despotic regime in Uganda. New Parks remained aloof and largely unchanged. Then things went badly wrong.

*

In 1987, Greville Janner, Barnett Janner's son and like him a Labour Party MP representing Leicester, told the House of Commons that New Parks and nearby estates were plagued by crime. Vandalism and disorder had become so common that older residents were too scared to walk the streets. This was chiefly the fault of young hooligans and their parents, he explained. But it was Britain's fault, too. Households in estates like New Parks were being crushed by poverty: national unemployment was close to 10 per cent at the time. They needed more police, more attention from the government and more money. Inner-city council estates were at last getting some attention, Janner noted. Suburban ones were being ignored.

Around the same time, Father Kit Dunkley was hit on the head by burglars who had broken into St Aidan's, a church in New Parks designed by Basil Spence, who is best known for the wonderful Coventry Cathedral. By the time Heather Stephen turned up to interview him for the *Leicester Mercury* in 1996, Father Kit had installed panic buttons in the vicarage. Two curates who worked with him had also been assaulted, and the church windows had been smashed. In a different article, the reporter Paul Grinnell described New Parks as 'a crime-hit Leicester estate'. One seventy-seven-year-old resident said that she had been burgled seven times in the previous three years, and that her windows had been hit by airgun pellets. Another woman had opened her front door to two men who claimed that they had a shotgun. The council promised to erect six-feet-high security fencing in parts of New Parks, but the burglary victim reckoned that eight-feet fences were needed. She wanted all the bungalows fenced off, with lockable gates.

The fear and atomization that Matthews and Trickey described in 1992 did not dissipate over the following decade. A survey conducted for the Home Office in the early 2000s found that only half of residents felt safe walking the streets of New Parks after dark. Fewer than two fifths agreed that it was a close, tight-knit community. The estate's inhabitants were less trusting of their neighbours than people in eight similar places. Some awful incidents occurred. In 2006, two Rottweiler dogs that were often seen on the roof of the Rocket pub, where the criminologists had interviewed local burglars, got into a room with a baby and killed her. Just a few hours later, a mentally-ill man attacked the baby's grandfather and killed his partner. The Rocket closed, as did another pub, the Two Triangles. Today, New Parks has no pub at all. The last holdout, the Good Neighbours, was crushed by Covid-19.

I visited New Parks for the first time in 2006, in the company of a local councillor. He took me to see a married couple, Don and Doris Connolly, who had lived in the estate for decades and had worked hard to improve it. The Connollys, both of whom have since died, told me how lovely New Parks had been in its early years. By the time I met them, though, some of their neighbours struck them as 'funny'. They meant chaotic and disorderly, although they were far too polite to say so. While they had lived there, New Parks had turned from a model estate into a problem estate. Whist drives, Noël Coward and solidarity had given way to vandalism, violence and suspicion.

For the mostly white working-class inhabitants of New Parks, the promise of a dignified life had curdled. As they surveyed their estate, they might have wondered what on earth had gone wrong. The answer is: the same things that went wrong on lots of British council estates.

The local officials who built so many council homes after the Second World War often had two agendas. They wanted to create ideal communities dominated by well-paid working-class people who were committed to self-improvement and civic action – the sort of people who might stage a play or arrange a discussion of post-war Germany. They also wanted to knock down inner-city slums as quickly as possible. These agendas pulled them in different directions. The first impulse led them to screen tenants and charge high rents, thereby keeping the estates respectable, while the second pushed them to open the estates to poor slum-dwellers. At first, it was just about possible to pursue both aims at once. The pace of council-house building was so swift in the 1940s and 1950s that it was possible to reserve new suburban estates for affluent workers and move the poor into older ones. But, by the 1980s, it was impossible.

Several things had changed. The council-house-building spree of the mid-twentieth century had ended, largely because planning rules had tightened. For a couple of years in the early 1950s, councils and housing associations managed to put up more than 200,000 homes a year, but by the late 1970s they were managing only half that. Meanwhile, the national government was pushing a new approach to allocating council homes. Beginning with the homelessness act of 1977, local authorities were cajoled into giving priority to the neediest people. They started to put less emphasis on respectability and local connections, and more emphasis on rescuing people from overcrowding, domestic violence and home-lessness. Then, under a Conservative government led by Margaret Thatcher, came the right to buy. The Housing Act of 1980 allowed many tenants to purchase their properties for much less than the market price. Inhabitants of the best estates were quick to take advantage, so their homes were taken out of the councils' hands. Because councils were barred from using most of the proceeds from property sales to build new homes, the number of available properties dropped. In some cities it became almost impossible to obtain a council house unless you were in dire need.

Those three changes transformed Britain's council estates, making them much less socially varied. In 2007, a detailed report on social housing by John Hills, 'Ends and Means', uncovered the remarkable fact that, in the late 1970s, over 20 per cent of house-holds in the highest-earning tenth of the population rented their homes from the council. That was a smaller proportion than the 50 per cent in the lowest-earning tenth who did so, but it was hardly a negligible share. (I am always amused when British people in their sixties and seventies say 'I was brought up on a council estate' as though it establishes their proletarian roots – it doesn't.) By the late 1990s, fewer people at all income levels were renting from the council, but there had been an utter collapse among the richest tenth. Council housing had been 'residualized'. Once a normal, even an aspirational living situation, it had become a safety net for people who seemed likely otherwise to end up on the streets.

In 1998, the BBC radio journalist Jo Hollis interviewed Geraldine Woodland, who was born in 1945 and grew up in New Parks. She remembered the estate as a 'wonderful' place that had repaid the residents' pride and care: 'you looked after it and you were really privileged'. Her parents' council house had a generous hallway and an indoor bathroom, and her neighbours were a good social mix, with only one family 'dead scruffy'. Woodland was horrified when her parents moved out of New Parks to a terraced house that they had bought. Not only was the new house smaller, it had a stone sink and an outdoor toilet – exactly the things that the people who moved from slums to the new council estates had been so delighted to leave behind. But she understood her parents' reasons. Owning a house meant that they would not have to pay rent in retirement. Besides, she said, it seemed like the right thing to do for families that had 'gumption'. And how did the New Parks estate seem to Woodland in 1998? 'Oh, it's gone downhill now,' she said. It had gone downhill partly because families like hers had left.

For everyone who remained living in suburban council estates like New Parks, their sharp deterioration in the last decades of the twentieth century was a tragedy. People cannot easily move away from declining estates. If they want to remain council tenants, they must either join a waiting list for a new property, which may be long, or arrange to swap homes with another tenant. Swaps can be vetoed by councils or housing associations if a family tries to obtain a property that seems too large or too small for its needs. In any case, nobody finds it easy to settle in a new place, and the fewer resources people possess, the harder they find it. Many of the estate-dwellers were stuck.

But the decline of Britain's suburban estates affected white working-class people in particular. They were unusually likely to live on such estates, partly because the working-class population of Britain had been largely white when many of the suburban estates were being built and populated, and partly because local councils had deliberately allocated homes on the estates to them. Particularly before the 1970s, housing officers often reserved homes on desirable estates for long-established residents – which is to say, not immigrants – or simply did not offer them to non-white people. And if bureaucratic discrimination was not enough to keep estates overwhelmingly white, their inhabitants fought hard, and in some cases viciously, to ensure it.

*

Anybody who feels a twinge of nostalgia for 1980s Britain might take a look at a report published by the Commission for Racial Equality in 1987. 'Living in Terror' describes in detail the treatment meted out to black and Asian people who were allocated to predominantly white council estates, and it curdles the blood. Excrement and lighted paper were pushed through people's letter-boxes. Pet cats were killed and skinned. Children were attacked, stripped of their clothes and dumped into communal dustbins. Some families perished in arson attacks, and many more were so terrified that they fled mostly white estates or did not seek homes outside ethnically mixed neighbourhoods. The London borough of Newham told the commission that it had rehoused fifty-one families in an eight-month period as a result of harassment. In the neighbouring borough of Tower Hamlets, an Asian family that was being relocated for that very reason went to view a flat on the Exmouth estate, south of Whitechapel. Soon after the family departed, the flat was daubed with National Front graffiti and adorned with pigs' trotters.

The official response to horrors like these was dispiriting. Tenants' associations insisted that nothing was amiss, or argued that crime and violence were commonplace in estates and that introducing measures to tackle racial harassment would be a form of special treatment for black and Asian people. Some councils denied the existence of racial harassment altogether, only for community groups to produce long lists of incidents. Housing officers quietly carved cities up, in effect keeping suburban estates white. The commission summed up: 'Far too often we hear of an "outer-city ring" or whole sections of a local authority area where housing officers say they are reluctant to make offers to black people because of potential harassment.'

Although the worst atrocities were in east London, Leicester was touched by violence. In 1972, the *Leicester Mercury* reported that one young man had tried to drive his Indian neighbours out of the street by setting fire to their front door. Ajmal Butt, who grew up (and now runs a boxing club) in Beaumont Leys, the estate just north of New Parks, remembers bricks crashing through his windows when he was a child; on one occasion, his father, an Asian man who had moved to Britain from Kenya, ran out of the house and threatened his assailants with a spear. In 1987, Marian Fitzgerald, a criminologist, surveyed 102 Asian residents of two Leicester housing estates for a report that was never published. More than a quarter said they had experienced harassment, and two fifths knew of others who had suffered it. The Asian residents set a pretty high bar for what constituted harassment. Having their cars smashed up didn't count, for example.

New Parks seems to have been quieter than some of Leicester's other council estates, although that may have been because very few black or Asian people even tried to move there. On several occasions young men from the estate were prosecuted for attacking Asian people in the city centre. In December 1977, the

Mercury reported that four New Parks residents had been hauled before magistrates after viciously beating an Indian chef near the restaurant where he worked. In 1985, Leicester's housing director, Peter Graham, observed that some Asian families in the city were waiting for large council houses. Estates like New Parks had many large homes, he noted, but the Asian families seemed not to want them. Graham thought that the problem could be a lack of cultural amenities, and suggested that the council might build temples and mosques to entice the families. There are more obvious explanations for their reluctance to move to the estate.

Whether they occurred in Leicester or in London, the attacks that took place were plainly racist. But it was racism of a specific kind, rooted in white working-class people's feelings of entitlement to superior council properties. A small number of attackers expressed what many seem to have felt – that the better estates had been promised to them, and ought not to be given to anybody else. The strength of that belief was especially clear on the Exmouth estate in Tower Hamlets. After the flat that had been shown to an Asian family was vandalized, dozens of residents petitioned the Greater London Council, the city's administrative body at the time, asking it to desist from housing Asian families there. In Leicester, Fitzgerald found that more than half of white council tenants believed the council was actually discriminating in favour of black and Asian people.

White council-estate residents argued then, and have argued since, that they were not racist but merely insular. As a woman in the Castle Vale estate in Birmingham told some academics who were researching a report for the government in 2009: 'It's not so much about race, it's about new people coming in.' And it is true that white Britons in highly desirable estates have sometimes resisted incursions by other white Britons, albeit far less violently than they have opposed black and Asian people. The historian Harold Carter has shown that rows over allocation policies broke out in the inner-London borough of Southwark as early as the 1950s, when the area was overwhelmingly white. Families who had been bombed out of their homes by the Luftwaffe felt more entitled to homes on new estates than slum-dwelling families whose homes were being knocked down by the council. Two clergymen who became involved in the Southwark row described the slum-dwellers in scathing terms: 'non-rent payers, disturbers of the peace, unmarried mothers'. The dispute only grew uglier as the borough became more ethnically mixed.

The combination of violence, the threat of violence, and bureaucratic discrimination kept many suburban council estates largely white until recently. Black and Asian families were forced into cramped council flats in city centres or into private rented accommodation, which cost more than council housing and was often worse quality. The 'Ends and Means' report noted that, although council *houses* were overwhelmingly white, council *flats* were much less so. The geographer Danny Dorling and others found in 2007 that children living on or above the fifth floor of buildings were seven times more likely to be of minority ethnic heritage than children living closer to the ground. Britain had become segregated by elevation.

The estate-dwellers who successfully repelled immigrants and minority ethnic people won a peculiar sort of victory. On the one hand, suburban council estates are usually more pleasant than inner-city ones. The air is cleaner, the noise level is lower, and families are able to light barbecues on summer evenings and let their pets run around. On the other hand, suburban estates are frequently further from jobs than the inner-city estates where black and Asian people are more likely to live. And the cost of living on suburban estates can be high, largely because they are so sprawling. It is hard for a family to live comfortably in New

Parks without a car or even two. People often walk out of the Co-op on Aikman Avenue with their shopping bags, pull out mobile phones and call minicabs to take them home.

Researchers sometimes wonder whether social housing is actually bad for its inhabitants, at least in an economic sense. Not surprisingly, people who live in social housing are much more likely to be economically inactive (that is, neither working nor looking for work) than people who rent privately or own their homes. That is mostly because social-housing residents are older, sicker and less educated than average. But some researchers argue that, even after you account for these things, people who live in social housing seem oddly inactive. It could be that the economists cannot control for everything, and that the social-housing residents are disadvantaged in ways that are hard to measure, such as experiencing greater anxiety or having needier children. Alternatively, it could be that their homes are actually holding them back. Perhaps the problem is that social tenants find it hard to move to places with more work, or perhaps it is tough to find a job if you are surrounded by people who are not working. Working-class white Britons saw off competitors for social housing, and may have harmed themselves in the process.

One thing is certain: the New Parks council estate would not be built today. Very few homes for social rent are constructed nowadays: councils and housing associations together manage to put up only about 30,000 a year in England. When such homes are built, they are generally in small developments, or deliberately interspersed with private houses. I have been shown around new suburban housing estates by commercial developers who point proudly to the few social homes they have built, and assure me that nobody can tell the difference between those homes and the private houses that surround them. Council homes are OK, it seems, as long as they are not obviously council homes.

Many people who live in New Parks speak scathingly of the estate today. One woman, who worked in a hosiery factory and as a care worker and has lived in the estate for five decades, offers this dismal account of decline during her lifetime: 'It was lovely. It was clean, and there were lots of buses. It was a nice estate. Everyone was very friendly; everyone knew each other. But it's got bad. You can see for yourself the litter, the dereliction. It's as though nobody cares about it . . . It's a horrible estate, it really is.' A group of teenagers who are chatting next to a football pitch in New Parks, vaping and occasionally disappearing to smoke something stronger, describe it as 'a shithole', a word seemingly always on the tongues of estate residents. I ask them what the residents of other estates might say, if I were to solicit their views on New Parks. 'Lots of crime,' one of them suggests. 'You'll get stabbed.'

They know more than I do. All the same, I think they are describing the estate's reputation better than its reality. New Parks is certainly run-down. Many of the houses have grown shabby, and a few too many residents seem to think that front gardens are for storing unwanted furniture. The security fences around St Aidan's Church and the empty Good Neighbours pub are depressing. But burglaries are much rarer than they used to be, and police statistics suggest that the overall crime rate in and around New Parks is about average for west Leicester. The teenagers who assure me that it is lawless drop their expensive-looking bikes on the ground without locking them, and leave their bags on benches as they wander off to chat. They think nothing of going home alone in the dark.

New Parks still contains many people who are determined to make the estate better, with whatever meagre resources they can mobilize. A group known as the Forum meets regularly in the local library, where it airs and tries to solve local problems, much as the tenants' association did in the 1940s. Jo Johnson, who says that she was once one of the teenage girls hanging out by the Co-op in Aikman Avenue, went on to run an adventure playground in the estate. Operating on a painfully small budget, she provides children with a place to hang out and takes them on trips. Shaun Hunt gathers dads and their offspring for a weekly Saturday-morning kick about.

Most impressive of all is Joanne Randall, who presides over a building in the centre of New Parks known as the Hub. Randall lives on the estate, in a former council house that she bought on the open market after being told that her chance of getting a council property was slim because she was living with her partner and working. She acquired the Hub building from the council, only to discover that it needed a new roof. Randall launched an online appeal, and the people of New Parks responded generously. The Hub offers a mixture of dance classes, children's play sessions, food, football and bingo. Its car park is frequently full.

*

Meanwhile, another great change is taking place in the estate. Steadily, and without much trouble in the past few years, New Parks is becoming more ethnically mixed. Asian families now occupy many houses; in a few corners of the estate, they account for one third of the population. More black families are moving into the flats along Aikman Avenue. 'It used to be a no-go area for Somali families,' says Abdikayf Farah of the Somali Community Parents' Association, a group based in central Leicester. Today, he rarely hears accounts of harassment in New Parks.

The woman who used to work in a hosiery factory and as a care worker tells me that Leicester is being ruined by one particular group of people, which is far too large and seems to be spreading in an uncontrolled way. Those people are students.

As for Asian and black people, several have moved into the cul-de-sac where she lives. She describes them as lovely, largely because their children are well behaved and because they talk to her when she is working in her front garden. Anyway, she argues, ethnic mixing is a good thing in itself: 'It's not good for Leicester to be split into whites, blacks, Asians, Chinese or whatever.'

Not everyone is so sanguine about the growing diversity of the estate. Residents sometimes gripe when destitute refugees are offered homes ahead of local families who have been waiting for years. Questionable rumours circulate: I have been assured, for example, that some homes built in the late twentieth century were reserved for Afro-Caribbean families. But the sharp edge of resentment and hostility has gone, which is something to be mightily thankful for. Muttering and ill-founded rumours are greatly preferable to skinned cats and racist graffiti. And it is worth remembering that lots of people in Britain, not just white working-class council-estate residents, trade dubious stories about newcomers. In my mostly middle-class neighbourhood, newly arrived Hongkongers are said to be pushing house prices out of the reach of more established residents.

The quiet integration of previously white housing estates like New Parks is one of the unheralded triumphs of the past couple of decades. It is also something of a mystery. Less than two generations ago, black and Asian families who attempted to move into white estates were viciously repulsed. How exactly did such estates go from extreme knee-jerk violence to quiet, if occasionally sullen, acceptance?

One possible explanation is that council-house allocations policies have changed. Before the 1970s, local authorities explicitly favoured well-to-do families with deep roots in the area; then they swung towards favouring needy people; recently, they have swung back a bit. Changes to housing law since 2010 have made it easier for councils to bar newcomers (whether they come from another country or from another part of Britain) from social rented homes, and many have done so. Leicester currently has a two-year residency requirement.

Another possibility is that the policy of selling council homes to their tenants, which helped to cause such a dire shortage of properties, has muddled the picture in a benign way. In the 1970s, a black or Asian family that had just appeared on an estate was almost certainly renting a home from the council. They were likely to be viewed as competitors for a scarce resource. These days, a family might have bought a former council house on the open market or might be renting from a private landlord. Or they might be living in a privately built home that has been squeezed into a council estate. At the northern edge of New Parks, an area of land that was once intended for allotment gardens was later developed, and the houses sold on the open market. That area is more ethnically diverse than anywhere else in the estate.

Much the same thing is happening in Wythenshawe, near the southern edge of Manchester. Although Wythenshawe was built as a council estate, it has always contained some streets of private homes, and many of those are now occupied by Asian families. The black and Asian residents of Wythenshawe have good jobs; a housing officer describes them to me, with wonderful delicacy, as 'a more economically active community'. The Office for National Statistics has produced a series of neighbourhood maps using data from the 2021 census, which reveal a remarkable pattern. The least-white parts of Wythenshawe tend to have the highest rates of home ownership, the biggest proportions of highly educated inhabitants and the lowest rates of unemployment. Middle-class homeowners from minority ethnic backgrounds might encounter racist aggression, but they are likely to have more resources for dealing with it.

Yet another explanation for the calming of suburban housing estates, which I think most important of all, is that white working-class people's attitudes have changed. Hostility towards immigrants and minority ethnic people in council estates is not produced automatically by housing policies, in the way that heavy rain leads to flooding. Rather, the hostility is expressed by humans with many thoughts in their heads. If white working-class people have become more open-minded in general, and less likely to view themselves as a distinct group opposed to other groups, they will be less likely to kick out against black and Asian people over social housing or indeed over anything else. And that appears to have happened. In Chapter Five, I will describe the change in attitudes and explain what has caused it.

Chapter Four

Fast, furious and female

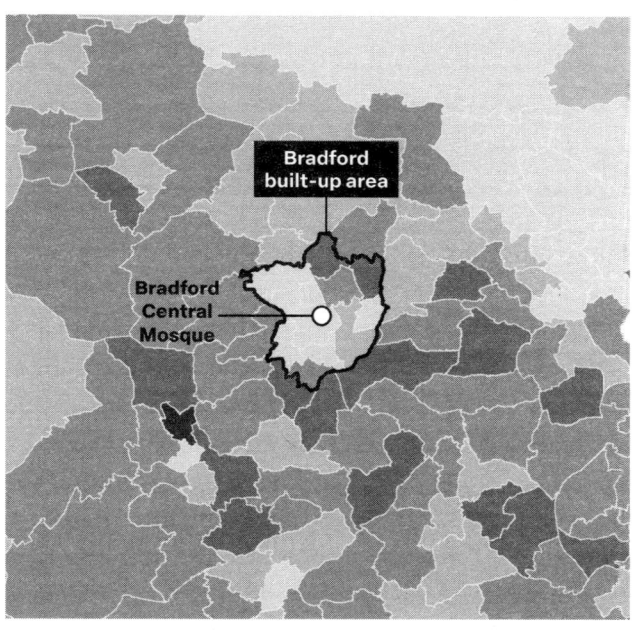

I often hear them before I see them. Sometimes the first hint is the squeal of tyres in a suburban street; sometimes it's a bass exhaust rumble; sometimes it's frantic revving in a motorway tunnel. Then the cars appear. Not uncommonly, they proceed to do something obnoxious. A strange-looking grey Audi overtakes me on the right, then quickly turns left, trailing a Victorian quantity of smoke. A black-and-white car, so low to the ground that I can see no light under the body, goes past me on the A1 motorway and lets out a shotgun blast from its exhaust.

I used to snigger at such machines, contemplate my low annual insurance premium and reflect on the fact that I will almost certainly reach my destination without killing myself or anyone else. Now, before the modified cars disappear ahead, I try to work out what their owners have done. Is that a real carbon-fibre spoiler? Those look like tinted tail-lights. How did they get the body so low to the ground, and how do they cope with speed bumps? I wonder what cost more, the vehicle or the pop-and-bang remap. I look for stickers in the windows. Does the driver belong to any car club I know?

A modified car is an ordinary factory-built car that someone has altered, usually after buying it second- or third-hand. It is likely to have new, eye-catching wheels and a wide exhaust pipe. Almost certainly, special springs have been installed to set the body of the vehicle closer to the ground. It probably has a spoiler, or, if the car rolled off the production line with one, a bigger spoiler. Its engine may have been retuned. The car may have a front splitter – a plastic or fibreglass part that makes the vehicle look lower than it really is. It might have special lights, a new cold-air intake, wind deflectors, racing pedals, a decorative wrap, an upgraded sound system, or any number of other wild and wonderful adjustments.

Ask the driver of a highly modified vehicle how it has been altered and, unless you know a great deal about cars, your head will spin. At one gathering of petrolheads in Bradford, called a meet, I spot a beautiful blue Opel. The bonnet is open, and half a dozen people are admiring the engine. I ask the owner, a beanie-hatted mechanic, what he has done to his car. His answer is so quick and complicated that, owing to a combination of technical ignorance and inept shorthand, I capture only a small fraction of his words. I catch 'rods and pistons', 'valve springs', 'bonnet extension', 'door mirrors', 'calipers' and 'anti-roll bar'. Then, thankfully more slowly, he explains the point of his labours. He has turned an old, modestly priced car into a powerful machine that turns people's heads, for much less money than it would have cost to buy a newer car with those characteristics. He describes the result as 'a sports car for the working class'.

As we are talking, a bright green convertible appears. I think it is a Ford Escort, although the car has been altered so heavily that it is hard to be sure. 'Ooh, that's quite nice,' says the mechanic. He explains that the car has been modified completely differently from his vehicle, to a different purpose. Whereas the Opel's engine has been tweaked and tuned to the maximum, the convertible's does not even appear to be turbocharged. Instead, the owner has lavished attention and money on fittings, such as an astoundingly colourful dashboard. It is all style and no performance. The convertible trundles slowly around the car park, then drives off.

Nobody knows how many Britons modify their cars. I tried asking Adrian Flux, a company that specializes in insuring them. It wasn't able to help me. As a very, very rough guide, I would guess that between one in every fifty and one in every 150 cars has been substantially altered, in a way that seeks to draw attention to the vehicle (a vanity plate doesn't count). In some places around the UK, the share is higher. I am always a little surprised when I see a modified car parked in an affluent urban neighbourhood. I am never surprised to see one parked in a seaside town or a suburban council estate.

This being Britain, many sports and leisure activities bear social-class labels. Snooker, darts, boxing, greyhound racing, punk rock and bingo have different social connotations from cricket, sailing, fly fishing, contract bridge, dressage and jazz. Before the Second World War, football was an overwhelmingly working-class sport. During the war, the authorities agonized: should manual workers be allowed to gather in their tens of thousands to watch games, in places and at times known to German bomber pilots?

Eventually, it was decided that they should. Football was too important to the masses.

Football is not an especially working-class sport today, although you might not guess that from the effort politicians put into talking about it, in order to burnish their images as men – and, occasionally, women – of the people. English Premier League fans actually skew middle class, not surprisingly considering the price of match tickets and sport TV channels. Nor are some other activities quite as working class as their reputations suggest. You will find snooker tables in grand country houses. Punk was created by art students as well as school dropouts.

Car modification really is a distinctively white working-class activity. It is, as one enthusiast put it to me, 'more common in your low-profit areas'. It is a phenomenon of places with poor public transport, quiet roads and plentiful parking spaces – of suburbs and small towns rather than densely populated inner-city neighbourhoods. The culture is especially strong in working-class places that have a bit of money. One of Britain's most enduring modified-car scenes is in Aberdeen, a Scottish city with good manual jobs in the oil-and-gas industry. Another is on the Essex coast. And I have never seen so many modified cars anywhere as I have in the Medway towns of Kent, east of London. That area is working-class, but not poor.

Most of the car modifiers who I have met are skilled manual workers or clerical workers, putting them somewhere near the boundary between the working class and the lower middle class. They have money to spend on cars, but not so much that they can afford to waste it. They tell me how they obtained a part cheaply by cannibalizing a different make of car, or persuaded a mate to work on their motor in exchange for some favour. Many of the men are mechanics, or do jobs that are somehow linked to vehicles. A driver of a modified Ford Focus installs bollards for a living; a driver of a modified VW Golf operates a forklift in a paper factory. Another man, who has lovingly altered a Renault 5, is a joiner.

To a man and indeed a woman, they are enthusiastic about meddling with cars, bordering on obsessive. As soon as they have altered one thing, they notice something else that could be improved. When they have changed one car to their satisfaction, they are likely to sell it and buy another to work on. The joiner thinks he has owned nine cars, an impressive total given that he is only twenty-two. Another man, who is not much older, reckons he has owned twenty. Modifiers burn through cars because they want to, not because it brings in any money. When talking about their hobby, they use words like 'addiction' and 'hooked'. Sometimes they scorn drivers of ordinary, unaltered cars, but more often they struggle to understand how anybody could resist the temptation to meddle. At one car meet, a young woman asks me about my own car. It's a Honda, I say, but I haven't modified it in any way. 'Not yet,' she retorts.

Car modification provides a rare opportunity for white working-class Britons to flaunt their artistry and skill, and lord it over everyone else. Someone who is prepared to put in the hours of informal research that are necessary to understand how a car works and which modifications are considered appropriate, and is then prepared to put in the money to do the modifications and pay a higher insurance premium, will be able to create an object that his or her peers consider to be beautiful. Other people will notice the car when it is on the road and, it is hoped, envy it. A working-class modifier might not have a more expensive car than a middle-class driver. But a faster car, a more distinctive car, a louder car? Certainly.

That element of peacocking distinguishes car modification from some other cultures created largely by white working-class Britons.

The rave scene that emerged in the 1980s allowed young people to join a joyous, music- and dance-loving community, and helped them to get through the tedium of a working week. But raves took place away from the rest of society, in abandoned warehouses and fields. Car modification is public. It allows participants to strut and show off to everyone else. At many gatherings of car modifiers, working-class people set the rules and run the show. A person who does a low-status job might be the driving force behind a big event that makes the local news. I can no more escape writing about the modified-car scene than I can escape the smell of burning petrol when someone decides to rev their remapped engine. Nor would I want to, because car modifiers are a delightful bunch.

To some extent, the point of altering a car is to deceive people. Some modifiers aim to create 'sleepers', which look ordinary but, in their owners' imaginations at least, are capable of outrunning a supercar. Others work hard to achieve the opposite effect. One middle-aged Yorkshireman, who works in a care home, has lowered his pale-blue Honda, replaced the steering wheel and wrapped the bonnet, among many other changes. His car has the air of speediness, and nothing more. 'Mine looks like it's got the power,' he tells me at a car meet. 'But it hasn't.' And in one sense the entire modified-car scene is deceptive.

Ask a man at a car meet how he got into modifying, and he is likely to tell you that he learned about it from a car-tinkering father or male friend, or from his job in the car industry. Ask a woman, and she might well explain that she is there with her boyfriend. This is misleading. The culture of car modification used to be male-dominated and macho, but these days some of the most important figures on the scene are women. Like the white working class as a whole, car modification might appear hidebound at first glance. In fact it is adaptable and forward-looking. Car modification is not just a largely white working-class activity; it also reveals the flexibility and openness of white working-class people.

*

Although people have modified cars for as long as cars have existed, the handbrake really came off in the late 1990s. Without warning, enthusiasts began to hold enormous 'cruises' in suburban retail parks and seaside towns. At one point, some 2,000 vehicles turned up in Bristol, according to the police. Drivers did 'burn-outs' (spinning the wheels while remaining stationary, which wears the tyres and creates smoke) and 'doughnuts' (rotating one end of the car around the other while spinning the wheels). A car park that had been visited by car cruisers ended up with thick black circles in the tarmac.

Several things caused the acceleration. Cars became cheaper around the turn of the century, and credit more accessible. In 2001, Universal Pictures released *The Fast and the Furious*, the first in a string of successful films featuring good-looking actors, powerful modified cars and increasingly daft plots. But the crucial factor in Britain was a magazine. When petrolheads talk about the wild years in the late 1990s and early 2000s, they do not give dates. Instead, they say: 'in the *Max Power* days'.

Picking up a copy of *Max Power* from its heyday – which I can do because, delightfully, the British Library has preserved them for posterity – provokes mixed feelings. One is envy. I became a journalist in 2001, when the internet had begun to compete for people's attention and advertisers' cash, so I missed the era when print adverts flowed like water. *Max Power* and competitors such as *Redline* were amazingly hefty publications in their prime, stuffed with adverts and editorial copy. The other feeling is despair, because, unfortunately, *Max Power* was poorly written and stultifyingly masculine even by the standards of the day. The issue of March 1997 is typical. It contains a feature about a Peugeot 205, which a man named Paul has modified into 'an aggressive machine'. This was at the behest of his friends, who told him 'it should be lowered before people started calling Paul a lesbian'. Many other cars are featured, all of them owned and modified by men, although one owner's wife is pictured, wearing leather trousers and smoking a cigarette. An editorial complains about people who drive too slowly on icy roads, such as 'Derek the Daewoo driver listening to Radio 2' and 'Denise the demented housewife popping down to Tesco'. And so on, for page after lavishly printed page.

Turgid and laddish though it was, *Max Power* helped to define a British approach to car modification that was different from the glamorous scene portrayed in *The Fast and the Furious*. That film depicts powerful saloon cars and coupes, which their owners had made still more powerful. Young working-class Britons could not possibly afford such motors. Instead, they got hold of humble second-hand hatchbacks, like the Peugeot 205, the Renault Clio and the Vauxhall Corsa, which had often been marketed to women (people who watched television in the 1980s may remember a string of adverts for the Clio featuring the winsome Nicole and her papa). Then, following suggestions in the car magazines, they went to work. Drivers bought body kits that drastically changed the look of their cars. Hatchbacks were 'slammed' – lowered so far that the side skirts almost touched the ground. 'It was often silly. Let's have a bonnet that opens the wrong way! Let's put Jaguar lights on a Corsa!' says James Burr, known as Midge, a mechanic and a veteran of the car scene who writes for Influx, a blog.

The March 1997 issue of *Max Power* also reported on a cruise in Chesterfield, south of Sheffield. The magazine printed lots of pictures of men admiring each other's cars, burnouts, and a woman flashing her bra. It noted with a twinge of disappointment that no 'rozzers', or police, had turned up to shut down the gathering. *Max Power* went on to cover many other cruises and car meets. It was soon scoring them according to fixed criteria: 'motors', 'burnouts', 'rozzers', (men's) 'arses', and 'birds'. The magazine was not just reporting on the modified-car scene. By creating the benchmarks by which cars and car gatherings were judged, it was shaping it.

People were desperate to get their cars into the magazines. Zannagh Hatton, who ingratiated herself with a group of modified-car enthusiasts in Cornwall and went on to produce one of the most entertaining PhD theses I have ever read, observed that they would drive a hundred miles to a cruise if they thought a photographer might be present. Cruise organizers informed the car magazines of their plans, by phone or occasionally by fax. And the presence of magazine journalists and photographers at cruises encouraged car modifiers to behave in all the expected ways. 'Everyone came alive when we arrived,' wrote 'Clifty', a reporter for *Redline*, of a car meet in Crewe in 2000. 'We were greeted with displays of synchronized reverse doughnuts topped off with a burnout or two.'

It seemed at the time as though the wheels would never stop turning. And yet, within a few years, they almost did. *Max Power* and *Redline* both went into decline and ceased regular publication in 2011. The specialist garages and car-parts retailers that had taken out so many adverts in their pages scaled back their operations, and in some cases vanished. And the big, unruly cruises ceased. Never again would thousands of people take over a town or a suburban shopping centre before the police or the local authorities knew what was happening. The car-modification scene that exists today is smaller and more timid than the one that existed in the late 1990s and early 2000s. It is also more interesting.

Underdogs

Many things conspired to harm the modified-car culture that had grown along with *Max Power*. The police got much cleverer. The huge illicit car cruises had flummoxed officers, who didn't know whether to treat them as traffic problems or crowd problems. As the Avon and Somerset Constabulary put it in 2002, in a write-up of their work that was submitted for an award, car meets took place at 'this crazy interface between Traffic and Disorder'. The traffic intelligence officer in that force did not even have access to the internet, so he had little sense of what the petrol-heads were planning. As soon as he got access, he began shooting off cautionary emails to people who were arranging events.

Parliament handed powerful legal weapons to local councils and the police. If they spotted two or more people causing alarm, harassment or distress to others, or even behaving in a way that was likely to cause such upset, they could hand out dispersal orders that forced people away from the area. Since cruises involved lots of people, and were often noisy, that was an easy bar to clear. And the police found reconnaissance and evidence-gathering easy. Modified-car enthusiasts are not like criminals, who live in the shadows. To many of them, scrutiny and publicity are the whole point of getting together. An undercover police officer with a camera is not only unlikely to arouse their suspicions, he or she actually makes a cruise seem more legitimate. In 2003, a plain-clothes officer turned up at a meet in Surrey carrying a Sony Handycam and telling people that he was a web designer. 'There are lots of people down here filming and taking pictures all the time,' he explained to *Jane's Police Review*, a coppers' trade magazine, afterwards. Later that night, his colleagues blocked the road, scanned number plates and handed out thirty-nine official warnings to drivers.

Then there was Ali G. The gormless white rapper created by Sacha Baron-Cohen, an actor and comedian, naturally drove a heavily modified car with a boot full of bass speakers. His bright yellow Renault 5 GT appears in the 2002 film *Ali G Indahouse*, cruising around the safe suburban streets of Surrey, blasting drum and bass. It was a devastating visual joke. A Renault 5 is objectively a small vehicle, but Baron-Cohen is so tall that he made it look like a clown car. Released just a year after *The Fast and the Furious*, *Ali G Indahouse* cruelly deflated the fantasy that your souped-up Corsa made you look like Michelle Rodriguez or Vin Diesel.

Troubles piled upon troubles. Cars became harder to alter: vehicles were increasingly controlled by computers and required the attentions of qualified mechanics. Jamie Brett of the Museum of Youth Culture, who spent many hours working on second-hand BMWs, remembers the proliferation of engine warning lights from the late 1990s, which he likens to in-car policemen. Insurance companies insisted on being informed of even minor adjustments, and sometimes refused to cover modified cars altogether. In 2009, the government launched a scrappage scheme, which eradicated many of the older, cheaper cars that modifiers loved to work on. A proud culture became an endangered subculture.

Some of the assault on car modifiers looks to me like an attempt to put young working-class people in their place. All were labelled 'boy racers', a term that once referred just to joyriders or dangerous drivers. Some of the more respectable car modifiers responded by explaining that they were not boy racers, but the young men who drove cheap cars (that is, men with less money) were. Occasionally the authorities seem to have worried as much about the preservation of property values as about safety. In Aberdeen, a long-established, largely working-class group of car cruisers known as the 'Bouley Bashers' came under sustained pressure when the area of the city where they gathered became middle class, with more expensive homes. And, although it is true that many modified cars were (and are) noisy and polluting, it is worth remembering that certain other vehicles with the same characteristics are treated far more gently by the authorities. Classic cars, which are often owned by older middle-class people, may be exempt from MOTs, road taxes and London's ultra-low emissions rules. Farmers are allowed to fill their tractors with red diesel (the same as regular diesel, but dyed red), which attracts much lower fuel duty.

Rave, that other mostly young, mostly white working-class scene, was firmly crushed. The Criminal Justice and Public Order Act of 1994 banned groups of more than twenty people from gathering at night in the open air, if the music at their gatherings was 'characterized by the emission of a succession of repetitive beats'. Ravers were herded into legitimate clubs, which were more easily controlled and more expensive. Later, the clubs began to decline. Car cruisers were sometimes likened to ravers: one 1999 article in the *Weston & Worle News*, a local newspaper, called a car meet a 'rave on wheels'. Within a few years, it seemed as though their culture might be crushed, too. But the scene has proved resilient. It never completely disappeared, and now it is coming back.

*

One showery summer evening, hundreds of modified cars arrive at the Meadowhall Retail Park in Sheffield. The meet has been organized by a group called Lowdown VW, which has been around since 2006 – an eternity in the fast-moving modified-car world. As you might expect from the name, it has a fair few Volkswagens, including a grey Polo with wheels that are extremely negatively cambered, or splayed out, which makes the car appear drunk. It also has Hondas, Toyotas, Fords (clustered together, as Fords often are), BMWs, Mazdas, Mercedes-Benzes and just about every other make of car. The owners of the most unusual, beautiful vehicles have staked out positions near the Pizza Hut, or have parked diagonally across two spaces. Look at *this*, they seem to say.

It is a 'static' meet, different from a 'Mexico' meet, where drivers race each other until the police turn up, or a car show, which charges admission. It isn't perfectly static, though, and it isn't at all quiet. Cars crawl around, looking for parking spaces or trying to attract attention. Some drivers rev their engines madly, producing all kinds of sounds, including explosions (if you should ever want to shoot somebody, do it at a car meet – nobody will know). The revving acts like a mating call, drawing crowds of young men and women to a car. It also seems to draw the police. The coppers cruise around the car park a few times, have a good-natured chat with the petrolheads, then zoom off, blue lights flashing, presumably in response to an actual crime.

The car modifiers return to their conversations. Here, and at other car meets, they mostly talk about cars and other car gatherings. It means a lot to them. 'It's like a giant, messed-up friend group,' says one young man, with a sly grin. Despite their loud, antisocial image, car modifiers are often shy when not behind the wheel. Several tell me that they suffer from social anxiety, which is so extreme in one man's case that he cannot work. Car meets help bring them out of their shells and make them feel proud of themselves. To learn how to do something difficult, to do it, to be commended by your peers for doing it well – it's a moving experience.

As the sun sets, two construction workers who have been digging in another part of the car park parade around in their filthy dumper, fists in the air, to laughter from the car modifiers. At about 9 p.m. some drivers open the boots of their vehicles and push their sound systems to the limit. Soon after, people begin to drive away. As the cars leave, they pass a group of people filming with their mobile phones, who encourage the drivers to rev their engines again. All in all, it has been a satisfying evening. '*Every single car* is good,' comments one man to another. 'Best meet I've been to in ages.' There will be another one in a month.

Many of the cars on display in Sheffield and at other meets have been amended more subtly than the exuberant machines that people created two or three decades ago. One mechanic has altered his VW Polo in numerous ways. He has lowered the body; upgraded the brakes; added parts, including a spoiler, new alloy wheels, a carbon-fibre steering wheel and new lights; and has 'de-chromed' the vehicle, removing many of its shiny metal parts. Like almost every car modifier I have ever spoken to, he says that he is nowhere close to being finished. He still intends to replace the bonnet, among other things. But all of his changes so far have been subtle. It is as though he has produced the car that Volkswagen ought to have made in the first place, if its budget had been a little bigger and its designers' eyes a little sharper. He describes the look of his car as 'quite OEM'. That term, which stands for 'original equipment manufacturer', is thrown around a lot by car modifiers these days. A rough translation into non-car-speak would be 'tailored'.

Near Barnsley, in a workshop surrounded by lovely gardens and (of all things) emus, Stuart Allatt and Jane Allatt make high-quality car parts of fibreglass and carbon fibre, which they sell under the DeltaStyling brand. Few people know more about how car modification has changed over the years. The Allatts were part of the modified-car boom in the 1990s, they endured the bust, and they are now participating in the revival. Because they design and make car-body parts, they especially notice changes in how people want their vehicles to look.

During the 1990s boom, Delta specialized in making objects that profoundly changed the shape of cars. Their body parts, which were tailored for individual models of vehicle, turned boring, boxy hatchbacks into wild-looking machines. 'In the *Max Power* days,' says Jane, using the approved dating technique, 'we did big, wide arches and huge body kits.' 'Nothing subtle,' adds Stuart. 'Big replacement bumpers, big side skirts, all outrageous stuff. People wanted their cars to be unrecognizable as the original.' Their work was often featured in *Max Power*.

The crisis in Britain's modified-car scene in the noughties was so severe that the Allatts decided to change course. Their firm switched from the creative, outrageous stuff to making ordinary car parts for vehicles that were more than a decade old. More recently, as modified-car culture has revived, the Allatts have changed course again. DeltaStyling has returned to manufacturing parts that will change the appearance of a vehicle, though much less drastically than their kits once did. 'There's a little bit of an aggressive touch to it, but it's far more subtle,' explains Jane.

The truth is that cars require less modification than they used to. In the 1990s, vehicles often looked dull and had weak sound systems. These days, some cars leave the factory looking almost like modified cars: check out a Volkswagen Scirocco, a Toyota Yaris GR4, a Cupra Leon hatchback or a Honda Civic Type R. Some modern electric cars can go from zero to sixty miles per hour ludicrously quickly, with no engine retuning necessary – not that many car modifiers will suffer electric cars, which strike them as too quiet and high-tech. It is not surprising that some people now choose to make only minor cosmetic changes to their vehicles.

Modified cars often look more polite, these days. They do not sound more polite. Many people take their cars to garages that 'remap' the engine, in effect reprogramming it. Remapping can achieve various things, including greater power, but drivers often ask for 'pops and bangs'. When a driver revs a remapped engine hard and lifts the accelerator, fuel ignites in the exhaust system, causing explosions. The sound will wake every sleeping baby in the vicinity and, not infrequently, draw the police. And a pop-and-bang remap is even less neighbourly than it sounds. Explosions in the exhaust system tend to wreck catalytic converters, so garages recommend that the cats are removed before they go to work. Drivers who do that will end up releasing large quantities of dangerous pollutants such as carbon monoxide and nitrogen oxides into the air. In order to pass annual emissions tests, they may briefly reconnect their catalytic converters or go to a garage that is prepared to look the other way. Obnoxious noises, air pollution, corruption – it's not a great combination, really.

Some modified-car enthusiasts, particularly those over the age of about twenty-five, loathe pop-and-bang remaps. Because the remaps are done by experts with laptops, at considerable cost, they contravene the do-it-yourself ethos of car modification. Besides, some petrolheads have babies of their own. The first time I heard popping and banging at a car meet, I asked someone how it was achieved. 'A remap and lots of money,' he said, wearily. 'If you spend £40,000, you can make your whole car explode.' Some of the people who organize car meets have tried to ban popping and banging or ridicule it into oblivion, without much success.

Needless to say, loud bangs provide the authorities with yet another excuse to crack down on car modifiers and their gatherings. In the past few years, some local authorities have covered entire towns with injunctions and protection orders that ban obnoxious car-related behaviour. Great Yarmouth, a seaside town in Norfolk, has one that targets dropping litter from cars, playing amplified music in a way that seems likely to cause a nuisance, and doing wheel spins, which the council helpfully defines as: 'accelerating at speed which causes the wheels of the vehicle to spin in a manner a competent driver would expect not to happen in the normal course of driving'. Stevenage, a town in Hertfordshire, bans 'excessive noise' and 'revving engines'.

Fast, furious and female

Between the controversies over popping and banging, the technologically savvy coppers and the legally tooled-up local authorities, it is not easy to organize a car meet these days. In the *Max Power* era, you could put the word out via text messages and cruise websites and not bother obtaining permission. Try that today and you would be met with a barricaded car park, a line of police cars and perhaps an exclusion order. Some car groups have responded to the worsening climate by releasing locations at the last minute and hoping that the modified cars turn up before the police and the security guards do. Others take a more legitimate road. They obtain permission for their meets, try to persuade burger vans and other retailers to attend, deal politely with the police and attempt to impose some order on the proceedings. The best of these groups tend to have one thing in common. They are at least partly, and often largely, run by women.

*

Women have always been present at modified-car cruises and meets. But for years their allotted role was to sit in the passenger seat and to pose for magazine photographers, wearing as little clothing as possible. 'It's funny, you don't see many girls driving cars at cruises,' noted *Max Power* at one point, oblivious to its own role in pushing them to the kerb. Modified-car culture was overwhelmingly male, and frequently sexist. When Stuart Allatt and Jane Allatt (who are father- and daughter-in-law) went to car shows, they noticed that the petrolheads would try to talk to him rather than her.

In 2020, Misha Rogers started to create an online community of modified-car enthusiasts in and around Lancashire – online because the government had barred people from meeting in groups lest they spread Covid-19. Rogers kept herself anonymous for months. She had previously gone to car meets and felt unwelcome, whether because of her sex or her car, a not-too-exciting Vauxhall Corsa, was hard to say. Now, without anonymity or apology, Rogers runs Midnight Lancs, one of the fastest-growing car clubs in Britain. She has also moved on to a better car: a black Toyota Celica, which she has modified and partially wrapped with a decorative film.

Midnight Lancs holds regular car meets and attends car shows, but it is as much an online community as a real-world one. On Facebook, the club holds regular 'cover competitions', inviting drivers to submit photos of their cars, then puts the best ones atop the club page. Members ask other members if they know a mechanic who could sort out their turbo or remove some dents cheaply. Like many modified-car clubs, Midnight Lancs sells stickers that members can put in their car windows. It uses those stickers to bind the community together. Anybody in the club who spots another car with a Midnight Lancs sticker may take a picture and post it online, which usually generates a warm response from the owner. People like to feel noticed and part of a group.

Managing a website, a social-media presence and regular car meets takes a good deal of time and effort. 'I used to take it all on myself, but I've learned that, to grow, you need to delegate,' says Rogers. Midnight Lancs has had different numbers of admin-istrators over the years, who take on various tasks; when I meet Rogers, it has eight or nine. Other car clubs are even more formally organized. At a modified-car event in Staffordshire, I meet Marie Wiseman, who has quickly built an impressive outfit known as Purely Static, which focuses on car shows. Her club has a recruiter, a merchandiser, a photographer, a content creator and several social-media managers. 'It's like a company – everyone has their own role,' she says.

I ask Rogers why women have become so much more prominent

in the car scene. She isn't sure, although she points out that, to run a successful club, you need to pay close attention to members' moods and wishes. Whether women are inherently more socially astute than men is a question I will leave to the psychologists. What is certainly true is that women are more likely to work as secretaries or administrators, or in the caring professions (Rogers works for a health-care company; Wiseman is a freight settlement specialist at a logistics firm). Jobs like that strengthen the social and managerial muscles that are required to run a modified-car club in an era of enormous challenge and complexity. Working as a mechanic might not.

One evening, I go to a car meet on the outskirts of Rotherham in South Yorkshire, run by a group known as Renegades. One of the founders, Tara Beaumont, greets me. For the next two hours, she does not rest. She deals with a bearded, oil-stained man who incessantly demonstrates the loud explosions that his car can produce. She deals with the police, who seem not to like the explosions. She deals with a yellow-vested security guard who turns up, unannounced, and starts photographing vendors. She deals with an angry crowd of car modifiers, who take umbrage at the security guard's behaviour. At one point, somebody complains to her that a four-by-four is being driven dangerously, and she deals with them. She deals with me. It is an impressive, exhausting display of competence and tact under pressure. Beaumont tells me that she doesn't know a huge amount about cars, but does know how to organize things. I don't believe her on the first point, but I believe her on the second.

I have described car modification as a facet of white British working-class culture. It is, but they are not the only people who do it. Midge, who has been around the car scene for a long time, is struck by its growing ethnic diversity. I have yet to attend a modified-car meet or a car show where no British Asians have been present. Car modification is especially popular among working-class Asian Muslims – perhaps even more popular than it is among working-class white people. As one Muslim man explains to me at a car meet: 'We can't go clubbing; we can't drink. What else are we going to spend our money on?'

The car meet where I spot the blue Opel has been organized by Bradford Modified Club. That outfit is run by a man named Mo Ali, who is too absorbed with his DJing responsibilities to talk to me (perhaps he should have a word with Rogers about delegation). It takes place in Manningham, just up the road from Bradford Central Mosque – the very heart of Pakistani Bradford. The event is billed as an 'Eid Extravaganza'. Not surprisingly, given the location and the billing, the crowd is mostly Asian. But it isn't entirely Asian. Working-class white men and women have also turned up to show off their cars and admire other people's. People mix easily, and obey the stewards, who are a mixture of Asian and white, male and female. No alcohol is present to offend anyone's religious sensibilities. It rarely is at car meets, whoever organizes them. Considering the attention that police officers lavish on car modifiers, you would have to be very stupid to drive away from a meet with alcohol in your bloodstream.

Bradford is the city where, in July 2001, white and Asian youths violently confronted each other and the police. Manningham Ward Labour Club was firebombed, causing the terrified occupants to retreat to the basement; businesses were attacked; many police officers were injured. Afterwards, an official investigation led by Ted Cantle, formerly the chief executive of Nottingham City Council, concluded that whites and Asians were living 'parallel lives' in Bradford and other northern cities. Cantle's report argued for more diversity training and a string of rather worthy measures to reduce cultural segregation. It did not anticipate that working-class Asian and white people might find common ground in their love of alloy wheels, enormous spoilers and pop-and-bang remaps. Yet that is what has happened.

Journalists have not paid much attention to the modified-car scene, beyond reporting on the injuries and deaths that sometimes occur at Mexico meets. They ought to reconsider, if only because attending a car meet as a journalist is such a pleasurable experience. 'Are you a poet?' asks one young man, who has spotted me scribbling some notes after an interview. 'Or . . . a journalist?' His evident delight at my answer is a lovely contrast to the usual reactions I receive when I reveal my trade, which tend to range from wariness to hostility. I will always think fondly of the car modifiers, even as I wince at their infernal exploding exhausts and look forward, one day, to acquiring my first electric car.

Chapter Five

The art of ventriloquized xenophobia

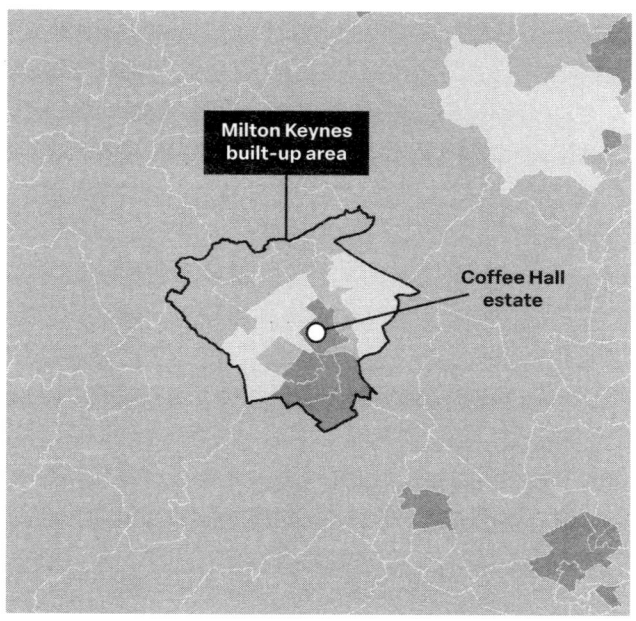

'It's got worse and worse as the years have gone on,' a middle-aged white woman tells me. 'It's just literally the volume. There's too many.' Asylum-seekers are treating Britain as 'treasure island', she continues, by sucking up resources that ought to be going to natives. 'We're not looking after our own,' she says. A man assures me, with heavy emphasis, that mass immigration has turned a nearby city into 'a very *dark* place'. He too is furious about the number of asylum-seekers crossing the English Channel in inflatable boats, and thinks that the boats ought to be sunk. Another man reckons that most asylum-seekers come to Britain not because they are in danger, but because they 'want a bit of lifestyle'.

Unemployed ex-miners in a depressed pit village in Yorkshire? The working-class inhabitants of a decaying seaside town? No. The people I have quoted are middle class. I met them in Market Harborough, a pleasant, wealthy market town that was chosen to represent the East Midlands in the 2023 Britain in Bloom competition, run by the Royal Horticultural Society. It is a reminder that Britons from more than one walk of life are capable of talking sharply about immigrants, and particularly asylum-seekers, if you assure them that you will not ask their names. But middle-class people should hardly need reminding of that. They might think back to the rows over current affairs that have erupted at their family gatherings, and what those rows were about.

British attitudes to immigration are like a tornado – furious, unpredictable and extremely dangerous to be around, especially if you are a politician. The subject can fade in importance, then come roaring back. Opinions move suddenly and unexpectedly. Although Britons can distinguish between different kinds of immigrant, national attention tends to light on one group at a time: the 'Windrush generation' of Caribbean workers in the 1950s and 1960s, Asians fleeing east Africa in the 1970s, Eastern Europeans in the 2000s, asylum-seekers today. Britons are liable to conclude that the entire immigration system is broken if just part of it is. People's views on immigration bleed into their views on ethnic diversity, and vice versa. The subject occupies far more space in some minds than in others. People who are relaxed about immigration, or want more of it, tend not to see it as terribly important. Those who firmly oppose immigration think it is very important indeed.

I will show in this chapter that white working-class Britons are more opposed to immigration and more sceptical about efforts to assist members of minority ethnic groups than white middle-class Britons are. Both groups take a harder view of immigration than ethnic-minority people do. But white working-class people are not of one mind. Opinions within the group vary hugely, from extreme xenophobia and racism to extreme liberalism. And social class is not overwhelmingly important. If you want to predict a white Briton's attitude to immigration and diversity, their class is not what you really need to know about them.

If these conclusions seem surprising, it could be because British politicians have for many years insisted that profound differences exist. White working-class people are believed to hold distinctive, hard-edged opinions on immigration and race. It is also widely believed that their views spring from their social and economic circumstances. Their experiences as workers in industries that have been permeated by immigrants, and as residents in neighbourhoods that have been flooded with immigrants, are said to have made them hostile. That these arguments have been aired so frequently does not make them correct, however. The truth about class, ethnicity and attitudes to immigration in Britain is different from the familiar story. In my opinion, it is more hopeful.

*

John (not his real name) seems at first to conform perfectly to the stereotype of the xenophobic white working-class man. He lives in a council estate in Leicester. A former building labourer, he is in his sixties and is in poor health. When I first met him, several years ago, he walked me round the estate, reminiscing about old shops and schoolmates and describing the many changes he had seen. These days, he finds walking difficult, so we sit in his garden. I ask him how the neighbourhood has altered, and especially how its population has changed.

His answer is long and detailed, spanning five decades. For

many years, he says, his estate was far more homogeneous than Leicester as a whole. Even as the city centre grew more ethnically diverse from the early 1970s, and a few Asian boys turned up in his school, the local streets remained overwhelmingly white and British until the very end of the twentieth century. Then immigrants began to arrive from Poland, Somalia and other countries. As a result, he says, 'it's a different vibe now'. White Britons see that council houses are being rented to immigrants and ethnic minorities while their own children are denied homes, and they deeply resent it. 'The feeling is,' he says, 'they can come over here and get whatever they want, but if we want something, we don't get it.' He believes that people who have lived on the estate for years should get 'first dibs' on homes.

John argues that immigration has turned Leicester's city centre into a foreign land and has smothered a vibrant white working-class culture. 'The life of the normal British person in the estates doesn't exist now,' he says. Most of the pubs and clubs where white working-class people used to drink have shut, partly because they were poorly managed and charged too much for beer, but also because immigrants seldom patronize them. Gallingly, some of the defunct pubs and clubs have been turned into community centres for immigrants. And some of the newcomers behave in ways that John finds offensive, such as speaking foreign languages in shops. He sees almost no overlap between their interests and his. 'There's two sides now,' he says. 'There's the immigrants and there's the families that were born here.'

At times, John talks like a soldier cowering in a trench while shells explode around him. At other times, though, he seems to hover above the conflict. He can be cool, reflective and funny on the subject of immigration and how it is perceived by people like him. 'Britain's always been a racist country – anyone who says not is lying,' he says. 'The English working class thought they were a cut above the Irish, then above the Windrush, then above the Asians.' He believes that their resentment – his resentment – of immigrants and ethnic minorities is based partly on misunderstandings and lies. At one point, he starts telling me that some of the immigrants who have moved to his estate are 'the dregs' and criminals. Then he stops himself and admits that, actually, there were plenty of criminals around when the estate was almost entirely white and British.

He doesn't think he is racist, he tells me several times. But his children think he is, because of the way he talks. John and his friends sometimes use words that the younger generation finds ridiculous or offensive, such as 'chinky' for a Chinese takeaway. He cannot help it. He explains that he picked up the words, and acquired his us-versus-them attitude to immigrants, as a young man, and he is too old to change now. Sometimes John seems to me like someone fighting a forgotten war. It is as though he is slogging away at the front, long after most of his army has given up and gone home. He flicks back and forth between arguing that all white working-class people in his estate feel angry and betrayed, and wondering whether only he and his friends feel that way.

One word that social scientists use to describe people like John is 'ethnocentric'. This refers to the tendency to put one's own ethnic group at the centre of the world, and to judge other groups in relation to it (generally negatively). It isn't a perfect fit for his views. John's central belief is not that white Britons are superior but that all ethnic and national groups have distinct interests, which inevitably bring them into conflict. He notes with satisfaction that some Asian taxi drivers in Leicester also rail against recent immigrants. Although he firmly takes a side – that of white working-class Britons raised in his estate – he is able to rise above the fray and see it as silly and probably short-lived. It is a peculiar mixture of views. But other people who have interviewed middle-aged and old white working-class Britons about immigration and ethnic change in their neighbourhoods have picked up a similar combination of hostility, reflection and sympathy.

If older white working-class people like John suspect that young people do not share their views, they are right. Just how far out of whack the two groups have become is suggested by a conversation with a second white working-class man, in Southampton. Like John, he lives on a council estate that is growing more ethnically mixed. It looks tatty, and feels more dangerous than John's estate. He likes it all the same, and hopes to stick around. 'The houses are pretty good,' he says, with a sly smile; 'the people who live in them, not always so good.' He is in his late teens and is immensely fit. I interview him in a boxing club, as he punches a bag in a quiet corner next to the ring. If I ask a question that he finds difficult, he steadies the bag and thinks for a moment before responding. I notice that he doesn't find questions about immigration or ethnic change difficult.

How, I ask, have people who were brought up in the estate responded to the arrival of immigrants and non-white people? 'It's all right, really – it's not a big deal,' he says, blithely. He says that the estate is not trouble-free, neither is the school he attends, but the divisions that exist do not run along ethnic lines. (This wasn't true a few decades ago: a middle-aged coach at the boxing club remembers when racist skinheads would loiter outside the local shops.) His close friend, an immigrant from the Balkans, seems to experience no animosity from other teenagers. And the issue of immigration does not exercise him personally. 'It doesn't bother me at all,' he says. 'As long as they're legal or whatever, it's fine.' He expects to become a carpenter or some other kind of builder, and does not worry that he will be competing against immigrant workers. He even has a vague notion that he might become an immigrant one day, in America. He is particularly keen on the idea of moving to California or Florida. Both of those states are quite a bit more ethnically varied than Southampton.

My conversations with young white working-class Britons, both male and female, tend to run along these lines. They are largely unbothered by immigration and ethnic diversity. They don't have particularly strong views on the matter, nor do most of the young people they know. At first, I found this frustrating. I wanted clear statements of liberalism or illiberalism, and did not get them. I suspected that my interviewees might be shy, and hesitant to express views that could be construed as racist or xenophobic. They probably are shy, given the strength of anti-racist norms in schools, colleges and other places where young people spend much of their time (at the Southampton boxing club, I am handed a cup of tea in a mug with 'zero discrimination' printed on the side). But I think the main reason is simpler. Many young white working-class people are just not very interested in immigration and ethnic change. I might as well be asking for their opinions on the disappearance of defined-benefit pension schemes.

*

The impression I get from talking to people, of a chasm between the views of old and young white working-class people, is backed up by data. With James Fransham, a colleague from *The Economist*, I have analysed a poll of 30,000 people conducted in 2022, part of a long-running series known as the British Election Study. Because of the enormous sample, far larger than an ordinary poll, the BES allows you to see not only how opinions vary by ethnicity and social class, but also how different groups within the white working class think. The poll included several questions designed to tease out people's views of immigration and race. One of them is particularly revealing. Do you think, people were asked, that attempts to help ethnic minorities in Britain have gone too far or not far enough?

The responses to that question show that, among white Britons, attitudes vary by class. Among white people from the A, B and C1 social groups (the middle class, more or less), 33 per cent think that efforts to give equal opportunities to ethnic minorities have not gone far enough, 34 per cent think the efforts have been about right, 23 per cent think they have gone too far, and the rest don't know. Subtracting the people who think that efforts have gone too far from the people who think they have not gone far enough, that is a balance of plus 10 per cent – a slight progressive tilt. White Britons from the C2, D and E social groups lean gently the other way. Among them, the balance of opinion is minus 4 per cent. That is, 4 per cent more white working-class people think that efforts to help ethnic minorities have gone too far than think the opposite.

That is a significant difference, but hardly an enormous one. And the averages obscure a good deal of overlap between individual working-class and middle-class white people. White working-class Britons do not reliably have harder views on ethnicity, in the way that summers are reliably warmer than winters. They have harder views on average. It is more like the longevity of women and men: women live longer on average, but every woman does not live longer than every man.

The pattern becomes more interesting, and more stark, when you consider age as well as class. The British Election Study poll shows that white working-class Britons aged eighteen to twenty-five are highly progressive. Fully 41 per cent of them believe that efforts to provide equal opportunities to ethnic minorities have not gone far enough, whereas only 11 per cent believe the opposite. That is a hefty balance of plus 30 per cent – substantially higher than the figure for white middle-class Britons as a whole.

Among white working-class people over sixty-five, on the other hand, the balance of opinion is minus 18 per cent. Opinions harden relentlessly from age group to age group. White working-class people aged twenty-six to thirty-five are more conservative than those aged eighteen to twenty-five, but not as conservative as those aged thirty-six to forty-five, and so on.

Questions about immigration reveal similarly enormous differences among white working-class people of different ages. The British Election Study asked people whether they thought immigration was good or bad for the economy, offering a seven-point scale, where 1 meant very bad and 7 meant very good. Among eighteen- to twenty-five-year-old white Britons from the C2, D and E social groups, just 13 per cent picked options 1, 2 or 3, suggesting they thought immigration was bad for the economy. Among white Britons aged over sixty-five, 46 per cent picked one of those three options.

Age is at least as important as social class. If you should ever be asked to guess somebody's views on race or immigration, and are given the choice of knowing only the person's rough age or knowing only their social class, you should pick age every time. Young white working-class people are not as liberal as young white middle-class people. But when it comes to immigration and race, they resemble them more closely than they resemble old white working-class people.

The fact that older white working-class people hold sharp views on immigration and race is politically important because, as I will show in Chapter Ten, they vote. But when it comes to daily life, young people's views matter more. In the days when black and Asian people were frequently attacked by racists who wanted to keep them out of particular streets and council estates, the people doing the attacking were often young white working-class men – perhaps the kind of young men who frequented boxing clubs. As the young have grown blasé, the streets have grown quiet. The large Crime Survey of England and Wales shows that, between 2007 and 2009, 2.1 per cent of Asian people and 1.7 per cent of black people were victims of a racially motivated hate crime. By the years 2017 to 2020, the proportions had roughly halved to 1 per cent and 0.9 per cent. The police are tallying more hate crimes than ever, but that does not mean more are occurring: levels of recorded crime are influenced by laws, changes in recording practices and levels of trust in the police.

A terrible exception to this happy trend occurred in the summer of 2024. Following false rumours that the killer of three children at a dance class was an asylum-seeker, rioting broke out in Southport in north-west England and quickly spread. Crowds of white people attacked mosques, hotels containing asylum-seekers, and ethnic-minority people who happened to be walking or driving nearby. The riots shook Britain. Months later, Ukrainians living hundreds of miles from the riots told me how scared they had been. As the alleged perpetrators were caught and charged, it became clear that many were working class; indeed, many were indigent. Strikingly, though, not all were young. An analysis by *The Guardian* found that 36 per cent of those charged were aged forty or over, compared with just 5 per cent of the people who were charged following riots in 2011, which were sparked by the police killing of a black Londoner. Some offenders were really old. 'Get off me, I'm fucking 70,' protested one man as he was arrested in 2024 (he was later convicted). 'Why are you at a fucking riot?' retorted a police officer.

In 2022, two political scientists, Jane Green and Roosmarijn de Geus, published a paper called 'Red wall, red herring?' They found, just as I did, that middle-aged and old people are hostile to immigration, particularly if they did not go to university. Green and de Geus also discovered something else. They measured people's level of economic security by asking whether they owned their homes and how easily they would cope if they suddenly had to pay £300 to cover some emergency. As you would expect, young people without university degrees are insecure. Old people without degrees are not, however. They tend to own their homes. They have steady (though often low) incomes from pensions. They're not likely to be blown into poverty by a sudden misfortune. By and large, the people who complain most loudly about immigration are not the people who live hand to mouth.

Britons have made two mistakes in thinking about ethnicity, class and attitudes to race and immigration. The first is the assumption that white working-class people think the same as each other, and unlike middle-class people. The second is the idea that white working-class people have derived their views from hard experience – that they are hostile to newcomers for pragmatic, self-interested reasons. These wrong ideas have been around for decades. But they took up residence in many people's minds at one moment: in the aftermath of the most famous speech by the greatest loudmouth ever to opine on the subject of race in Britain.

*

Enoch Powell's 'Rivers of Blood' speech, which he delivered to an audience in Wolverhampton in April 1968, is remembered as a searing attack on immigration. That isn't exactly right. True, Powell believed that British immigration policy was far too lax, and argued that immigrants should be encouraged to leave the country. But his main concern was not the porousness of the border. He had nothing against temporary migrants, including foreign students and doctors. Powell's real objection was to the growth of the non-white population, whether foreign- or British-born. He believed that black and Asian children who had been born in Britain were at least as hazardous as their parents, because they would grow up to have children of their own – they were 'the material of the future growth of the immigrant-descended population'. As the numbers of non-white people grew, Powell argued, so did the likelihood of riots like the ones that were then convulsing American cities following the murder of Martin Luther King Jr. He was apocalyptically gloomy about Britain's future: 'It is like watching a nation busily engaged in heaping up its own funeral pyre.'

If the growing non-white population of Britain was the pyre, Powell went on, racial equality was the match that would set it alight. He gave his speech on 20 April, knowing that it would be covered by newspapers the following day. Two days after that, on 23 April, the Race Relations Bill was debated in the House of Commons. That bill, which tightened racial discrimination laws, would in Powell's opinion empower black people against white people. In the most famous section of his speech, he claimed that a white old-age pensioner in Wolverhampton who was refusing to let rooms in her house to black people had already had her windows broken, and was harassed by 'wide-grinning piccaninnies' as she walked to the shops (a respected classical scholar and a poet, Powell flung insults deliberately, knowing the dehumanizing effect they would have). According to him, the pensioner feared that the new bill would result in her being sent to prison. The probable outcome of the new racial-equality legislation, as Powell put it in another famous passage, was that: 'in this country in fifteen or twenty years' time the black man will have the whip hand over the white man'.

Powell, who had once been health minister, was promptly sacked from the Conservative shadow cabinet and was never again a force in Parliament. He went on to endorse the Labour Party because of its opposition to European integration, then joined the Ulster Unionist Party. But the speech that ended his hopes of a plum job was a sensational success in its own right. The Commons debate on 23 April was taken up largely by discussion of Powell's views, just as he would have wished. Some of the talk was approving, some disapproving, some sniffy. The best quip came from Quintin Hogg, a Conservative MP from London, who said that, if Britain was really building its own funeral pyre, 'it might be thought a little careless to go about with a lighted cigarette in one's mouth, flicking the ash all over the place'.

Then, in response to Powell's sacking, came the strikes and the demonstrations. Some 1,000 workers in West India Dock failed to report on 23 April. The following day, another 500 walked out at two other London docks. Some of the dockers went to meet Powell, and emerged from the room saying that the experience had made them feel proud to be British. Meat porters from Smithfield market marched on Parliament in white coats, carrying a sign: 'We back Enoch'. There were strikes and demonstrations at a tyre factory in Gateshead, at a power station in Staffordshire and at a factory in the West Midlands that made HP Sauce.

Powell had not appealed specifically to white working-class people. He claimed that most Britons agreed with him, and he described the views of two constituents. One, who had told Powell he was so scared of the prospect of black domination that he wanted to settle his children overseas, the MP described as 'a middle-aged, quite ordinary working man employed in one of our nationalized industries'. The other person Powell mentioned was the landlady in Wolverhampton. Whereas the man sounds working class, the woman – who owned outright a seven-bedroom house on a 'respectable' street – sounds solidly middle class. In another speech, Powell fretted that immigration was reducing property values, a classic middle-class concern. He was trying to speak for all white people, but the people marching in the streets were mostly working class. Were they the only ones who agreed with him?

They were not. Middle-class white Britons also supported Powell. They just expressed it differently. On 23 April, *The Scotsman* printed a letter from a vicar, who echoed Powell's warnings and compared anti-racists to the pacifists who had refused to stand up to German aggression before the Second World War. *The Birmingham Daily Post* reported that the managing director of an agricultural machinery plant in Huntingdon congratulated workers who walked out to express their support for Powell. Opinion polls revealed strong middle-class assent. Soon after the speech, Gallup showed that 70 per cent of people belonging to the A, B and C1 social groups agreed with Powell's views, compared with 75 per cent in the C2 group and 78 per cent in the DE group. Another poll by NOP put the proportions at 66 per cent, 71 per cent and 63 per cent. Powell was preaching to an enormous congregation, which included a majority of people from all classes. A book published in 1977, *Enoch Powell and the Powellites*, described his supporters as 'distinctive for their lack of distinctiveness'.

Manual workers were not always as solid for Powell as they appeared. Some strongly agreed with his racial views. 'Docklands always feels it worst,' Harry Pennington, a leader of the Royal Docks strike, told *The Times*. 'You have every colour in God's earth down there. We've got as many Chinese as Mao and we're getting a bit browned off.' Others did not. Some dockers disagreed with Powell, but could not bear to cross the picket line that their Powellite colleagues had set up. One man who made that choice was a card-carrying member of the Campaign Against Racial Discrimination. He was so disgusted with his own behaviour that he tore up his card. Some unions took firmly anti-Powell positions. The general secretary of the Scottish Mineworkers' Union railed against a 'pathetically misguided minority of the working class'.

The events of April 1968 did not show that white working-class Britons held uniquely hostile views on immigration and race. But they did show that many people dearly wanted to believe this. Opinion polls and dog-collared letter-writers notwithstanding, the public discussion of Powell's speech focused on how and why *working-class* white people were so keen on it. Middle-class people sought to explain that support in a particular way. Those who agreed with Powell argued that poor East Enders were righteously angry about the presence of foreigners in their neighbourhoods. Those who opposed Powell, including Ian Mikardo, a Labour MP, suggested that the London dockers had been unsettled by the threat of redundancy. All agreed that working-class people's experiences and economic concerns drove their protests. And some white working-class people made the same arguments.

Powell received more than 100,000 letters following his speech, most of them fawning. Demonstrating impressive stamina, the historian Amy Whipple read some 2,000 of them for an article published in 2009. She found that many of Powell's working-class admirers cited their experiences to justify their racial views. 'Ordinary "white folk" . . . have to contend with working and living next door to Indians, Jamaicans, and God knows what other coloured people,' wrote one. 'At last someone speaks for the working day man who has to live with these people,' wrote another. They were reading into Powell's speech something that was not there. He had argued that the rising black and Asian population threatened all white Britons. His working-class admirers saw it as a problem for them specifically, and claimed that other politicians had ignored it because it did not touch them personally.

Educated xenophobes had made similar arguments before. Opponents of Jewish and Italian migration in the nineteenth century had also claimed to be motivated by the desire to protect British workers. In 1965, the peer Lord Godfrey Elton published

141

a book called *The Unarmed Invasion*, in which he argued that immigration challenged 'the fragile but intensely precious homogeneity of a sparingly-educated urban community' of white natives. But the reaction to the 'Rivers of Blood' speech turned up the volume on this argument, and taught politicians an important lesson. A good way to express hostile views on immigration and race is to voice them not as your own opinions (which might get you labelled a xenophobe or a racist, and get you sacked), but as the opinions of vulnerable white working-class people who have acquired them through hard experience. A good way to attack people with more liberal views is to argue that they do not appreciate the negative effects of immigration because they do not experience them.

In 1978, Margaret Thatcher, then leader of the Conservative opposition, went on a television programme called *World in Action* and declared that Britons feared being 'rather swamped by people with a different culture'. Thatcher knew exactly what she was doing (she said 'swamped' twice, to be sure people heard) and the effect on public opinion was dramatic. The Conservative Party jumped in the polls. Looking back, in the mid-1990s, Thatcher explained that she had been thinking about working-class people. It is one thing, she wrote, for a well-heeled politician to preach the virtues of open borders before returning to 'a comfortable home in a tranquil road in one of the more respectable suburbs'. It is quite another for poorer people to watch their neighbourhoods changing in alarming ways. The politician's job, she explained, is to stand up for the powerless.

Politicians who agree on little else have echoed this opinion. 'Crudely expressed,' said John Denham, then the Labour Party communities secretary, in 2009, 'the higher you are in the pecking order, the more likely you are to benefit from immigration.' In 2014, James Brokenshire, a Conservative minister, explained that mass immigration was good for bosses who want 'an easy supply of cheap labour' and for members of the wealthy metropolitan elite who want 'cheap tradesmen and services'. It was not good for 'the ordinary, hardworking people of this country'. In 2016, during her unhappy spell as prime minister, Theresa May lamented that immigration had 'put a downward pressure on wages for working-class people'.

This often-repeated story of working-class white Britons resenting immigrants for rational, self-interested reasons has a couple of plot holes, though. One is that the economic evidence about immigration and wages isn't clear-cut. Although it might seem intuitive that increasing the supply of working-class immigrants would depress working-class wages, it is remarkably hard to see this happening in practice. American economists have argued for decades about an episode that ought to have provided a splendid case study: the moment in 1980 when many working-class Cubans suddenly migrated to Miami, swelling its labour force. To the extent that a consensus about immigration and working-class wages exists among economists, it is that any effect is small – smaller than the effect of policies like the minimum wage. And immigrants bring hidden benefits. Because new arrivals tend to pay more in taxes than they receive in benefits, it is likely that taxes – including taxes on working-class people – would be higher if they had not come.

A second problem with the familiar story is that, if immigration has a bad effect on other workers, this effect is not felt strongly by the people who are grumpiest about immigration. Immigrants tend to be young, and they often work in industries that employ lots of young Britons, such as hospitality. You might, therefore, expect that young white working-class people would be particularly hostile to immigrants. And you might expect that working-class ethnic minorities would be even more hostile, since immigrants not only compete against them for jobs but frequently settle in their neighbourhoods. The opposite is true. Old white working-class Britons are the most hostile group, even though immigrants compete with them hardly at all. Retired white people depend on new arrivals to fund the state pension system and look after them in hospitals and care homes. Having to listen to them chatting in foreign languages once in a while might seem a small price to pay. But apparently not.

Why are we so attached to the idea that hard life experiences lead to hard attitudes? One possibility is that it is nearly accurate. It could be that older white working-class people are angry not because they have been harmed by immigration, but because they believe their children and grandchildren have been harmed. In Leicester, John has a pretty cushy housing situation, but he claims to be angry on behalf of his friends' children. Another possibility is that conservative populists are being crafty. In an era of strong anti-racist norms, it would be unwise for a politician to appeal openly to white people's racial prejudices. Better to couch an appeal in terms of economic self-interest. 'It has suited the radical right to say: "you've got a legitimate reason to be angry and fearful"', Jane Green says.

I'm going to suggest another, more cynical explanation. My analysis of the British Election Study shows that white middle-class Britons are sharply divided by age, just as white working-class Britons are. The young are very progressive about race and very relaxed about immigration. Older white middle-class people are illiberal, though not quite as illiberal as older white working-class people. They too are aware of anti-racist norms, not least because their children harangue them on the subject, and they are keen to smuggle their own prejudices into the mouths of others. Please understand, it isn't that I detest ethnic diversity or mass immigration, they say. But white working-class people do detest it, and their views ought to be respected. In this way, the prejudices of the suburban golf club are imputed to the council-estate boxing club. It is a kind of ventriloquized xenophobia.

*

Why do the old and the young think so differently from each other? The answer offered by conservative populists is that many (indeed, far too many) young people go to university, where they have their heads filled with what they would call woke nonsense. There is a grain of truth in that, but no more than a grain. Going to university does not in itself make young people much more liberal; rather, young people with liberal instincts tend to go to university. And even young school-leavers somehow manage to develop fairly tolerant views. Young white people who did not go to university are, for example, more willing to accept a minority ethnic in-law than old white people who did go to university.

The most likely explanation for the age divide is familiarity. Thanks to research on the censuses by Migration Watch, a think tank opposed to mass immigration, it is clear just how different the generations' experiences have been. A person who was born in 1951 grew up in a land where 4 per cent of people had been born abroad. In the year this person turned twenty, the proportion was only slightly higher, at 6 per cent. A person who was born in 2001, on the other hand, entered a land in which 9 per cent of the population was foreign-born. By the time they reached the age of twenty, in 2021, the share was 17 per cent. Less is known about the growth of the minority ethnic population, because the census did not ask about ethnicity until 1991. But the trend is probably similar: a gentle rise in diversity in the late twentieth century, followed by a rapid rise in the twenty-first.

The 'contact hypothesis' is a fancy academic term for a simple idea: that people who grow up in a diverse country are more comfortable with diversity. Lauren McLaren, who studies the subject at the University of Leicester, thinks that the teenage years are especially important. She has calculated that, controlling for other things, if the share of the foreign-born population is 1 per cent higher when a cohort of people is aged fifteen to twenty, that cohort will be 0.2 points more relaxed about immigration on a one-to-ten scale. Going to mixed schools and colleges makes white Britons more accepting, and they stay that way.

As I showed in Chapter One, many white working-class people live in small towns where few immigrants or non-white people are seen. But few is more than none. The white British share of the population is falling almost everywhere as immigrants and minority ethnic Britons venture beyond cities and large towns. At the same time, a more subtle change is occurring. Some places that used to contain lots of white Britons and lots of one other group, and may have felt sharply divided along ethnic lines as a result, are now a more complex mix. The 2002 film *Bend It Like Beckham*, which is set in the west London borough of Hounslow, makes much of the mutual incomprehension of the white British and Indian communities. Half of Hounslow's population is now neither white British nor Indian.

Besides, it is not necessary to live next door to people of a different ethnicity or national origin in order to be exposed to them. In sport, politics and the media, diversity has grown hugely over the years. It is sometimes hard to believe how recent the changes have been. The men's England football team is often said to have got its first black player, Viv Anderson, in 1978, although another man, the Plymouth Argyle player Jack Leslie, was called up to the national team five decades earlier, only to be dropped when officials learned of his ethnicity. Just six ethnic-minority MPs were elected in 1992; ninety were elected in 2024. *Coronation Street*, a TV soap opera set in a working-class neighbourhood somewhere in Manchester, acquired its first Asian family in 1999 and its first black family in 2019.

A woman who was born in 1951 will have seen every one of these changes during her adult life. If she is well disposed towards immigrants and ethnic minorities, she may feel that Britain has become more interesting as a result. If not, she is likely to resent the change and may want to reverse it. The young have had a very different experience. For them, diversity is a fact of life. They have never known anything other. Their parents' and grandparents' tales of an overwhelmingly white, British country are curious but irrelevant, rather like their tales of life before the internet. The young might dislike some aspects of modern, ethnically diverse Britain, just as they might dislike some aspects of the internet. They do not believe it can be wished away.

You are only young once, of course. Middle-aged and old white Britons had the experience of growing up in a homogeneous country, and they cannot re-enter adolescence now that Britain is more mixed. But does that mean they will remain forever uncomfortable with diversity? Some researchers have argued that ethnocentrism is a stable aspect of people's personalities, and that attitudes change mostly because older generations die and younger ones replace them. Yet attitudes to some things, such as inter-ethnic marriage, have softened in every cohort, including the oldest. And even older people who are consistently suspicious of immigrants sometimes modulate their views in subtle but important ways. I found that process underway in a council estate in one of my favourite cities: Milton Keynes.

*

Coffee Hall is one of the oldest housing estates in one of Britain's youngest cities. It was built in the 1970s, at a time when Milton Keynes was a modernist architectural showcase rather than the conventional house-builders' paradise that it became. The estate is rigorously gridded, with streets running north–south and east–west in the American style. It has enormously wide, straight roads. The houses, many of them bungalows, have generous front gardens and tiny rear gardens, which, as one resident tells me, makes them feel back to front. They feature innovative though ill-advised building materials, such as breeze blocks. Coffee Hall is not even the most architecturally notable estate in the area. The next-door estate, Beanhill, was designed by a young Norman Foster.

Since the 1970s, Milton Keynes has changed from being overwhelmingly white to one of Britain's more mixed cities. The 2021 census showed it to be 62 per cent white and British. The other 38 per cent are a mixture of Asian and black people, non-British whites and mixed-heritage people, with no noticeable concentrations of ethnic-minority groups anywhere. Coffee Hall is much like the rest of the city, but is even more diverse. I ask a middle-aged white resident who has lived on the estate for many years how this change has gone down. It's been absolutely fine, she says. There have been no problems. Only, she adds, the older residents sometimes grumble about immigrants and ethnic minorities. I soon discover what she means.

When I visit, during a pay-what-you-can lunch at the local community centre, Coffee Hall is suffering from two problems. The first is parking. A popular mosque has opened on one edge of the estate and, during Friday prayers, the streets are clogged with cars. Many people complain about this, but, for one retired woman, the crush of Muslim drivers is a sign of a bigger problem. The population of the estate is changing too quickly, she says. Whenever a house comes on the market, it seems to be bought by an investor, chopped up and rented to immigrants. 'I want the estate to remain a mixed estate, and it might just become a mosque estate,' she says.

The second, more alarming problem in Coffee Hall is rats. I am told that the estate has a lot of them, and that they are becoming so brazen that they saunter through front gardens in the middle of the day. 'The pied piper has got nothing on it,' a man tells me. 'It's as though they're part of the estate.' And this problem, like the parking problem, strikes some of the residents as a by-product of changes in the human population. 'I don't want to sound racist, but a lot of people have moved into the estate who are not from Britain, shall we say. And they don't understand,' an old woman tells me. 'I'm not sure how to put this, but they're not white,' adds her middle-aged friend. What the immigrants (or non-white people) do not understand, according to these residents, is that, on rubbish-collection day, you must not put out your bags of rubbish too early. If you do, the rats will munch the contents and multiply.

Stories like this, of immigrants or ethnic minorities failing to understand some unwritten local rule, are told in many parts of Britain. In Higher Blackley, a suburb of Manchester, researchers listened to people complaining that immigrants were not inviting the neighbours round to admire their newborn babies, as custom demanded. In Waltham Forest, a north London borough, working-class white people complained about spitting in the street. Such tales are suffused with a subtle double standard. A white British resident who puts the rubbish out too early, fails to invite the neighbours to admire a baby, or spits in the street is an ill-mannered individual. When an immigrant or a non-white person does it, an entire group is tarnished.

The double standards are depressing. But gripes about people's behaviour can be dealt with more easily than objections to their mere presence. It should not be beyond the city of Milton Keynes to deal with a parking problem or a rat problem on the Coffee Hall estate. A residents' parking zone for the whole area, or white

149

lines indicating that you cannot park directly in front of people's driveways, would go a long way to ameliorating the Friday crush. As for the rats, the solution is thick plastic wheelie bins that cannot be gnawed through. Although these would not be in keeping with the original modernist vision for the estate, I doubt the architects envisaged a plague of rats either. In the autumn of 2023, the council started to provide bins. If the rat problem can be alleviated, local white people will have one less reason to complain about newcomers.

I went to Coffee Hall for a reason. In 2008, four researchers were commissioned by the National Community Forum, an organization set up by the government, to go around council estates and find out why some white working-class people were resentful. They visited Runcorn near Liverpool, Castle Vale in Birmingham, Thetford in Norfolk, and Milton Keynes. They found the Milton Keynes estates more run-down (even though the city is not poor) and more furious than the others. The residents of Coffee Hall told them something extraordinary. The council had offered to demolish their homes and build better ones for them, but they had refused to budge. If the residents moved out, even temporarily, they might lose their places in the estate to immigrants. Better a cold, draughty house than that.

I ask half a dozen people who have lived on the Coffee Hall estate since the noughties about this episode. They remember it completely differently. The residents say they were indeed wary of the council's plans for their estate, but they say nothing about the threat of losing their places to immigrants. What people now remember is that they feared ending up with less space. The council wanted to move them to 'titchy little box houses', says one woman. Another recalls that some people were happy to trade large old properties for smaller modern ones, but 'the rest of us were thinking, What's going to come of our gardens?' I do not believe the researchers misheard local people in 2008. Rather, I think the locals have chosen to remember a conflict with the authorities in a way that minimizes their own xenophobia. The new story, which revolves around a desire not to compromise on the size of their properties or their gardens, is more socially acceptable than a story about fearing and resenting immigrants. It is a small, subtle example of fading ethnocentrism.

It is possible that grievances against newcomers only move from subject to subject, and never disappear. Perhaps the residents of Coffee Hall will go from worrying about being displaced by immigrants, to complaining that immigrants don't handle their rubbish properly, to blaming them for something else. But I'm not sure that will happen. They have already taken an important step, from complaining about the mere presence of immigrants to complaining about their behaviour. And the hesitancy with which they express their views ('I'm not sure how to put this') suggests that the window of acceptable complaint is shrinking. People's words may have changed more than their attitudes, but words matter.

Here are some predictions, if anybody would like to visit Coffee Hall in about the year 2040. The parking problem will be partly solved. People will still be complaining about the Friday crush, but some means will have been found to preserve a space for everyone. The rat problem will be almost completely solved. The older residents of the estate will remember the rats. But they will not remember that some of them once blamed the infestation on immigrants and non-white people. And I am confident of one more thing. Most of the residents, of all ethnicities, will still like living in Coffee Hall. It will be a quiet, decent place, just as it is today. As one resident told me: 'It's not a glamorous estate. But we've got something here.'

Chapter Six

A refreshing breeze from the east

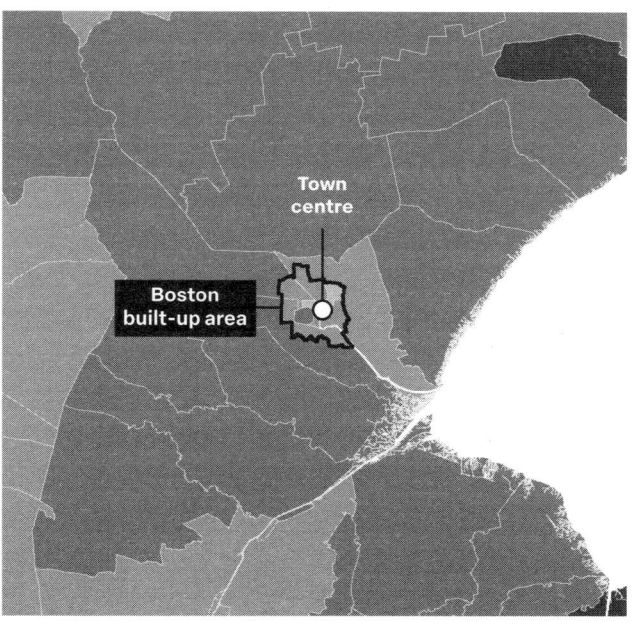

Britons often talk about the north–south divide, but, when it comes to farming, the most important divide is between west and east. In the west, from Cornwall all the way to Sutherland in Scotland, the soil is indifferent, the hills are high and the precipitation is heavy. 'Devon, lovely Devon,' goes the rhyme. 'Rains six days out of seven.' It is a mostly pastoral region of grass, sheep, cattle and Romantic poets. By comparison, the east is flat and dry. Fields are large and filled with cereal crops, fruit and vegetables. The east is Britain's larder and, unfortunately, it looks like it.

In the Fenland region of England, around the towns of Ely, Chatteris, March, Wisbech, Spalding and Boston, eastern arable farming reaches its apogee. The highly fertile soil is dark brown, and in places almost black. Crops press up close to roads and towns: this is valuable growing land and little goes to waste. Whereas you can walk for hours in the western countryside and not see a farmer, Fenland fields are busy with workers hoeing, cutting and loading. In large, cool sheds, other workers trim vegetables and send them down conveyor belts to be packaged. From there, they go to warehouses and supermarkets.

Much of Fenland used to be under water. It was drained at huge cost, beginning in the early seventeenth century, to the fury of local people, who were accustomed to fishing and hunting birds in the marshes. Today, many of the rivers are dead straight, as are the field edges. But this man-made landscape is largely devoid of resident men: Fenland has fewer villages than other parts of England. Farmers in the region have long relied on workers from nearby towns, and on the people who hire and transport those workers to them. In towns like Boston, it sometimes seems as though every other business is an agricultural employment agency. From high-street premises and suburban front rooms, these agents offer field and food-processing jobs paying the national minimum wage or a shade higher. Packing line, day shift, £11.44 per hour; warehouse, night shift, £13.33 per hour.

Although they detest the analogy, modern agricultural employment agents are descended from a notorious group of people known as gangmasters. They were a Fenland fixture by the nineteenth century. In *Capital*, his exploration of the drivers of capitalism, Karl Marx described a typical Lincolnshire gangmaster as 'a bad lot, a scapegrace, unsteady, drunken, but with a dash of enterprise and *savoir-faire*'. After contracting with a farmer, he marched workers (many of them young children) from town to field and back.

Labouring in a gang was hard, although it was leavened by a kind of outlaw jolliness and by drink. Marx, who liked a tipple himself, wrote delightfully about that: 'Generally the gangmaster pays up in a public house; then he returns home at the head of the procession reeling drunk, propped up right and left by a stalwart virago, while children and young persons bring up the rear, boisterous, and singing chaffing and bawdy songs.'

These days, the children are in school, the journeys to the fields and food-processing factories are in cars and minivans, and the after-work boozing has been drastically curtailed. But the fundamental facts of Fenland agriculture have not changed much since the nineteenth century. The industry still requires large numbers of people to do basic jobs, and is not prepared to pay them much. It has a well-oiled system for transporting workers to and fro. As a result, Fenland is a magnet for young immigrants who lack useful qualifications and speak little English. Over the past two decades, it has mostly drawn Eastern Europeans.

Even before eight Baltic and Eastern European countries joined the EU in 2004, a few of their citizens were working illicitly in Fenland fields. Then Britain opened its labour market to citizens of the accession countries, and a rush began. Today, the district of Boston has a higher share of people born in the countries that joined the union in 2004 than any other local authority in England or Wales. Peterborough, which is west of Fenland but within easy driving distance, comes second; South Holland, which lies between Boston and Peterborough, is third. A map of England and Wales showing the proportion of people born in Eastern European and Baltic countries looks remarkably like the inverse of a national rainfall map. The lower the average annual precipitation, the more cereal crops and vegetables are grown, the more Eastern Europeans live in the area.

In the spring of 2005, a man who I will call Lukas travelled from Lithuania to Peterborough. He was nineteen and had just finished school. He was due to enrol in the Lithuanian army later in the year and hoped to make a career as a soldier. But his brother, who had moved to Peterborough as soon as it became legal to work in Britain, encouraged him to come to England for a few months. Lukas agreed to try it. 'It was simple,' he remembers. 'I had no money.'

Lukas's first job was in a food-processing factory. For six days a week, he trimmed and packaged carrots, onions and tomatoes for a supermarket chain, travelling to and from the factory in a co-worker's car. In a little over a week, he earned as much money as he might have made in a month in Lithuania. His family had not been well off when he was growing up, and he found the pay astonishing. 'I was young – I could get crazy with this money,' he says, grinning at the memory. His plan to return to Lithuania and join the army was quietly set aside. Then, step by step, Lukas began to ascend Britain's occupational ladder.

His next job was for another supermarket, Morrisons. At first, he stacked potatoes, carrots and onions on pallets, but he soon learned to drive a forklift. Encouraged by a friendly British supervisor, he also began to learn English in earnest. Eventually, he left Morrisons and started working as a coach driver, taking schoolchildren on weekend trips. After he became a father, he sought a job with normal hours, and found one training other bus drivers. His English improved rapidly, not least because he asked his British students to correct his mistakes. He went on to set up a driving school. It had been a remarkable journey. In one and a half decades, Lukas had progressed from doing one of the most remedial jobs in Britain to skilled manual work, then into running a small business. From the lower reaches of the working class, he was knocking on the door of the middle class.

*

Until now, this book has focused on people who are incontrovertibly British. The people I have described and quoted tend to speak one language fluently. Migrating across national borders to live and work is less something they do than something they have opinions about. But the British white working class is only one part, albeit by far the largest part, of the white working class in Britain. A white person who recently moved from Lithuania or Italy and does a working-class job belongs to the second group, and may join the first in time. As I argued in the Introduction, people's ethnic identities are not always fixed, nor are their national identities. You can become a white Briton. You can also be a white Briton in some contexts but not in others. The white British working class is entirely capable of absorbing people from other countries and their children. If it could not, it would be a lot smaller and less varied than it actually is.

In the twentieth century, large numbers of working-class people migrated from Ireland to mainland Britain, continuing the toing and froing between the two islands that had occurred before Ireland became independent. They settled in some of the places where immigrants often end up – London, Birmingham, Manchester – but also in western Scotland. At the peak, in 1971, about 900,000 people who had been born in Ireland or Northern Ireland lived in England and Wales. They amounted to a little under 2 per cent of the population. In that year, London contained more people born in Ireland than in India, Pakistan or the Caribbean.

As Enda Delaney, a historian of Ireland and its diaspora, has shown in several illuminating books, the migrants frequently did hard, dirty jobs that the natives did not want. They were often looked down upon. One report for the Home Office in the 1920s called them 'almost a class of helots living in an alien land' and claimed that they were responsible for a large proportion of the crimes that took place in Scotland. In the late 1930s, following a bombing campaign by the Irish Republican Army, they were required to register with the police. Aircraft workers marched in Coventry, demanding that employers stop giving jobs to Irish workers. After the Second World War, landlords and publicans put up signs reading 'No Irish' or 'No work boots'. Since many Irish men worked in the construction industry, those signs amounted to more or less the same thing. As a child in 1970s London, I learned many rude jokes about Irish people, which I assume arrived in my school via parents and older brothers. I was too clueless to realize that some of my classmates were the children of Irish migrants.

Yet almost all of the migrants were white and English-speaking. Some of them could pass as white Britons, as migrants from Commonwealth countries generally could not, and their children and grandchildren found it easy. With greater or lesser comfort and difficulty, Irish migrants and their descendants have folded themselves into the majority ethnic group. As a result, Britain now contains an enormous number of people who are white, working class, and some combination of British and Irish. Exactly how many varies, based on the question and the context in which it is asked. An opinion poll in 2001 reported that a quarter of the population claimed to have Irish ancestry. But in the 2021 census of England and Wales, just 507,000 people described themselves as having a white Irish ethnicity – and more than half of those people had been born in Ireland. Despite campaigns by Irish groups to encourage people with Irish heritage to 'tick the box' in the census, and slogans like 'Feel Irish? Be Irish', most people descended from Irish migrants have become British for most purposes.

It has not always been an easy, painless process. Noreen Hill, who left Ireland during the Second World War to work in an aircraft factory in Leicester (and married an Englishman), was distressed by the ease with which her children became English. She even told an interviewer who was collecting Irish women's stories for a 1988 book called *Across the Water* that she envied Asian people for their distinctive languages and appearance, which she believed helped to preserve a sense of difference.

Nor is assimilation a predictable, one-way process. In a 2016 article, Ludi Simpson of the University of Manchester and others studied how people describe their ethnicity in censuses of England and Wales. By linking the censuses to a second survey that covers 1 per cent of the population, they found 4,069 people who described themselves as white Irish in the 2001 census and went on to fill in the 2011 census. Of that group, 1,008 (or almost a quarter) had become white British in the intervening decade. Some went the other way. Out of 370,669 people in the sample who called themselves white Britons in the 2001 census, 689 had become white Irish by 2011. Even people with almost identical backgrounds and experiences can make different decisions about their identities. Liam and Noel Gallagher, from the rock band Oasis, were held up as exemplars of working-class Englishness in the 'Cool Britannia' era of the 1990s. The British-born sons of Irish migrants, the two brothers firmly identify (respectively) as Irish and 'very English'.

Eastern Europeans are now going through a process that will eventually make many of them British. Like those who crossed the Irish Sea in the twentieth century, these twenty-first-century migrants are largely working class, and they have taken some of the worst jobs in the country. Also like the Irish, they have often been given the cold shoulder. The backlash against them, which culminated in the 2016 Brexit referendum, has had enormous consequences for them and for Britain.

They are not the same as the Irish. One difference is that the Eastern Europeans must overcome a language barrier. Another is that their legal status has changed profoundly. Many arrived under

EU freedom-of-movement rules but are now subject to special regulations, whereas citizens of Ireland have always been free to live and work in Britain. The two groups are concentrated in different parts of the country. That many Eastern Europeans will follow the Irish in joining the white British working class is certain. But they will give it an accent that it has never had before.

According to the 2021 census, 1.9 million people living in England and Wales were born in the eight countries that joined the EU in 2004 (the Czech Republic, Estonia, Hungary, Latvia, Lithuania, Poland, Slovakia and Slovenia) or the two that joined three years later (Bulgaria and Romania). Most migrated to Britain after their countries joined the union. The three biggest groups are Lithuanians, Poles and Romanians. In this chapter, I focus on working-class Lithuanians and Poles, because they have been around for longer. Although Romania joined the EU in 2007, its citizens have only been able to work freely in Britain since 2014. The Lithuanians' and Poles' experiences are varied, as you would expect from such a large group. I will show later in this chapter that some, notably women living near London, are faring well. But I will start with the people who do the sort of hard, undesirable jobs that Lukas took when he first arrived, and who are living in much the same place.

*

Boston was once a wealthy town with a busy port. Its parish church, known to local people as 'the stump', is almost cathedral-sized and would dominate the skyline even if the surrounding landscape were not so flat. In the seventeenth century, the town supplied the Massachusetts Bay Colony with several prominent figures, and that state's largest city with its name. These days, it is an unprepossessing place, with an unnerving ambience at night and a surprising number of betting shops. Throughout the Boston local authority area, average incomes are below the English and Welsh average.

The town does, however, contain an impressive institution that caters to migrants. In a warren of rooms, the Boston Lithuanian community group teaches English to migrants and Lithuanian to their British-born children. It also organizes traditional dances and festivals, translates documents, and tries to help people with their many problems. The school is overseen by Jurate Matulioniene, a university graduate who moved to Britain in 2010 with her husband, who had taken a job with a retail chain. 'I said, "I'm not going to work in a food factory," she remembers. Not many of the migrants she assists have the qualifications or the confidence in English that would allow them to make that decision.

Over a couple of days, the community group helps many people who work in food-processing factories around Boston. Apart from one man, who had been unemployed in Lithuania and very much enjoys his new life in Fenland, they are disgruntled. One woman works night shifts, going wherever an employment agency sends her. She hates working nights, and is paid only one pound per hour more than if she worked the day shift. She has nonetheless been doing it for nine years. Another factory worker, who had been an accountant in Lithuania, was treated so badly by her British supervisors – who, as well as screaming abuse at her, would not allow her to sit down when heavily pregnant – that she cannot bear to return to work. A third woman cares for dementia patients, who often threaten to kill her. She suffers from panic attacks, and has considered returning to her old factory job. Her friends are trying to talk her out of that.

In Peterborough, Lukas was able to climb from job to better job. If there is an employment ladder for Lithuanian factory workers in Boston, it seems to be missing every rung apart from the bottom one. The workers' pay hardly increases, and when it does, it is usually because they earn the national minimum wage, and that wage has been bumped up. They learn English painfully slowly, partly because hardly any native Britons work in the factories. 'I have got much better at speaking Russian and Polish,' says one Lithuanian woman, wryly. Nor can they easily train to do something else. 'When you're working sixteen hours a day, six days a week, you don't have time to go to college,' says the accountant-turned-vegetable-trimmer. They are stuck.

Speaking another language is partly a matter of confidence. Lukas says that his English improved dramatically when he started training Britons, which suggests that it was linked to his promotion – he gained control of the language at the same time as he gained more control over his work environment. His English is still far from perfect. And the Boston factory workers' English is not at all bad: the words I have quoted were spoken to me in English, not translated from Lithuanian. Their problem is less a lack of facility with the language than the fact that they have been so beaten down and demoralized by their work.

Naturally, their children are in a different position. Even those who spent their first few years in Lithuania speak perfect English, with an accent that is part Lincolnshire, part Multicultural London English. They also speak some Russian, which helps them communicate with immigrants from other Baltic and Eastern European countries. This is true across Britain. As one Lithuania-born student in London, the son of a cleaner and a construction worker, explains to me: 'We speak two and a half languages, English being the half. We might as well use our second language.' The Turkish managers of a new nightclub in Boston, Club Medusa, say they hear a lot of Russian on the dance floor, and will sometimes even end the night with a Russian song. But most of the music they play is what they call 'English music', and the English know as pop, house and R & B.

For the Lithuanian migrants, the linguistic prowess of their children is a mixed blessing. Some feel embarrassed when they have to rely on their offspring to communicate with Britons; woundingly, their children sometimes ask them not to speak English in public because their failings in the language are so evident. On the other hand, Lithuanian parents take great satisfaction in knowing that their children's working lives will probably be happier than theirs. 'They speak perfect English, so they're not going to be working in a factory in the damp and cold,' says one mother.

Exactly how the new generation is going to earn a living is not always clear. They have grown up in a small town that is not exactly stuffed with good jobs. Their parents are hardly well connected. And Lithuanians seem to face discrimination in the skilled labour market: Matulioniene tells me that one young woman who was struggling to find a job got on much better after she changed her name to an English-sounding one. I would not be surprised if many of the young Lithuanians who remain in and around Boston end up doing working-class jobs. But the jobs will probably be easier than the ones their parents do. And not all of the Lithuanians will stay in Boston.

One young man who came to Lincolnshire as a small child, whose mother drives workers to and from factories, has finished school and is currently 'taking a break'. But he is clear about one thing, he tells me over a cup of coffee in the town centre. Although he identifies strongly as Lithuanian ('where you were born, that's what you are, it's just a fact'), he has no intention whatsoever of leaving Britain to go and live in Lithuania. 'What's the point?' he asks, rather crossly. 'What's so good about it?'

*

Every Saturday morning, a parallel education system cranks into action in British cities. In churches, community centres and schools, children are taught the languages that their immigrant parents speak fluently. They struggle with grammar, play games, sing songs from the mother country and learn a little history. Polish supplementary schools are more common than any other kind – about 130 around the country are associated with the Polish Educational Society, a venerable organization that was founded in Britain soon after the Second World War. There are also Latvian schools, Lithuanian schools, Romanian schools and even Ukrainian schools. Not all Eastern European children attend: the majority have made it clear to their parents just how enthusiastic they are about being stuck in a classroom on a Saturday. The schools are nonetheless among the most important institutions created by the Eastern European diaspora in Britain.

In Welwyn Garden City, north of London, the Polish school has more than a hundred pupils in eight year groups. It was created in 2013 to cater to a community that was then growing quickly. Many Poles were being hired by local warehouses or moving out of the capital in search of a better quality of life. The school's head is Iwona Pniewska, who on weekdays works as a physical-education teacher in a school for the deaf. She says that the Polish school would find it hard to take on a larger number of children. The youngest often rock up with excellent English but little knowledge of the Polish language, and every new cohort seems to need more remedial help than the one that came before. I spend some delightful hours at the school, asking tweens and teenagers about their lives and their identities.

Insofar as any twelve- or thirteen-year-old understands what their parents do for a living, most of the children in the Welwyn Garden City Polish school come from working-class households. Many say that their fathers work in construction – Welwyn is close enough to London to enable quick commuting. Their mothers are cleaners, shop workers and carers. But there are a few exceptions. One boy says that his mother works 'on a computer', whereas his father is a cook in a cafe. Another says that his mother is training to be a mental-health nurse and that his father works in a factory. 'My mum's an accountant and my dad's a builder,' says a third child.

Women born in Eastern Europe are more likely to be employed than women born in Britain, and much more likely than women from traditionalist Muslim countries such as Bangladesh and Pakistan. Most do working-class jobs. But, as the children in Welwyn Garden City have noticed, Eastern European women are a little less likely to do working-class jobs than Eastern European men are. The 2021 census reveals that 22 per cent of Polish-born women have professional or managerial jobs, compared with 16 per cent of Polish-born men. That makes them unusual. Among other groups, including white Britons, men are more likely than women to hold professional or managerial jobs. Eastern European women do not necessarily earn more than Eastern European men: an accountant may well bring in less money than a builder. Measured by their jobs, though, they are a little less working class.

In the mid-2000s, the stereotypical Polish man in Britain was a plumber, and this was not completely inaccurate. Many men did in fact take construction jobs, which were reasonably well paid and required little English. Some have stayed in the industry, often setting up businesses of their own. Their English may have improved only slowly, especially if they employ other Eastern Europeans. Polish women, by contrast, have ended up in industries like care, retail and hospitality, where language skills are crucial. Their children notice the effect. 'My dad works on building sites where lots of other people are Polish. He speaks broken English. My mum works in a beauty shop with lots of other English people, and she speaks it well,' explains one girl at the school.

Some of the women who migrated from Eastern Europe to Britain have found an even more pressing reason to learn English:

they have fallen in love with people who cannot understand their native language. In 2022, women born in Poland gave birth to 11,100 babies in England and Wales. Of those babies, 6,400 (or 58 per cent) had Polish-born fathers. With the exception of 400 births where the father's country of birth was not recorded, all the other fathers were born somewhere else. Most, not surprisingly, were born in Britain, but several hundred babies had fathers from Africa, Asia or the Middle East.

Eastern European men have been less romantically adventurous. In 84 per cent of cases where Polish-born men became fathers in 2022, the baby's mother was also born in Poland. The same imbalance between men and women can be seen among Romanians and among Eastern Europeans as a whole. And that might explain something about the Eastern European population of Britain. Although many of the earliest migrants were single men, today there are tens of thousands more Polish women than Polish men in England and Wales, and tens of thousands more Lithuanian women than Lithuanian men. I cannot be sure, but I suspect that some of the pattern can be explained by selective reverse migration. Especially since Brexit, some Eastern Europeans have returned to the countries where they were born. For women with British husbands or lovers, let alone Kenyan ones, that option seems less appealing.

In the Polish school in Welwyn Garden City, many children know of their parents' desires to return to the countries of their birth. They have mixed feelings about it. Some are keen on Poland, which they judge to be a well-off country (as it is, these days), with noticeably less street litter than Britain. 'Poland's really rich,' asserts one teenage girl, confidently. Others have warm feelings about the country, but they are wise enough to understand that they might be confusing the delightfulness of Poland with the delightfulness of holidays, cousins and doting grandparents. Most seem committed to Britain. 'Sometimes my parents talk about moving back to Poland, but I'm not really keen on the idea,' says one girl. By their own accounts, their friends at school are largely the children of Britons, not Poles.

Whatever their feelings about the mother country, and no matter how much or how little they hang out with Poles of their own age, to a boy and a girl the Saturday school pupils think of themselves as Polish. 'I have an English passport and a Polish passport, but I would say I'm more Polish,' explains one boy. 'I think I would say I'm Polish because both of my parents are Polish, and I like Polish food,' a girl says. Some say they have come to feel increasingly Polish as they have grown older. 'When I was younger, I was like: "I'm English! I'm English!"' says another boy. 'But then I was told that I'm Polish.' I suggest to the children that perhaps they feel fully Polish and also fully British. With just one exception, they not only reject this suggestion but also the term 'British'. To them, and to adult Lithuanians in Boston, the native-born ethnic majority is invariably known as 'the English'.

The first few times I heard young British-raised Lithuanians and Poles describe their identities this way, I was distressed. I have spent a decade of my adult life in America, where many people happily walk around with hyphenated identities: Irish-American, Italian-American and so forth. Many non-white Britons confidently express pride in their foreign roots without compromising their Britishness. The idea that identity is a zero-sum game is normally associated with out-and-out racists. Why do so many Eastern European migrants and their children feel obliged to choose between one identity and another?

I am calmer these days, for a couple of reasons. The first is that the young people I talk to are calm. They do not feel excluded from British life because of their passports or their parentage, so they do not have to assert their right to belong (the children of Romanian immigrants, who have for no good reason been stereotyped as criminals and welfare cheats, may well feel differently). Sometimes their names mark them as foreign, but not always. Many Eastern European migrants have given their children English names, or names that the natives can pronounce easily. Anyway, school classrooms are full of interesting names. Amid all the Islas, Avas, Freyas, Esmes, Arlos, Jaxons and Kais, a Jurate or a Jan does not stick out. And the second reason I have learned not to worry is that working-class Eastern Europeans are in practice creating a hybrid culture that incorporates British elements. They might describe themselves simply as Lithuanian or Polish, as though they have just stepped off a cross-channel ferry. Their actions say otherwise.

*

In a Unitarian meeting house near the middle of Boston, Mantas Grauzinis teaches local children and the odd brave adult how to move. He learned street dance – a loose family of hip-hop influenced styles including breakdancing – in Lithuania, and expected to find a thriving dance scene when he arrived in famously multicultural Britain. When he didn't, he created one. His dance studio, known as Kast, is Eastern European in the sense that it is run by Eastern Europeans and is attended largely by Eastern Europeans. It is also Eastern European, according to Grauzinis, in the sense that it emphasizes hard work: unlike many dance clubs, children generally attend twice a week. Yet the dance style is international, and the instruction (which is sometimes given by guest teachers from outside Boston) is entirely in English. At the end of one dance session, I ask two happy, sweaty teenage girls about themselves. Both are the children of Lithuanian factory workers, and both speak only Lithuanian at home. I ask what language they think in, and they look horrified. Of course they think in English.

In Peterborough, an even more ambitious project is underway.

Lukasz Stachowiak, a warehouse worker who migrated from Poland as a teenager, and Dawid Jedrychowski, who arrived from Poland as a young man and now drives a road-sweeping machine, have gone into sport. They trained as football coaches, but could not find jobs at established clubs, so, in 2022, they decided to set up one of their own. Be Active Football Academy now has dozens of young players and excellent facilities, thanks to a deal with Peterborough United, a League One team. Stachowiak and Jedrychowski hope to create five or six teams in the city, then expand to other British cities, then abroad. Their none-too-modest aim is to be better than every other football club.

Many of the children they train in Peterborough are the offspring of Polish migrants. But they also work with Lithuanians, Romanians, Portuguese and Hongkongers. The language of instruction is firmly English. The two men wanted to avoid creating the sort of cliquish club where all the players speak Polish. And they reckoned it would be foolish to limit their appeal, especially at a time when Polish families seem to be drifting out of Peterborough to other British cities or back to Poland. 'I used to run a clothing shop just for Polish people,' Jedrychowski says, 'but it didn't work. So I decided I should make something for everyone.'

Such is the culture that working-class migrants and their children are making. It is not entirely British, nor is it entirely Polish or Lithuanian. Instead, it is a mixture of the two. In addition to British and Eastern European elements, it sweeps up things from other parts of the world – black American music and fashion, kids from Portugal and Hong Kong. A lovely mess is being created in the Fenland's rigid, rectangular landscape.

*

The language that Britons use to describe migration is often watery. People flow into and out of the country; a wave of immigrants arrives; politicians are accused of opening the taps. The statistic that politicians and reporters tend to focus on is net migration, as though immigrants are fished out of the seas. Perhaps Britons are drawn to these metaphors because their islands are surrounded by water. I'm going to use a liquid metaphor, too, but a more precise one. The migration of people from Eastern Europe and the Baltic countries to Britain strikes me as being like flood irrigation – the old-fashioned practice, still used in many countries, of inundating fields with fresh water.

It is like flood irrigation partly because it was done deliberately. The British government could have imposed transitional controls on the countries that joined the EU in 2004, and prevented their citizens from working for several years. Most other European countries did just that, and Britain would do so a few years later when Bulgaria and Romania joined the union. It decided not to impose controls in 2004 because, as the prime minister Tony Blair explained at the time, Britain had a strong economy and a pressing need for more workers, and also because barring Eastern Europeans from the legitimate labour market would probably drive some of them into the black economy. Blair's Labour government greatly underestimated how many people would take up the offer. The farmer opened the floodgate and got more water than he expected.

The migration of Eastern Europeans was also like flood irrigation because it was a one-off. Between 2001 and 2011, the number of Polish-born people in England and Wales shot up from 58,000 to 579,000. In 2010, more babies were born to women from Poland than to women from any other foreign country. Poles would hold that record until 2020, when they were overtaken by women from both Pakistan and Romania. But the Brexit vote in 2016 crushed the pound, making Britain less attractive to economic migrants. And when Britain left the EU, it enacted a new immigration system, which treated continental European workers the same as everyone else. Just like Indians or Nigerians, Lithuanians and Poles who want to migrate to Britain today must generally be students or workers who can clear the salary thresholds that the government has set up. Obtaining a work visa is not cheap. In 2023, a mere 2,000 entry-clearance visas were issued to Polish workers and students, and another 300 to Lithuanians. By contrast, Indians received 323,000 visas. Polish women have fallen to fourth position in the baby league table. Those Eastern Europeans who have not headed back across the English Channel are quietly seeping into British soil. Now that Britain has left the EU and Eastern Europe has grown richer, a further inundation seems very unlikely.

Lukas is one of the migrants who drifted away. Having climbed from humdrum work into running a small business, he began to look for new opportunities in Britain. He studied with the Open University and discovered that he enjoyed writing. But when he looked for more challenging work, he could not find a job that paid enough to support his family. Then a job came up in Lithuania that was ideal for him, so he went home. He now travels outside Europe, assessing lorry drivers who are seeking visas to work in the EU. His competence in English, his experience training bus drivers in Britain and his experience as an immigrant prepared him well. And he has found, to his delight, that housing is a good deal cheaper in Lithuania than it is in Britain.

'England taught me a lot,' he says. 'I am where I am now because I came to England.' Still, he never felt entirely at home. Even when he had a job and a family in Peterborough, he always felt that he belonged to Lithuania. Only once, while preparing to return to England after a trip to Lithuania, did he catch himself thinking that he was going home. 'It's easy to cross a border, but not in your heart,' he says. That is the thing about the working-class

Eastern Europeans who migrated to Britain. They can seem settled; they can weave themselves ever more tightly into British life. But they have another option, and occasionally they exercise it. Irish people would understand that. Many of them returned from Britain in the 1990s and 2000s as the Celtic tiger's economy roared.

I am disappointed by Lukas's departure, not so much because Britain has lost an exceptionally determined, dynamic person (I tell myself that my country's loss is Lithuania's gain), but because it suggests that Britain is failing to create enough of the well-paid, interesting jobs that might have bound him to the country. Still, the reverse migration of some Eastern European migrants may be speeding a process that I see as benign. If the people who are leaving tend to be those who viewed Britain mostly as a workplace, who did not marry or have children with Britons, the ones who remain will be the ones who do see the country as home. Eastern Europeans might become more committed to Britain simply by a process of subtraction. And they were becoming more committed to the country anyway.

As well as dry weather and European migrants, eastern England is notable for its large population of Leave voters. In the referendum of June 2016, 76 per cent of the vote in Boston was for Brexit – the highest proportion anywhere in Britain. South Holland ranked second. You can travel all the way down the east coast of England, from Berwick-upon-Tweed in Northumberland to Eastbourne in East Sussex, without passing through a single local authority where the majority of people voted to remain in the EU. In the 2024 general election, the voters of Boston and Skegness elected Richard Tice, from the anti-immigration Reform UK Party. Three of that party's five seats are on the east coast of England.

The 2016 referendum was lopsided. British citizens were able to vote as long as they lived in Britain – or, for complicated reasons, in Gibraltar. Citizens of Lithuania, Poland and other EU countries living in Britain were not allowed to vote. Migrants could have taken out British citizenship before the vote, and a few did. But the Home Office had made the process of acquiring citizenship costly and cumbersome, and for some people it would have meant ditching their existing citizenships. In towns like Boston, the Brexit vote was an argument with no riposte. Natives were, in effect, invited to deliver their opinions on the migrants who had settled among them.

For Eastern Europeans, the referendum was shattering. Britain had welcomed them in 2004, and in effect promised them a life in a fully European country. Suddenly, it seemed to be telling them to clear off. Jakub Krupa, a journalist and activist, met many Poles in 2016 who wondered whether they were still welcome. Yet the referendum appears to have made Poles and other Eastern Europeans more welcome in Britain, not less. Soon after the vote, public opinion swung in favour of immigration and against some of the people most associated with the Leave campaign, such as Nigel Farage – a pattern that some observers described as a 'populist paradox'. Perhaps Leave voters felt they had made their point. Perhaps they were stung by insinuations that they had been motivated by racism and xenophobia, and wanted to show that they weren't. Whatever the reason, they calmed down.

The vast majority of Britons, including big majorities of Leave voters and working-class people, wanted the government to allow Europeans to stay in their country (which it proceeded to do). And Eastern Europeans have been made to feel more welcome, not least by white working-class Britons. I have often noticed that, although migrants and their children tend to describe themselves simply as 'Polish' and 'Lithuanian', white working-class Britons do not use such stark words. They describe the people who have turned up in their streets and council estates as being 'from Poland' or, still more delicately, as 'originally from Poland'. In Peterborough, Jedrychowski senses that British people have become more welcoming in the past few years. They now seem to view him as one of them, he says, rather than as a worker filling a gap in the labour market. One unfortunate sign of assimilation is that some Poles have adopted prejudiced views of black and Asian people.

Time will continue to grind the edges off Britons' feelings about Eastern Europeans, just as it has done to their feelings about people from Ireland and many other countries. And the process of turning British will roll on. Every day, the Eastern European migrants' English grows a little better and their children's Lithuanian and Polish grows a little worse. They may gradually be surprised to find themselves becoming British, in feeling if not in law. They will still have hard-to-pronounce surnames, but the natives will probably get used to those, just as they got used to saying 'Doherty' and 'Mahmood'. Many will eventually merge into the British white working class, making it more complex, dynamic and interesting. That is another way in which the migration of working-class Eastern Europeans is like flood irrigation: it has benefited Britain.

Chapter Seven

Bye-bye, Billy Elliot

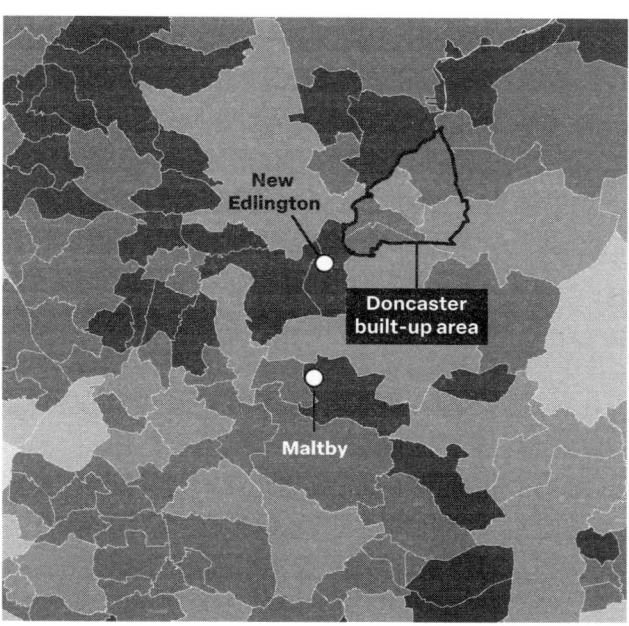

In 2000, a scratchy little film opened in British cinemas. *Billy Elliot* is about a boy from a pit town in County Durham who dreams of becoming a ballet dancer. The film opens in the midst of the mid-1980s miners' strike. Billy's mother is dead; his father is on strike and running short of money; his older brother is fighting the police. At first it seems highly unlikely that Billy's desperate, hidebound family will let him pursue his dream, and still less likely that he will catch it. But, this being cinema, everything turns out well in the end. Billy ends up in London, dancing in *Swan Lake*.

Underdogs

Many people enjoyed *Billy Elliot*, which was turned into a successful stage musical five years later. It is just tough enough, and funny enough, to prevent the improbable sweetness of the plot from coating the whole film in sticky toffee. But few people loved the film more than John Prescott, a long-serving cabinet minister in Tony Blair's governments. He watched it repeatedly, and confessed that it made him cry. Prescott had a couple of things in common with Billy, and also with Lee Hall, who wrote the screenplay. All were born into working-class families and migrated long distances within Britain. Prescott left North Wales as a child, moved around England and ended up in Kingston upon Hull, where he became an MP. Hall left Newcastle for Cambridge University. Among other things, *Billy Elliot* is a film about the pain and the necessity of working-class migration.

At one point in the film, Billy's father says that he has never been to London, and cannot see why he should go, since there are no coal mines there. He comes to understand that Billy will have to move to the capital if he is to have any chance of becoming a dancer. He even tries to cross the miners' picket line, to earn some money for his son's trip. The musical hits this note hard, with a song called 'He Could Be a Star', in which Billy's father sorrowfully decides to let him go. Billy's friend Michael, who is gay, also seems to leave north-east England for the big city, in the film at least. The message is clear. Family is important, but if you want to get on in life and become the person you were meant to be, you must get out.

Nothing dates *Billy Elliot* more than that confidently expressed notion. Today, it is not at all expected that working-class people living in the poorer parts of Britain ought to move. 'Levelling up', the folksy name for regional economic development that was supposedly the top domestic priority of the government headed by Boris Johnson between 2019 and 2022, was all about bringing opportunities to people. 'For many, if you want to get on you need to get out,' explained the government in its main document on the matter. 'Levelling up is a mission . . . to change that for good.' Meanwhile, the Labour Party promised to create 'jobs that mean a young person who wants to get on in life no longer has to get out of their hometown'. Rachel Reeves, the chancellor, lamented that her working-class grandparents had to leave their home in South Wales to find decent jobs.

Politicians are only telling people what they want to hear. An opinion poll in 2021 by Public First shows that few Britons expect to move for a new job: just 12 per cent think it very likely they will do so in the next ten years. One fifth think it fair that young people should have to move for work, whereas two fifths think it unfair; the rest are unsure or sit on the fence. Opinion would be even more lopsided were it not for Londoners. By a small margin, they are inclined to believe that young people should move. Londoners are also the most likely to think that they will move themselves, and (rather bizarrely, given high London wages) the most likely to believe that they could boost their own incomes by doing so. British opinion has divided in a peculiar way. People living in the metropolis that offers the greatest economic opportunities are fairly keen on moving, and expect to do it themselves. Outside London, few people see the point.

Britain has less good data on domestic migration than on many other aspects of life. But the data that exist suggest it has slowed over the decades. In 2018, the geographers Ian Shuttleworth, Thomas Cooke and Tony Champion showed that 52 per cent of people in England and Wales had changed address between the censuses of 1971 and 1981. Between 2001 and 2011, 41 per cent did. Almost everybody is moving less: immigrants, natives, men, women, the young, the old, professionals, manual workers, even people in the armed forces. There are some intriguing regional patterns, though. Migration has slowed most among people living in Wales and the north of England – *Billy Elliot* country. And working-class people are less mobile than middle-class people. Just 35 per cent of unskilled workers moved in the noughties, down from 49 per cent in the 1970s. The 2021 census suggests that the overall slowdown has continued, although it is hard to interpret, given the disruption caused by Covid.

British people sometimes complain about a 'brain drain' from poorer parts of the country. The young are said to leave for university, take jobs in rich cities and not return. The truth is rather different, as some amazingly detailed data released by the Office of National Statistics in 2024 shows. In fact, young people from poor places nearly always stick around. Look at Sunderland in north-east England. Of 8,500 teenagers who took GCSE exams there between 2008 and 2011, 26 per cent went on to graduate from university. Of the graduates, fully 76 per cent were still living in Sunderland in their mid-twenties. Those who gained vocational qualifications were even more likely to stay put. In the wealthy town of Sevenoaks in Kent, by contrast, 54 per cent of young people went on to get degrees, and only 57 per cent of the graduates ended up living in Sevenoaks. Wealthy small towns and villages, not poor ones, lose the highest proportions of young people. Nobody worries about this, because the leavers are replaced by other highly qualified people moving in. By contrast, outsiders with degrees seldom move to Sunderland.

It is a similar story in Scotland. The national records office estimates that out-migration from the country peaked in 1987–8, when 65,000 Scots left for England or another part of the United Kingdom. A few years later, Tennent Caledonian, a brewer, ran an advert that showed a Scot suffering through a day in London, where he endures a packed Tube carriage, a confused man who might be a foreigner, and disputatious cockneys. At the end of the advert, he chucks his briefcase away and returns to a friendly pub in his homeland. The experience of working in England was common enough at the time that many Scots could have identified with the man. It is rarer now. Out-migration from Scotland has not exceeded 50,000 per year since the turn of the century, despite the country's growing population.

Britain has gone from being a nation of movers to a nation of stayers-at-home. And this seems to be especially true of working-class people. Whereas highly educated middle-class people often travel long distances for university and early jobs, working-class people stay. They are assured that this is perfectly fine, even admirable. Politicians of the left and the right alike promise that opportunities can be brought to people in deprived areas rather than the other way around. Books like *The Road to Somewhere* by David Goodhart, published in 2017, praise the people who stick around. If there is a modern equivalent of *Billy Elliot* it is the 2018 film *Wild Rose*, in which a working-class Glaswegian woman travels to Nashville to pursue her dream of becoming a country-and-western singer, only to realize that she really belongs in Glasgow. The final song in that film insists there is no place like home.

The great slowing of Britain is a big change, which has also occurred in other rich countries. And policy has changed even more than personal behaviour. Within living memory, the official view was that working-class people damn well ought to move around the country. Strenuous efforts were made to bring this about, which gave rise to large migrations and entirely new towns. The current fashion for immobility raises several questions. Why did Britain turn against domestic migration, in practice and as a matter of policy? Is the new consensus right? And if people are really going to stay put in struggling areas, how can opportunities be brought to them?

All of these questions are especially pertinent for white working-class Britons. That isn't because they are the least mobile people in Britain. Members of ethnic-minority groups often move even less, especially if you exclude recent immigrants. Bangladeshi, Indian and Pakistani men without degrees are extremely unlikely to move by the age of twenty-seven, although women are a little more footloose, possibly because of subcontinental traditions of moving into your husband's home upon marriage. Even getting a degree does not greatly encourage Asian men to move around the country.

Compared with white working-class people, though, they simply have less need to move. England and Wales contain 9.6 million people who describe themselves as black, Asian or mixed ethnicity. Of them, 4.3 million live in just three cities: London, Birmingham and Manchester. Many others live within a short commute of those cities. They do not feel compelled to move to a great city because they already live in one. That fact probably helps them a good deal. In their 2022 book *Streets of Gold*, the American academics Ran Abramitzky and Leah Boustan show that much of the success of immigrants in that country comes down to the fact that they usually arrive in places where jobs are plentiful – thriving cities and suburbs rather than decaying small towns. The same is likely to be true of Britain. There are some exceptions, such as the Pakistanis who arrived in Bradford and other northern mill towns in the 1960s, just before the textile industry collapsed, and the asylum-seekers who are forcefully shunted to the poorest parts of the country today. But the general pattern holds. Whereas immigrants and minority ethnic people tend to live in or near big cities with diverse economies, white working-class Britons tend not to. If lack of movement is a problem for anyone, it is especially a problem for them.

White working-class Britons are unusual in another way. In

the days when domestic migration was seen as desirable, strenuous efforts were made to move them around. Many white working-class Britons live where they do because they, a parent, or a grandparent moved there from another part of Britain, quite likely encouraged by the state. In the past few decades, they have experienced a political and rhetorical whiplash, from pro-migration to pro-staying-put. Nowhere is that whiplash more evident than in the coalfields.

*

Edlington, south-west of central Doncaster, takes every opportunity to remind you of its mining heritage. The town sign features a winding wheel, part of the machine that transported miners up and down the pit, which was known as Yorkshire Main. It has a small, sweet garden with a monument to the 144 miners who died in industrial accidents between 1909, when digging began, and 1985, when the pit closed for good. Yorkshire Main Football Club is the local team. There is a Yorkshire Main Sports and Social Club, a Yorkshire Main Officials Club and even a Yorkshire Main Motors ('MOTs, servicing, repairs') with another image of a winding wheel on its sign. Walk into the Martinwells Centre, which contains the town library and a couple of medical practices, and you will see two large banners. One reads: 'Edlington women against pit closures'. The other is a National Union of Mineworkers banner, with local scenes painted onto red cloth.

The town remembers mining partly for the same reason that the small city where I live remembers the Romans. Without coal, Edlington would not exist. At the beginning of the twentieth century, there was only a tiny village just south of the present town – a village now known as Old Edlington. The area currently occupied by Edlington proper was farmland. Then, in 1909, the Staveley Coal and Iron Company sank the first shaft towards the

Barnsley Seam. Coal was soon flowing, and men dying. At first, miners lived in wooden huts, but the company soon contracted a builder to create brick homes and roads, starting with one named Staveley Street. The town grew incredibly quickly. By the 1920s, it had a cinema that could hold 900 people. And those people came from all over.

A memoir published in 1940 gives a flavour of the extraordinary human churn that occurred in South Yorkshire towns like Edlington in the first half of the twentieth century. *Brother to the Ox* was written by Fred Kitchen, a son and grandson of farm labourers, who began working as a cowman at the age of thirteen. The early chapters of his book describe traditional farm life. Then the railway arrived in South Yorkshire, 'like a long shiny snake across the fields'. With it came navvies, a discombobulatingly diverse lot who were nicknamed for the places where they came from – 'Scotty', 'Lincoln', 'Brum' and so forth. 'Never since the time of the Danes had our village suffered such an invasion,' wrote Kitchen. Before, everybody had known everybody, and it was foolish to criticize any man behind his back, since he was probably related to the person you were talking to. It quickly became a community of strangers.

Coal mining brought many more people to South Yorkshire, including migrants from Ireland, and yet more changes. Kitchen spent six years away from the village he calls Little Norwood (it is actually Maltby, just up the road from Edlington). By the time he returned, the settlement had exploded in size, 'as though a town of bricks had been carried bodily through the air and dropped'. Kitchen was sucked into the expanding industrial economy by the promise of higher wages. He became a building labourer, then worked at the local colliery, but he eventually grew tired of the industrial hurly-burly and went back to farm work. The success of *Brother to the Ox* allowed him to concentrate on writing, which he did with amazing vigour. He died in 1969, after a life of almost non-stop movement and change.

I ask a group of local people who have gathered to chat about the history of Edlington in the Helping Hands Community Centre whether they remember the days of churn. They do. A retired nurse whose grandparents migrated from Ireland describes the building of a new housing estate in the 1960s. It was occupied by miners from Scotland, and became known, rudely, as Jock Town. 'When they first came, we couldn't understand a word they were saying,' she recalls. She muttered resentfully about the new arrivals until her father, a miner, rebuked her, telling her that unemployment and poverty had forced them to move. Others remember that groups of native-born Yorkshiremen, Scots and Geordies kept to themselves, forming little clumps in Edlington's pubs. But they soon found common ground in work, in sport and in rivalries with nearby Yorkshire towns. Besides, the inhabitants of Edlington shared an awareness that many of them had come from somewhere else, or were the children or grandchildren of people who had. They still have that sense today. 'We're all half-breeds here,' says a former miner, cheerfully. 'Mongrels.'

The town isn't quite what it seems. Following the typology of places that I created in Chapter One, Edlington looks at first like a heartland town. It is overwhelmingly white and working class, and, despite some modest signs of growing diversity such as a shop in the high street selling African and Caribbean goods, seems very likely to stay that way. But it also has some of the flavour of a colony like Thetford. The people of Edlington came from all over Britain and Ireland, and forged a common culture around coal mining. After the mine closed, they built a culture on what was left, including the memory of coal mining.

Working-class Britons moved to towns like Edlington not only because they wanted well-paying jobs, but also because officials

183

prodded them. Miners were shoved about the country with great vigour. As early as the 1920s, state 'transference' offices organized the movement of men from regions where pits were struggling to regions where they were booming. The Ministry of Labour paid for train tickets and shelled out the equivalent of up to half a year's rent to encourage people to explore new places. The war brought an end to that particular scheme, but the National Coal Board did much the same afterwards. Meanwhile, local authorities across Britain pushed working-class people out of city centres into suburban council estates, new towns and 'expansion towns'. Whether you were unemployed or happily employed, if you were working class, an official somewhere probably had a plan to move you.

These efforts were not always popular, to put it mildly. In 1944, the researcher Margaret Attlee asked local authorities how people had responded to the transference boards' attempts to move them around. Her report on the subject, 'Mobility of Labour', was discouraging. Miners seemed reluctant to move, owing to 'their strong local traditions and pride'. When they did move, they were not always welcomed. In Watford, on the edge of London, Welsh migrants encountered a gang of local men armed with razors and lead pipes. Overall, about a quarter of movers quickly returned to the places they had come from. Some coal miners from Cumbria who had been transferred to pits in Kent were so disgruntled that they walked home – a journey of about 300 miles. South Yorkshire was an easier place to settle, perhaps because it had become so used to human churn. One official told Attlee that the region had 'received many immigrants and assimilated them successfully'. Still, the fact that white Britons moving within their own country were described with words like 'immigrants' and 'assimilated', which are now applied to foreign migrants, hints at the strain.

*

The closure of Yorkshire Main in 1985 pulled the heart out of Edlington. The town lost its reason for being, its social as well as its economic centre. The community of miners had largely policed itself: a teenage tearaway could expect someone to have a discreet word with his father in the pit or the pub. After the mine closed, chaos grew. By the 1990s, Edlington was generating a remarkably large number of awful headlines, considering its small size. A petrol bomb was thrown into a moving car. A television shop was burgled eleven times in three years, prompting the owner to declare that a handful of miscreants were holding the village to ransom. 'Running a business in Edlington has cost me my livelihood and my health,' she complained to the *Doncaster Star*. In 2009, two children in Edlington were abducted by two other children, brutally beaten and set on fire. Yet most people stayed.

The pit closure did not cause an exodus even among people who had migrated to work in it. One woman remembers that her father had 'upped sticks' and moved the family from Scotland to South Yorkshire when she was a young child so he could work in the mine. The move was abrupt: 'It was just "we're moving" and that's it.' But almost her entire extended family stayed in and around Edlington after Yorkshire Main closed, and it is still there. Others tell me the same thing. I meet and hear about a few exceptions, such as a woman who recently arrived from northeast England to be close to her son, and a man who left Britain after joining the army, but they seem unusual. These days, only about one in twelve people move into or out of Doncaster (the local authority area that includes Edlington) every year. That is low by national standards – in fast-moving places like Cambridge, one in four comes or goes. Doncaster sees almost as little movement in or out as the Isle of Wight, which has the excuse of being surrounded by water.

Coal miners moved less in the 1980s than they had in the 1970s, even though job losses were heavier in the 1980s. Very few made long-distance moves from one British region to another. There was little point. In the mid-twentieth century, miners could still move from places where coal seams were becoming exhausted, in Scotland and north-east England, to places where mines were still humming, such as Yorkshire. By the 1980s, mining was declining everywhere. And other businesses were emerging in the coalfields to offer work that was less dangerous, if often less well paid, than going down the pit. Some laid-off Edlington miners went to work at Pegler or Polypipe, respectively makers of plumbing valves and plastic pipes.

Women seem to have been slower to enter the workforce in Yorkshire than in much of southern England, especially if they were married. The local culture was rather traditional, involving a strict division of labour. And being a miner's wife was an onerous job in itself. Alice Rodgers, a former teacher who is now involved with the Maltby Historical Society, says that, before the creation of proper pit baths, wives would have spent much of their time cleaning. But by the 1980s, women were rushing into employment, in part to compensate for their husbands' slimmer pay packets. The rise of women's paid work helped bind families to towns like Edlington. It is much easier to up sticks if you only have to worry about one person's job. Meanwhile, the growth of car ownership made it easier to switch jobs without moving home. Edlington is utterly car-dependent today.

Local people offer other explanations for the lack of move-ment. At a weekly food market run by the Edlington Community Organisation, an excellent local charity, I meet a man who says he has so many relatives in the area that he does not know them all. He is a welder – 'not the healthiest of jobs, but you fall back on what you know'. He expects to stay around the area and guesses that his children will, too. Their school is pretty good, he says, and, although Edlington and nearby towns have some bad neighbourhoods, they also have some good ones. He suggests a couple of reasons why local people tend not to move. First, he says, they fear the unknown. Second, they lack the means. To move from one place to another, he says, 'you need money behind you'.

That seems to be the most important reason why working-class people stay in small towns such as Edlington even after the main employer has disappeared. It isn't so much that they are deeply fond of their neighbourhoods or cannot bear to leave Mum, although those things may be true. It is more that the economics of moving do not work out for them. The cost is large, and the rewards are not obvious. The reasons for that do not only lie in small towns like Edlington. They also lie in big cities, and in Britain's planning rules.

*

Sheffield is about half an hour's drive away from Edlington. It feels like a very different place. With more than half a million residents, it is almost fifty times as populous. It has two large universities, a tram system and a small but growing grove of high-rise buildings in the centre. To the west are pretty stone-built suburbs such as Crookes, which contains a great many students, a health-food store, a vegan cafe and a shop selling extremely small plants. Loitering in such an area, it would be easy to get the impression that Sheffield is much better off than Edlington. It isn't.

Britain has a strange pattern of economic strength and weakness, which is often misunderstood even by the British. Other countries tend to have urban–rural divides. Metropolises, especially large ones, are usually better off than small towns and villages. Take America and the city of Pittsburgh, which is similar to Sheffield in that it had a large steel industry and lost it. According to the OECD, GDP per head in Pittsburgh and its surrounding suburbs was $77,546 in 2022. In the state of Pennsylvania as a whole, GDP per head was lower, at $70,290. In an era when wealth is created more by brainpower than by manpower, that is what you would expect. Cities like Pittsburgh bring huge numbers of people together, where they can learn from each other and come up with brilliant innovations. Small towns might be nice places to live, but they cannot hope to compete economically.

Britain does not conform to this pattern. It has one spectacularly successful big city in London, and one pretty successful one in Edinburgh. London is so successful that it scatters economic fairy dust over the whole of south-east England. Villages and towns near the capital are for the most part well off. Even Luton, an erstwhile car-making powerhouse north of London that suffered an industrial decline as bad as many northern or Midlands cities, is better off than Sheffield. The OECD calculates that GDP per head in Sheffield was just $47,439 in 2022, which is startlingly lower than Pittsburgh (the OECD's figures use 'purchasing-power parity', so the huge gap between the two cities is not caused simply by the weakness of the pound). Sheffield is neither poorer nor richer than the region of Yorkshire and the Humber. In 2022, the region's GDP per head was almost identical to the city's, at $47,192.

As Philip McCann, an economist at the Alliance Manchester Business School, puts it, Britain does not really have an urban–rural divide. Instead, it has a core–periphery divide. It has a wealthy mega-region in the south-east that contains successful cities, successful towns and successful villages. Beyond that charmed zone lie many poor regions that contain mostly poor cities, poor towns and poor villages. No big city in the north of

England, the Midlands or Wales has a really strong economy. Birmingham and Greater Manchester are doing better than Sheffield, but not much better.

The great conurbations of the Midlands and North are economically weak for many reasons. Their traditional industries have been gutted. Manufacturing has declined in many rich countries over the past half-century, but the decline in Britain has been especially steep. Most English conurbations also have lousy public transport, especially compared with continental European cities. That makes them less productive, because it means that companies can draw on a smaller pool of workers. In effect, a big English city becomes a small city at rush hour. And cities have neither the resources nor the power to change their fortunes. Buy a chocolate bar or a house in Sheffield, and all the tax you pay goes to the Treasury in London. So does all your income tax. The money is then redistributed (northern England overall gets more cash from the Treasury than it contributes in taxes), but it is not necessarily spent on the sort of things that local politicians and officials might wish. If the officials want to do anything ambitious, such as building a new tramline or even a large roundabout, they usually have to go cap-in-hand to London.

It seems unlikely that a town like Edlington will thrive while the nearest big city does not. A small industrial town that was built in a hurry might fare well if its urban neighbours are successful – Luton and Thetford are never going to be very poor while London and Cambridge are so wealthy – but, if it is in a poor region, forget it. The experts who the last Conservative government drafted to help it create a plan for 'levelling up' Britain's poor regions understood that. Andy Haldane, a Yorkshire-born economist who wrote the first part of the government's main levelling-up report in 2022, pushed politicians to focus on metropoles. Make the big cities more productive, he and others argued, and the small towns around them will be able to share in their success.

Unfortunately, politicians have often pushed back against this advice. They have their reasons. Big cities are seldom politically competitive – they tend to be firmly Labour – whereas towns often are. Edlington was part of the Don Valley constituency, which flipped from Labour to Conservative in 2019. Following a boundary change, it became part of Rawmarsh and Conisbrough, which is a Labour seat. It is tempting for politicians to court voters by insisting that such places deserve a larger piece of the pie: instead of spending money on trams in Sheffield, let's fill some potholes in a pit town. And there is another big obstacle in the way of making cities and their hinterlands more productive. Although people who live in cities and towns say they love new jobs and economic growth, they often don't love the things that tend to come along with growth.

For a century, the burghers of Sheffield have tried to prevent their city from expanding too much. In 1924, the Sheffield Association for the Protection of Local Scenery was created. Local worthies, including a formidable woman with the formidable name of Ethel Haythornthwaite, bought up land west of the city, in what is now the Peak District, before builders could plonk houses on it. Sheffield girdled itself with a green belt, and nearby local authorities followed. Eventually, all these preservationist efforts cohered into a giant protected area. The South and West Yorkshire Green Belt is a colossal 950 square miles in size, which means it accounts for 2 per cent of the entire land area of England. It extends so far west that it touches the (equally huge) green belt around Manchester and Liverpool. It extends so far east that it wraps around Edlington.

Local governments in Britain are toothless in many ways. But they have a good deal of power to stop things from being built, and goodness do they use it. Today, anybody trying to put up homes in most of the South Yorkshire green belt would be run out of town. It is an accepted principle, as though carved in stone tablets, that Sheffield must not merge with neighbouring towns such as Rotherham. The same tablets state that Edlington must not merge with the built-up area of Doncaster. According to the town council, it should not even merge with Old Edlington. Edlington cannot make any change to the green belt – something that is reserved to a higher tier of government. But its town plan states, warningly, that the green belt has 'strong community support'.

In 1978, Robert Grainger, a local councillor, wrote a shrewd missive in a now-defunct magazine called *The Edlingtonian*. 'The growth of Edlington in the post war years has been without interruption,' he began. 'We have seen whole new estates put up to meet the needs of our own local people, or for the many friends who have made their homes here and are full members of our community.' But this could not go on for ever, because Edlington would soon reach the limit imposed by the green belt. What would it do then? Grainger laid out three options. It could cut into the green belt, it could accept that the town will stop growing, or it could convert land that was presently being used for something else into housing. 'It's worth thinking about,' he wrote, 'for the time is coming when decisions about land for housing are not going to be as easy as in the past.'

Edlington has followed the third suggestion. The closure of Yorkshire Main liberated some land for houses, which have been built in the style known as Tudorbethan, with red bricks and decorative half-timbering. (In one corner of that development, two concrete plugs mark the covered mineshafts.) Nearby, on the former spoil tip, a new housing estate is going up. But, once that is finished, Edlington will be pretty well done with building. Given the choice between Grainger's first two options, cutting into the green belt or accepting that the town will stop growing, Edlington seems to have plumped for the second.

Greenery is always nice. But the enormous difficulty of building on the fringes of cities and towns affects the residents of places such as Edlington in two ways, both of them bad. The first is that their town is isolated, and therefore not as productive as it could be. The towns and cities of South Yorkshire have been frozen in their mid-twentieth-century shapes – shapes that made some sense when mining and steel-making provided huge numbers of jobs, and many people walked to work, but do not make sense today. In a part of the country where settlements are so scattered, it would be hard to build a viable public-transport service even if lots of money were available (which it isn't). Public transport in London is so good that a business in the centre can easily draw workers from suburbs like Dartford and Watford, about fifteen miles away. A firm in central Sheffield would struggle to tap the skills of someone in Edlington, even though it is closer.

The second drawback of highly restrictive planning rules is that it is incredibly hard for people to move from a poor place like Edlington to a thriving city such as London. Homes are expensive everywhere in Britain, but they are ludicrously pricey in successful cities, partly because those cities are not allowed to expand. As a result, working-class people cannot access them. They tend to move sideways rather than up. One report on migration by the Social Mobility Commission divides the country into hot spots, cold spots and places in between, which might be called tepid spots. Hot spots are characterized by great social mobility: they have so many opportunities that people find it relatively easy to escape their social-class backgrounds. Cold spots have much less social mobility. Edlington lies in a cold spot, whereas almost all of London is a hot spot. The general pattern is that people from hot spots move to tepid spots or other hot spots, while people from cold spots move to tepid spots or other cold spots. In reality, few people are like Billy Elliot, moving from cold spots to hot spots.

Some people are more discouraged than others. To take an extreme case, a young man or woman who is born in Edlington and manages to earn a law degree from a prestigious university would be well advised to move. Their housing costs will be higher in London, or even in Leeds, but their salary will be so much higher that it will more than compensate. The main difference between rich parts of Britain and poor ones is not that low-paid people earn more in the rich parts – thanks to the national minimum wage, they don't. The difference is that highly paid people earn more. Professionals can do far better in or near the capital than anywhere else. So they move there, and complain about the high price of beer and the rapaciousness of their landlords, while working-class people stay in small towns. They have been left behind not as the result of a metropolitan conspiracy, but because of over-centralized government and planning rules that inflate house prices.

The pattern of movement and non-movement in Britain makes more sense if you think about it as a pragmatic issue rather than as a cultural or a moral one. I don't believe the country really has two tribes, which David Goodhart called 'Somewheres' and 'Anywheres' – one rooted and conservative, the other deracinated and liberal. If it did, how would we explain the fact that so many working-class Somewheres are descended from people who moved so energetically around the country? Nor do I think it is necessarily a sign of state failure when people move from one place to another, as politicians have argued. The opposite might be closer to the truth: a lack of movement is worrying, because it suggests that people cannot take advantage of opportunities. Somehow, we have turned an alarming trend into a virtue.

Some working-class people do leave the poor areas where they grew up and head for thriving places, armed with the vaguest of plans. The Isle of Wight hairdresser who I quoted in Chapter Two told me that he was preparing to leave for London because, as he explained, his flamboyant dress style made him stick out on the island. Don Paterson, who grew up in a council estate in Dundee, moved to London as a young man with a half-formed notion of becoming a jazz musician; he eventually became a poet and an editor. As Paterson put it in his memoir, *Toy Fights*, London was the place where a working-class Scot could rise or fall. Stay in Dundee and 'there was blessedly little risk of either success or failure'. But they are exceptional. Few people thrill to the prospect of a leap in the dark.

Chapter Eight

The world of the armed robbers

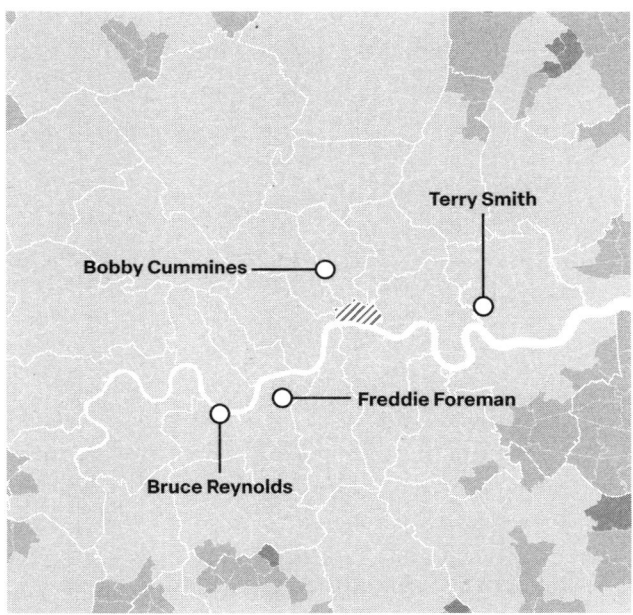

When I met Bobby Cummines a few years ago, over a glass of wine in London's Victoria railway station, he described himself as 'old school'. He meant, partly, the way he comports himself. Few men wear a suit with a pocket handkerchief these days, and fewer carry it off as well as Cummines does. He is a straight-backed man, short and lean; there is, as he puts it, more fat on a fried chip. But Cummines was also referring to his erstwhile career. He was once an old-school criminal – so old-school that he now seems like a historical relic.

For a spell in the 1970s, Cummines was one of the most feared men in London. He carried out a string of armed robberies, barging into banks with a sawn-off shotgun and a team of accomplices. During one robbery, a person died after being badly gagged. Cummines also extorted money from businesses and terrorized criminal rivals around his turf in north London. In the 1990s, following a long spell in prison, he went straight. Since then, he has tried to steer people away from crime and has campaigned for convicts to be allowed to open bank accounts. When I met him in Victoria, he was on the way to meet some bankers – sans shotgun.

It is hard to give up a career as a serious criminal. People can become addicted to crime and the apparently easy money that it brings. They can also become inured to prison, where they need not worry about straight-world annoyances like paying taxes and making appointments with doctors. They may have few friends who are not criminals. But giving up a career as an armed robber is perhaps a little easier than giving up other criminal trades, because of what has happened to armed robbery. It is finished, Cummines assured me. Well, hold on, I said. You still hear about the occasional armed robbery, so some people must be doing it. 'Only *lunatics*,' Cummines retorted. Nobody with half a brain would rob so much as a corner shop. As for robbing banks the way he used to do, threatening the cashiers as a getaway car waits outside: 'You might as well take out a gun and blow your own head off.'

Armed robbery was once almost routine. The 'supergrass' David Smith, who identified dozens of criminal associates in exchange for a lenient prison sentence, confessed to taking part in a staggering seventy-nine robberies in the late 1970s. As Cummines recalls in his 2014 autobiography, *I Am Not a Gangster*, he was once about to pull a gun on a cash-delivery man when he spotted another robber getting out of a car with a shotgun – a member of an East End gang after the same target. 'We had a laugh with them about it,' he remembered. In 1991, the Home Office tallied fully 1,395 armed robberies of banks and building societies in England and Wales.

Then the collapse began. By the late 1990s, the Home Office was recording only about 200 armed bank robberies per year. The British Bankers' Association reported a mere sixty-six in 2011. It stopped reporting armed robbery figures shortly afterwards and began to fret about online fraud, which would eventually grow into one of Britain's most intractable crimes. Armed robbery has become so rare, and professional robbers so peculiar, that banks were quickly alerted when a middle-aged bank robber called Michael Wheatley absconded from an open prison in Kent in 2014. Predictably, Wheatley soon robbed a building society in Sunbury-on-Thames (one that he had robbed before). Just as predictably, he was swiftly caught, charged, found guilty and sent back to prison with an increased sentence.

Like coal miners and professional typists, armed robbers are rapidly heading for extinction in Britain. That is nothing but good news, because armed robbers cause enormous harm. The cashiers and security guards who have guns pointed at them – or worse – can suffer life-ruining trauma. Although robbers have sometimes tried to excuse their crimes by saying that they only harm rich people and insurance companies, this is nonsense. Because insurance firms pass on their costs to businesses, which in turn pass them on to consumers, armed robbery affects everyone. And armed robbers often harm their own families through violence, neglect and awful example. The health secretary Wes Streeting, whose grandfather was an armed robber, writes well about that in his memoir, *One Boy, Two Bills and a Fry Up*.

But I think it is worth dwelling on armed robbery, even though I do not regret its passing in the least. Ugly though the robbers' role in post-war Britain was, they shone a sideways light on some important social and cultural changes that were sweeping the country. They appeared in the 1950s and 1960s, at a time when working-class life was roiling. The masked robber was the irresponsible, violent half-brother of a new type of working-class man who became prominent at that time, in fiction and in reality. And the subsequent decline of armed robbery at the end of the twentieth century tracks changes in working-class life, particularly in London. In the rise and fall of armed robbery is mirrored the rise and fall of a certain kind of white working-class city-dweller.

The armed robbers left behind more than shaken cashiers and elevated insurance premiums. Sometimes with the help of ghostwriters, they set down their thoughts and experiences in books. Those books are valuable because they are so unusual. Walk into a bookshop and you will find plenty of biographies of people who were born poor but later became rich and famous: footballers, singers, politicians, entrepreneurs. The authors' recollections of their working-class childhoods, though often vivid and compelling, are refracted through the glass of their subsequent achievements. Their stories of outdoor toilets and tin baths serve to show how far they have come.

Criminals' autobiographies are different. Most armed robbers were born working class and they remained working class through their adult lives. When they tried to do normal jobs, during (often brief) spells of going straight, they worked as house painters, street sweepers and the like. Cummines worked the night shift in a supermarket, stacking shelves. Crime boosted their fortunes only briefly and, if you count the long stretches they served in prison, it looks like a lousy career choice. 'As a criminal I have been a lamentable failure,' admitted John McVicar, an armed robber and frequent prison escapee, in his autobiography, *McVicar,*

By Himself. He estimated that he would have made twice as much money if he had worked as an honest labourer. If you want to read an account of an uninterrupted working-class life, albeit of a peculiarly irresponsible kind, head for the true-crime section of the bookshop.

*

Armed robbery became common in Britain because another type of crime had become too difficult. Before the 1960s, criminals who wanted loot went straight for the stuff, without tangling with human intermediaries. Working as solitary practitioners or in loose groups, they jimmied windows in grand country houses, smashed shop windows (sometimes after carefully sticking brown paper over them, so the glass would not fly everywhere) and drilled through walls. They went after jewellery, fur coats and, especially, safes.

Bruce Reynolds, a prominent member of the gang who stole £2.5 million from a mail train in 1963, started out as a safe-cracker. Using gelignite purloined from quarries, he drilled and packed and blew the doors off. He was not, he later insisted in his book *The Autobiography of a Thief*, a heavy criminal – nothing like the gangsters who ran protection rackets. More of a craftsman, really, who took pride in his work. But technological progress did to Reynolds' craft what it has done to so many others over the centuries. New safes appeared that could not be blown open, driving the safe-crackers out of business. Some villains then started going after money that was more vulnerable, because it was being moved or kept in a box to which someone – someone who could be threatened – had a key.

The pioneers of armed robbery in Britain were not always armed with guns. The train robbers carried coshes and pickaxe handles; others used socks filled with sand. They started out by targeting the men who delivered wage packets to factories – tough men, armed with truncheons, often four or five to a van, who were paid a little extra for carrying out a dangerous task. The robbers simply tried to overpower them. Even if they had guns, they intimidated the delivery men mostly through surprise and force of numbers. The boldest then took these techniques and adapted them to tougher targets such as banks.

In a classic 'banking hall robbery', to use the industry jargon, three or four masked men rushed into a bank. At least one of them held a sawn-off shotgun. He pointed the gun at a cashier or a customer while another man stuffed money into bags. 'A sawn-off shotgun is the perfect tool for armed robbery', explains the former armed robber Noel 'Razor' Smith in his 2004 auto-biography, *A Few Kind Words and a Loaded Gun*, 'because it is so frightening-looking, and putting the fear of God into those you are about to rob is essential.' Some robbers fired a shot into the ceiling to emphasize that they were serious. After collecting the money, the criminals ran outside to a waiting car, which had been stolen for the purpose. They turned a few corners before getting into another car, which they drove to a flat. There, they divided the money.

The people who did this were not particularly varied. In 1994, two criminologists, Shona Morrison and Ian O'Donnell, identified 214 armed robbers who had collectively committed more than 500 robberies in London, and interviewed many of them. The two researchers found that 72 per cent of the robbers were white and 90 per cent had been born in Britain, making them a little more ethnically diverse but a little more British-born than the city's population, as it was recorded in the 1991 census. A few years later, Roger Matthews, the same criminologist who studied the New Parks housing estate described in Chapter Three, went around English prisons interviewing 340 armed robbers. Only 5 per cent of the convicts in his sample were anything other than white. Even today, the mugshots that appear in the newspapers when some lunatics are convicted of armed robbery tend to show white faces.

Armed robbers share a few other characteristics besides an ethnicity and a country of birth. Needless to say, almost all are men. Most are Londoners. In the early 1980s, the Metropolitan Police estimated that 60 per cent of all serious armed robberies in England and Wales took place in the capital and that three quarters of robberies everywhere involved at least one Londoner. A few neighbourhoods have produced more than their fair share. One is Highbury, Bobby Cummines's old manor – a once rough, now pricey part of north London. But the most productive criminal nursery is in central London, within smelling distance of the Thames River.

Freddie Foreman, a former armed robber and gangster, grew up on the Wandsworth Road in south London. In his 1997 autobiography, *Respect*, he has a stab at explaining why so many heavy criminals were raised near the river. Foreman points out that the London docks had for decades provided opportunities to working-class men from that area. Dockers were comparatively well paid and were used to luxuries like televisions and fitted carpets. When the London docks closed in the 1960s and 1970s, some of the dockers' children attempted to recover their former lifestyle (or, as Foreman put it, 'go out and get big money') through crime.

There may be something to Foreman's theory, and it helps to explain something else about the armed robbers. Cummines, Smith and Foreman are all descended from Irish immigrants. So are the Bradish gang, who carried out a great many armed robberies in the 1990s, at a time when others were giving up. The Irish occupied an uncomfortable niche in post-war London.

Although they had one foot in the British white working class, they were stigmatized and discriminated against. They tended to take hard, undesirable jobs, seldom joined trade unions, and often cobbled together livelihoods through casual work and petty entrepreneurship. Men had reputations as drinkers and fighters, which were not altogether undeserved. Many ended up working in the docks. From that macho, pugnacious world sprang the men who would terrorize Britain.

Armed robbers were often descended from Irish migrants, but they were seldom migrants themselves. Noel Smith suggests to me that the people who actually crossed the Irish Sea were like many immigrants, in that they tried to keep their heads down and stay out of trouble. Their cocky British-born children were a different matter: 'They thought, this country is there for the taking.' Besides, people who are born outside Britain are likely to lack the extensive social networks that are necessary to pull off such a difficult crime. Armed robbery is considerably harder than it seems. You need a gun, for a start, and some sense of how to use it. You need reliable accomplices. You need information – which usually comes from unscrupulous employees – about when banks and shops empty their safes. You need to know the local streets, so you can make a quick getaway. You also need to be able to spend the money without attracting police attention, including money that has been stained by an exploding dye pack when the cash box containing it is forced open. To develop such contacts and knowledge, it helps to have grown up in Britain.

The most successful armed robbers had one more thing in common: they were prodigious spenders. Several of the men who went on to write autobiographies happily recall buying their first expensive suits with the proceeds from heists. Reynolds blew much of his money on cars and dining. This behaviour is more sensible than it might seem. Robbers cannot very well bank their loot, and there is not much point in holding on to the cash – other criminals will quickly beg or steal it from them. So they might as well spend it. Anyway, the robbers loved to swagger. The point of crime, Reynolds wrote, was 'swanking, of making out that I was someone'. McVicar called crime 'flattering'. He was not just after money, he wrote, but a superior lifestyle.

*

As some white working-class Londoners were pulling on masks and stuffing shotguns under their coats, others were throwing themselves into music, writing and art. The photographer David Bailey and the hairdresser Vidal Sassoon clawed their way into fashionable society through sheer talent and nerve. 'My mother used to say, "You'll end up like all of us, driving the 101 bus,"' Bailey remembered in his autobiography, *Look Again*. 'I thought, I fucking won't.'

Others sat down to write. The years 1955 to 1960 saw the appearance of the plays *Look Back in Anger* by John Osborne and *A Taste of Honey* by Shelagh Delaney, as well as the novels *A Kind of Loving* by Stan Barstow, *Room at the Top* by John Braine and *Saturday Night and Sunday Morning* by Alan Sillitoe. It was the era of skiffle, a British offshoot of blues and rockabilly that would eventually morph into rock and roll. Skiffle was proudly proletarian, with a strong do-it-yourself ethos. Observers of society were amazed. 'The entire English class system may be on the point of going into reverse,' gushed Raphael Samuel, a left-wing intellectual, in a letter to the sociologist Peter Willmott. 'The middle class plainly *wants* to identify with the working class.'

Underdogs

The new working-class man who arose in the 1950s and 1960s was epitomized by three fictional characters: Vic Brown in *A Kind of Loving*; Arthur Seaton, the hero of *Saturday Night and Sunday Morning*; and Joe Lambton in *Room at the Top*. These men were optimistic, believing that they could do better than their parents, but also worldly and cynical. They sneered both at middle-class life and at the working-class culture they had grown up with – the working men's clubs, the buttoned-down respectability. They did as they damn well chose. In an era of high employment, the men reckoned they could walk into and out of jobs easily. There is a wonderful scene in *A Kind of Loving* in which one character gets into a fight at work and is chastised by his boss. The man calmly picks up a newspaper and starts leafing through the job advertisements. Go ahead and sack me, he implies: I won't have any problem finding another job. Ideally the new working-class man of the era wouldn't work at all, but would just come into money somehow. As Joe Lambton put it: 'I wanted an Aston-Martin, I wanted a three-guinea linen shirt, I wanted a girl with a Riviera suntan – these were my rights, I felt, a signed and sealed legacy.'

Today there seems to be a world of difference between the armed robbers and the brash working-class men who strutted through post-war London and thundered through contemporary novels. But the criminal and creative worlds touched. Bailey photographed the Kray twins, helping to make those two gangsters more famous than they really deserved. Foreman hung out in Sibylla's, a nightclub partly owned by the Beatle George Harrison, and ran clubs of his own. The skiffle singer Adam Faith and the skiffle-turned-rock musician Roger Daltrey starred in a film about McVicar. Noel Smith led a rockabilly gang before he moved into armed robbery. John Bindon, who played mobsters in films, was no real-life angel. He was acquitted of the murder of a criminal in 1978, but was later jailed for threatening an off-duty police officer with a carving knife.

And although it now seems fair to view the armed robbers as predators who inhabited a shady world outside society and the working class, that is not quite how they saw themselves. In their books, they describe themselves as workers, and they frequently scorn gangsters, who (as they see it) do not work, but merely send underlings to collect protection money. In his book *Bad Business*, Dick Hobbs, the leading sociologist of heavy crime in Britain, quotes an armed robber who had been active in the 1950s and 1960s. The man described himself as a 'steady worker' and a dependable gang member. When robbing a bank, he explained, he would take charge of his environment and work quickly so that his victims would not be tempted to challenge him: 'The better you are at the job, the better they like it.' Another violent armed robber assured a nervous policeman who had been charged with accompanying him that he would not attack him. Violence was part of his work, the robber explained, but he was not working that day.

*

It didn't last – any more than the steelworks of Teesside or the potteries of Stoke-on-Trent lasted. Beginning in the 1970s, wave upon wave of change broke over the armed robbers. Bank and Post Office cashiers retreated behind security screens. Security technology improved, with new forensic 'taggants' that could tie a banknote to a specific cashbox, and therefore to a specific robbery. Then came 'hair samples, DNA, all that fucking stuff', remembers Cummines. Police officers got better at working with banks and security firms to prevent robberies. Testimony from supergrasses led to many armed robbers being locked up for long spells. There was no honour among thieves when the authorities came calling, promising shorter sentences in exchange for information.

Meanwhile, the riverine environment from which so many robbers had sprung began to change. Working-class white people drifted out of inner London to suburbs and estuary towns. Their old neighbourhoods were soon settled by immigrants and white middle-class adventurers. Some criminals who moved to suburbs and small towns in Essex and Kent tried hitting the local banks, but found it tricky. London's crowds and its dense street network make getaways easy. A robber who puts five miles' distance between himself and a bank along a rural road before the police turn up looks just as guilty as if he were standing right next to the bank. Besides, rural police forces are likely to throw lots of investigative resources at something as rare and exciting as a bank robbery.

Those who continued robbing in London sometimes encountered a new problem. Immigration was transforming the capital, making for an ever more unpredictable cultural environment in which to work. One bank robber interviewed in prison by Roger Matthews for his 2002 book *Armed Robbery* tried to coerce a cashier into giving him money by threatening a customer. He failed because the cashier, a South Asian, could not understand the customer, a West African. By the mid-1970s, Noel Smith had fallen to robbing corner shops. He was thwarted in one attempt when the shopkeeper, a South Asian Sikh, flatly refused to give him any money at all. Smith is the paramount writer among former armed robbers – he went on to edit a newspaper for prisoners. In *A Few Kind Words and a Loaded Gun*, he recounts what happened with flair:

He crossed his arms and leant back in his chair.

'I don't think so,' he said. 'In Uganda I saw many guns, and

206

I see that your gun is unloaded. You are minus the magazine.
And you swear far too much for such a young man.'

Smith grabbed a Mars bar and ran.

*

By the 1980s, armed robbery was becoming ever more difficult. But
some robbers refused to give up. The decade saw some spectacular
heists, including the Brink's-Mat robbery, in which roughly
£26 million in gold bullion was stolen from a warehouse in
Heathrow by men who threatened to murder the security guards
by burning them. There was a lucrative armed raid on safety
deposit boxes in Knightsbridge. And a new kind of armed robber
appeared, self-consciously different from those who had come
before and very much a man of his time. One of the shrewdest
of these men was Terry Smith.

Smith was born in Canning Town in east London, a neighbourhood that was then tied to the docks, but he has spent much
of his free life in Essex. He is part of the great migration of
working-class white people eastwards from London. I first interviewed him by telephone in 2005, when he was living in Canvey
Island. At the time, Smith had just embarked on a brief career as
a writer and pundit on armed robbery – brief because, in 2010,
he was convicted of conspiracy to rob and given an indeterminate
prison sentence. He is a shrewd analyst of serious crime. In that
interview, in books such as *The Art of Armed Robbery* and *Blaggers,
Inc*, and in letters to me from prison, he has explained how serious
armed robbery evolved in the 1980s, why it subsequently disappeared and what replaced it.

Like many others, Smith was introduced to armed robbery by
older men. They impressed upon him the necessity of wearing a
mask and the advantage of stealing your own getaway car rather

than getting one from a car thief (there is less risk of being informed upon that way). Under their tutelage, Smith became a competent pavement robber. Instead of barging into banks waving a gun, he intercepted cash-delivery men as they made the short, dangerous journey from security van to bank. But he quickly developed ideas of his own.

Smith decided that the criminals who had taught him were stuck in the 1960s. They assumed that four or five men were needed to rob a security van, because that had been the case when they learned the business. Guns had made such large teams unnecessary. Smith reckoned that two men were sufficient – one to commit the robbery, the second to watch his back. They could drive their own (stolen) car away from the scene of the crime or make off on motorbikes. Then they would only have to split the loot in two. Smith even carried out some robberies solo. He invokes a paranoid saying: if one person knows something, nobody knows; if two people know something, everybody knows.

Smith became famous not only for what he did, but also for something that was done to him. In 1984, he was being moved from one prison to another in a security van. Some of his associates, who were experts in holding up just that sort of vehicle, forced it off the road and plucked him out. Unfortunately, Smith was handcuffed to another prisoner, who had to be bundled into the getaway car and hidden along with him. This created a dilemma. Sending the man off on his own would be dangerous. If he was caught, he might reveal Smith's whereabouts. But bringing him along on robberies was just as dangerous. In the end, the gang decided to cut him loose. The new breed of armed robber would not work with anybody he had not known for years. Ideally, he would not work with anybody at all.

The shrinking of the robbery gang is one of the most relentless developments in British crime since the Second World War. Reynolds' gang of train robbers contained more than a dozen men, plus others on the fringes of the operation. True-crime writers have speculated for years that other men were involved in the robbery but were never caught. Soon, four-man gangs were the norm. Smith and his contemporaries shrank the unit to two. A statistical study of bank robberies published in 2012 reported that the mean average number of raiders had fallen to 1.6, and that six out of ten robberies were solo. A job that had once been done by a group of men became a family business, then a lone activity.

The move from large teams of armed robbers to smaller teams, then to solo operators, has some parallels in the world of legitimate work. At the end of the Second World War, almost every Briton with a job worked either for the state or for a company. In 1945, just 7 per cent were self-employed. The proportion of self-employed people rose in the 1980s – the era of Terry Smith – and again in the 2000s. Today, even people who do traditional working-class jobs in teams, such as factory workers, are often employed by agencies. They have little job security and possess few rights. Many working-class people, not just armed robbers, are in effect working for themselves.

To describe modern armed robbers as solo operators is to flatter some of them. Better words would be 'disorganized' and 'shambolic'. Two of the convicted armed robbers interviewed by Matthews in the early 1990s were caught after they handed threatening notes to cashiers that had their names written on the back. Other research has shown that most armed robbers do not carry loaded guns, and that a fair few are high on drink or drugs. Over time, the 'idiots', as one police officer scornfully described them to me, have become a larger and larger fraction of the shrinking population of armed robbers.

Underdogs

There has been but one big exception so far this century, and it proves the rule. In December 2004, two groups of robbers dressed as police officers entered the homes of executives working for Northern Bank in Belfast. They held the executives' families at gunpoint and instructed the men to go to work as normal. In the evening, the executives were forced to allow another group of robbers into a storage area containing more than £20 million in banknotes. It was the biggest robbery in Northern Irish history, and is unusual because it has not been solved. The bank attempted to render the stolen notes worthless by retiring all the bills in circulation and printing new ones with fresh designs. But much of the money had been laundered.

A couple of years after the Northern Bank robbery, I interviewed Sir Hugh Orde, who was then chief constable of Northern Ireland's police force. He showed me the new banknotes and explained how peculiar the robbery had been. The gunmen had left almost no evidence behind, he said. By contrast, the 2006 robbery of a Securitas depot in Kent, which also involved taking a family hostage, had left a good deal of evidence; several men were later convicted for that crime. The difference between the two crimes was plain, Sir Hugh said. The Kentish robbers were criminals, whereas the Belfast robbers were terrorists. He was convinced that the Irish Republican Army had carried out the crime. Naturally, the IRA denied having anything to do with it.

Nobody knows the truth about Northern Ireland's bank robbery except those who will not talk. But it says something about the decay of armed robbery that the police were so confident in asserting that conventional criminals were not capable of pulling off such a complex crime and getting away with it. They simply aren't up to the job any more. It was a similar story in 2015, when thieves broke into a vault in Hatton Garden in London and raided safe-deposit boxes. After that crime, the *Guardian* journalist Duncan Campbell was assured by two former criminals that the robbers might be Eastern Europeans, or perhaps people with military training. In fact, the Hatton Garden robbery was carried out by a group of elderly British men, who were soon caught and convicted. The message that safe-cracking had died out half a century earlier had somehow failed to reach them.

*

The armed robbers' story has a happy ending – for them, not for Britain. By the 1970s it was becoming clear that large sums of money could be made more easily than by running into banks with guns. A new group of criminal entrepreneurs had emerged to feed the growing British demand for heroin, cocaine and marijuana. At first, the armed robbers preyed on these men. Then, because so many traffickers were being robbed, they began to pay the gunmen to protect them. Eventually, some of the robbers went into the drugs business themselves.

As a criminal enterprise, drug importation has several advantages over armed robbery. It is policed by a variety of domestic and international organizations, which do not always cooperate brilliantly well. It is far less dangerous. Police officers do not normally open fire on drug traffickers, as they have done on bank robbers. And it is far more profitable. Some retired criminals have written of the buzz they got from robbing banks and security vans, which in some cases became almost addictive. Many others, however, have been keen to trade buzz for plentiful, less risky money.

The gunmen who went into the drug business found themselves in an open, competitive marketplace. Unlike armed robbery, the British drug market is not dominated by a single ethnic or national group. It is almost impossible to monopolize any aspect of importing or drug dealing: two traffickers could well be bringing shipments of cocaine through the same port without knowing of each other's activities. A reputation for violence can help in an enterprise where contracts are unenforceable in law, and armed robbers have such reputations. But violence is best avoided in the drug trade, because it attracts attention.

Most of the armed robbers who went into the drugs racket let their muscles and their violent reputations atrophy. 'They are fat old men with heart problems,' says Cummines, dismissively. 'All they worry about is how to keep their money.' But that is a nice problem to have.

Chapter Nine

In the family way

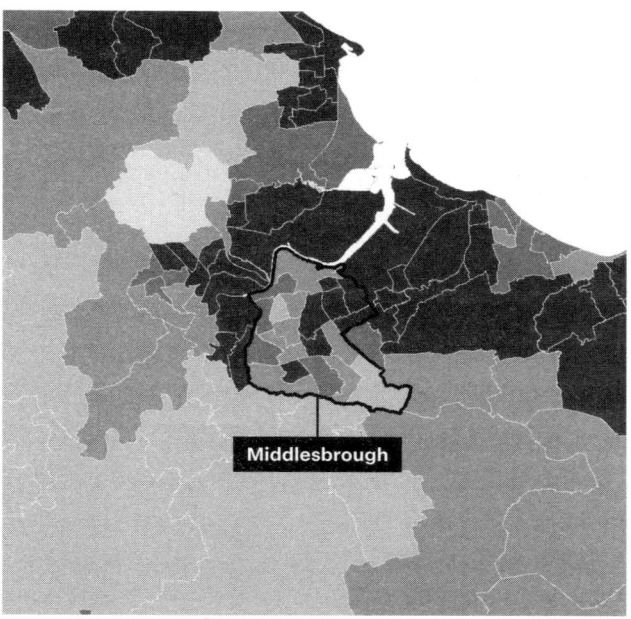

Middlesbrough

As I write, a mysterious group of people is approaching retirement age. Almost nobody knows who they are or where they live, although Kent would be a good guess. Many of them have probably forgotten that they belong to the group. Thanks to a sociologist named Ray Pahl, though, I do know how these people once imagined they would feel when they reached this point in their lives.

Most of them were just sixteen years old, and about to leave a secondary school in the Isle of Sheppey, on the Thames estuary's southern flank, when they were set an unusual task. Imagine you are old, they were told, and are reminiscing about your life. Write about what happened to you. Pahl, who was researching working-class lives in a place that had once been dominated by a Royal Navy dockyard, wanted to know how young people thought about work and family. He collected 154 essays in 1978, which are now in the care of the University of Essex. They open an extraordinary window into the minds of an earlier generation of working-class teenagers.

Almost all the teenagers took their assignment seriously, although some could barely write, suggesting a troubled schooling (one essay is titled 'My parst'). Rather than fantasizing about becoming professional footballers or film stars, they produced plausible accounts of ordinary lives. They imagined working as low-level engineers, lorry drivers, sewing machinists and secretaries. Some imagined languishing on the dole. An oddly large number anticipated that they, or members of their families, would be maimed in vehicle accidents. A few 1970s concerns waft through their essays – one mentions inflation, which was then high, while another alludes to contemporary worries about over-population. But most of the teenagers concentrated on the ordinary highlights of life. They expected to take jobs, get married and have children, in that order.

Reading the essays today, I am struck by how very regular, how clock-like, the teenagers expected their early adult lives to be. 'I met Dave and we got on really well straight away,' wrote one girl. 'After a year or so, we were engaged.' 'When I was exactly twenty, I proposed to my girlfriend,' wrote a boy. 'Two months later we were married. It was only a matter of a few months before my wife was pregnant.' Only later, in middle age, does that boy's imagined life take some unexpected turns. He is injured in a car accident, tries to make a career in music, turns to drugs, then finds God.

Many of the teenage girls seem to have bridled at the expectations on young women. They anticipated being pushed, not too happily, into housewifery, and expected to struggle with the trade-off between work and family life. One imagined turning down a marriage proposal at the age of twenty-one, although she accepted another at the age of thirty-five. Some anticipated marrying not because they were ready for it, but because their parents insisted or because they became pregnant. One girl imagined marrying in a hurry 'cos I was in the club', then discovering her husband in bed with 'a bird of eighteen'. Like one other girl and three boys, she imagined going through a divorce. But, of all the 154 essay writers, only one girl imagined having a baby out of wedlock. Hers is a wonderful tale involving two Frenchmen and a self-sacrificing mother. She is the author I would most love to meet.

So old-fashioned are the family lives most of the teenagers imagined for themselves that it can be hard to believe they were writing as late as 1978. 'It's the 1970s, but people are still living with some of the ideas of the 1950s,' says Dawn Lyon, a professor at the University of Kent who has studied the essays and tried to track down their authors, without much success. Sheppey seems to have been a gossipy, conventional place in the late 1970s, with lots of adults prying into young people's affairs. The teenagers had an itinerary drummed into them: work, court, marry, children. They chafed against society's expectations but could hardly imagine breaking them.

Unless the essay-writers were extremely unusual, though, their family lives will have turned out very differently from what they imagined in 1978. Almost certainly, a great many more than five have divorced. The essay-writers who imagined marrying at twenty would have walked up the aisle in 1982. Of the 342,000 marriages in England and Wales that year, one fifth would be broken by divorce before the couple's tenth anniversary, and more than two fifths would dissolve before their thirtieth anniversary. Meanwhile, another change was quietly gathering speed. In 1978, one out of every ten babies was born to an unmarried woman. Ten years later, one in four was.

Family life has kept on changing. Marriage has become quite a bit rarer. Just 220,000 weddings took place in England and Wales in 2019, including same-sex weddings. That was probably the lowest number since 1893 (figures are missing for many years in the early twentieth century), and there were even fewer weddings in 2020 because of the Covid pandemic. Living together before marriage has become completely normal: 85 per cent of people do it. Just over half of babies are now born to unmarried mothers. The birth rate has dropped, and the average first-time mum grows a little older every year. Twice as many babies are now born to women aged forty or older than to women under twenty.

These changes have swept Britain, along with many other rich countries. They are collectively known as the 'second demographic transition' and they seem almost as inexorable as the first demographic transition, which took countries from a terrifying equilibrium of high births and high mortality to a happier state of low births and low mortality. But the changes in family life over the past few decades have not touched everyone equally. Although the age of motherhood has risen for everyone, it has increased more slowly for less-educated women. Social class shapes patterns of marriage and parenthood: two thirds of births to women with routine jobs occur outside marriage, compared with one third for women who are managers or high-level administrators. And Britain as a whole stands out in one unhappy way. The Organisation for Economic Co-operation and Development collects data on family lives in thirty-three countries, most of them rich. The share of children living in single-parent households in Britain is the fifth highest, at 23 per cent. America comes top of that unhappy table.

New accents, new music and new fashions tend to emerge in big cities, then spread. The same has been true of new patterns of marriage and childbirth. At the turn of the century, all ten of the postcode areas in England and Wales with the highest proportion of births outside marriage were in or around Liverpool and Manchester in north-west England (counting only places with at least 100 births). By the late 2010s, only three of them were. The hotspot for unmarried motherhood has moved ninety-odd miles north-east, to the cluster of towns in the Tees Valley, which include some of the poorest places in England. Four of the ten postcode areas where unmarried births are most common are in and around Teesside – two in Middlesbrough, one in Hartlepool and one in Redcar and Cleveland. Two others are not far away, in County Durham and Sunderland.

Single-parent families have become common in the same places. The 2021 census showed that 36 per cent of children under sixteen in Middlesbrough live in single-parent households. The rate is about as high in Blackpool, a poor, mostly white town north of Liverpool, and in Merthyr Tydfil in South Wales. Inner-London boroughs like Lambeth and Southwark have even higher rates, but only barely. Single parenthood used to be associated mostly with ethnically diverse inner-city areas. These days, it is just as common in towns that are largely white and working-class. It has spread to the heartlands.

*

Teesside has enjoyed a few spells in the sun. It fared well in the early twentieth century, and again after the Second World War, when the expanding chemicals, steel and shipbuilding industries supplied local people with good jobs. But it has often slipped back into poverty and unemployment. It is poor today, with wages well below the national average and many young people working insecure jobs. Its inhabitants suffer from awful physical and mental health. The suicide rate in all of Teesside's local authorities is above the national average. A man born in Middlesbrough can expect to live fifty-six years before becoming disabled, meaning that he struggles to do something basic such as cleaning, gardening, lifting objects or remembering to pay a bill. A woman can expect fifty-five years. Nearby, in wealthier, mostly rural North Yorkshire, men get an extra nine years of good health and women get an extra seven.

Some erstwhile industrial powerhouses, such as Manchester and Newcastle, have reinvented themselves as hubs of culture and services. Teesside seems more reluctant to move on from manufacturing. Until 2022, the long, lovely beach in Redcar was incongruously backed by an enormous blast furnace – the remnant of a defunct steelworks – which some people fought to preserve. Offshore, easily visible from land, is a large wind farm. The elected mayor of the Tees Valley, Lord Ben Houchen, talks incessantly of bringing heavy industry back to the vast area where the steelworks stood. Though he trained as a lawyer, though he is a Conservative and though his political life began in a wealthy corner of Teesside, Houchen often sounds like a nicotine-stained Labour boss from decades ago. He bangs on about local 'grit', boasts that 'real jobs' are being created and promises to get 'a larger slice of the cake' from the government in Westminster. He is enormously popular in the area.

For a long time, Teesside also clung to an old-fashioned model of family life, with a male breadwinner and a stay-at-home wife. Sharon Birch was born in Hartlepool in 1965. Her father was a navy seaman, and as a result her mother sometimes resembled a single parent. That caused consternation, she says: 'When I went to school, I remember children asking, "Where's your dad? Is he in prison?" It was very unusual at the time.' Birch remembers that unmarried couples who lived together were still being frowned upon when she left Teesside in the mid-1980s to take a job with the London Metropolitan Police. And when she had children of her own and returned to Teesside a decade later, she noticed something else. In London, few people openly disapproved of working mothers. In Teesside, many did.

The change that has come over Teesside families in the last few decades, which has taken them from highly traditional to unusually fragile, has been incredibly fast and scary. 'Family life is not as we know it any more,' says Olwyn Peters, a former mayor who helps run the Whale Hill Community Centre in Middlesbrough. In the postcode area encompassing that building, just one quarter of babies were born to married parents in the late 2010s. Although many of the others were born to unmarried couples who were living together, a quarter of the babies were born to men and women who were living at different addresses. For a further one in ten, the father's name was not even recorded on the birth certificate.

A few miles from the community centre, I sit down for a long conversation with a middle-aged woman and her friend. She knows well how family life has changed in Teesside, because she has seen it in her own family. Her mother, a factory worker, got pregnant as an unmarried teenager and was promptly thrown out of the house. She then reconciled with her parents, married the father of her child practically at gunpoint and stayed married for the rest of her life. My interviewee also got pregnant in her teens, although things worked out slightly differently. She was strongly encouraged to marry her boyfriend, and she did, but the marriage ended in divorce. A few years ago, one of her own children gave birth when young and unmarried. The couple split quickly and have little to do with each other. 'It is very easy for a man to walk away,' she says. 'It doesn't help when children have children,' adds her friend, a little tactlessly.

To the west, in Stockton-on-Tees, I meet a charming young man who currently relies on benefits on account of ill health. He has a council house but no car – a great limitation in a corner of England with poor public transport. He is married to a woman who also subsists on benefits, and has two children. He delights in his marriage ('I'd be lost without her') and feels himself to be unusual among his neighbours. He is: at the last count, fewer than one third of babies in the local postcode area were born to married parents. When I ask him how family life in the area has changed, he begins by holding his hand horizontally in front of his face. In his grandparents' generation, he explains, marriage was common and families were resilient. In his parents' generation – he drops his hand to his chest – they were more likely to fall apart. And in his generation . . . his hand falls to his waist.

I have seen many family forms in my time as a journalist, from large families in rural Senegal to young couples cowed by overbearing mothers-in-law in the slums of north India. Although I know what kind of family life I prefer, I do not condemn anybody else's arrangements. I certainly do not look down on single parents in Britain, who do heroic work raising children in tough circumstances. But I am interested in children's fortunes, and in the ways that advantages and disadvantages are transmitted from generation to generation. Family arrangements matter to me not for how closely they adhere to an ideal, but for how they affect people who belong to families. And they do affect people. The poverty of white working-class people in Teesside is connected to the fragility of their families.

*

Britons are used to the idea that gender, ethnicity and social class hand large advantages and disadvantages to people. We are a little less familiar with the notion that family background can help or hinder; perhaps we are less comfortable with it. But the facts are clear. One 2016 study of the cohort of Britons who were born in 1970, by Fabrizio Bernardi and Diederik Boertien, found that the children of couples who divorce are one third less likely to obtain university degrees. Divorce itself seems to harm children's prospects: the pattern cannot be explained away by pointing out that divorcing couples tend to be less educated than couples who stay together. In 2013, a study of Californians reported that being the child of parents who divorce appears to shorten your life. Strikingly, separation seems to affect children's prospects today as much as it ever did. You might expect that divorce has become less harmful as it has grown more common, but that doesn't seem to be the case.

Researchers also think they have worked out why divorce and parental separation harm children. The answer is largely that it impoverishes them. Most children of separated parents live with their mothers, and they tend to suffer a sharp drop in household income as soon as their fathers leave. As it happens, middle-class households experience a bigger drop in income than working-class households do. More affluent households lose the men's often hefty earnings, and receive little by way of public assistance to compensate. Working-class mothers and children lose the men's earnings too, but those earnings are smaller, and they are able to make up more of the shortfall with welfare. Still, working-class mothers can ill afford to lose anything at all.

Splitting is far more common among parents who are not married. In a 2022 report for the Institute of Fiscal Studies, Kathleen Kiernan and other demographers and economists looked at what happened to babies born around the turn of the century. They found that 88 per cent of those who were born to married couples were still living with both parents at the age of five. Just 8 per cent were living with only one parent (the remaining few were living with one parent and a new partner, or had seen their parents separate and then reunite). Babies who were born to unmarried cohabiting parents experienced more disruption. Many of their parents stayed together, sometimes marrying, mostly not. But, at the age of five, 21 per cent of the children in that group were living in a single-parent household. And of the babies born to parents who were not living together, 42 per cent remained in single-parent households.

Some observers, such as the Centre for Social Justice, a conservative-leaning think tank, have looked at data like this and concluded that marriage glues couples together. They also argue that, given the egregious social consequences of family break-down, the British government ought to subsidize marriage far more generously than it does at the moment. That isn't necessarily right. Yes, married couples are far more stable than unmarried couples. And yes, that remains true (although it is less true) even when you take account of the fact that married couples tend to be wealthier and more educated. But it is still hard to say for sure that marriage holds couples together, because some very import-ant things – such as how much people love each other – cannot be measured easily. Statistically, the trouble with marriage is that it is subject to selection effects. If married couples are stronger, is that because marriage has strengthened their relationships or because people with strong relationships get married?

Demographers might soon be able to venture an answer to that question, partly because of the Covid pandemic, which wrecked many people's wedding plans, and partly because of the Hungarian government, which has pursued a fervently pro-marriage, pro-baby agenda since 2019. For now, my guess is that marriage does help to bind couples together. If it had no effect whatsoever, it would mean that all the effort and expense that couples and their families put into weddings – all the dresses, the flowers, the decisions about where to seat that difficult uncle – are for nothing. But, even if my guess is right, it still does not mean subsidizing marriage is a good idea. A government that does so will throw lots of money to couples (disproportionately, privileged couples) who would have married anyway. And I think that marriage boosters misunderstand the obstacles to stable, committed relationships, particularly in poor places like Teesside. The problem is not so much that working-class people living in post-industrial towns do not believe in commitment or marriage. As I will show, it is more that they do not believe in their partners.

*

Around 2010, Dawn Lyon tried to repeat Pahl's imaginative experiment in Sheppey, with a few differences. Instead of sixteen-year-olds, she focused on seventeen- and eighteen-year-olds, reflecting the fact that teenagers are supposed to study for longer. Rather than going into a school, she invited teenagers to write their essays in a community centre. It did not go brilliantly. The teenagers could refuse to participate, and some did. They also seemed uncomfortable with sitting down and writing, perhaps because they had grown up in a more digitally distracting, entertaining world. Their essays were shorter than the ones their predecessors had written in 1978. Still, Lyon managed to collect just over a hundred.

They were different from the essays written by the people now hitting retirement age. Many more of the teenagers mentioned going to university, taking professional jobs and travelling abroad, all things that are more common than they used to be. They also described family life differently. In 1978, 96 per cent of the girls had mentioned marriage; in 2010, 58 per cent did. Among boys, the proportion fell from 75 per cent to 55 per cent. And the number of teenagers who wrote with precision about their imagined unions – the age at which they met their partners, the length of time they courted, the age at which they married – plunged. The essays suggest that marriage has become less important to teenagers, and even less expected. The strict clock mechanism that had ruled their predecessors' early adult lives seems to have broken. Young people in Sheppey have not exactly turned against marriage on principle, though. In 1978, 5 per cent of the boys wrote that they would remain single. Three decades later, 4 per cent of boys wrote the same. No girl in either group imagined a single life.

National opinion polls tell a similar story, of marriage becoming only a little less popular but a lot less expected. In 2022, YouGov found that, among unmarried eighteen- to twenty-four-year-olds, those who want to marry at some point outnumber those who do not want to marry by a ratio of six to one. But the proportion of Britons who hold that people *ought* to marry before doing other things has fallen a great deal. The long-running British Social Attitudes survey shows that, in 1989, 70 per cent agreed with the statement that people who want children ought to marry. By 2022, just 24 per cent agreed. Although marriage remains an alluring ideal, people have come to see it as the capstone of a successful relationship and an excuse for a big party, rather than as the doorway to family life.

One person who has watched marriages change in Teesside is Gary Walsh, a photographer with a studio in Stockton-on-Tees. When he started shooting weddings in the early 1990s, couples usually tied the knot in local churches, then repaired to a nearby venue for the reception. They did not expect their families to travel far for a chicken dinner and a glass of bubbly. Weddings were usually paid for by parents, who kept control of the guest list. Today, weddings occur anywhere photogenic, and seldom in churches. Couples, who are usually in their thirties – not in their twenties, as they were when Walsh started photographing them – tend to pay for and run the entire show. They have homes of their own, and often children. 'House together, child and then wedding seems to be the way forward,' he says. A modern wedding says not 'we are beginning a new life together' but 'we have made it'.

Working-class Teessiders sometimes hold fast to old-fashioned views about commitment, marriage and childbearing, believing that children ought to be raised by couples who are firmly committed to each other, if not married. I ask one new mother, a tattoo artist who has been with her partner for more than a decade, why so many women in her neighbourhood end up raising children alone. She answers swiftly: 'I think a lot of couples aren't ready. They have a baby because they think it will save their relationship, and it doesn't work. Either that, or they're just not very careful.' 'A lot of babies are born out of lust, not out of love,' adds another woman, who has worked a variety of unskilled jobs. Her own family life has been complicated, to put it mildly. She has had several children by more than one man, some of whom have occasionally been removed from her by the state. She is now desperately trying to keep one of her teenage children from slipping down what she calls 'a dark path', by which she means drugs and drug dealing.

The problem that working-class women in Teesside face is that reality falls so far short of their ideals. They might believe it is best to raise children in a stable home, with a committed partner. They might believe that a strong relationship ought to culminate in marriage. But that does not change the fact that their lives, and the lives of the men they tend to end up with, are so often blighted by poverty, instability and addiction. Among the local pool of men, 'there are a lot of alcoholics, a lot of cokeheads,' says the woman who is trying to keep her son on the right path. I tell her that I admire her ability to raise children alone in a dangerous neighbourhood. Her retort is brutal and desperately sad: 'Even when I was with people, they were no help. They were a waste of space.'

One day, I drop into the Tees Valley Women's Centre, a charity in Middlesbrough. It is hosting an Access to Higher Education course – a two-year programme that prepares people who did not do well at school for university. All but one of the women on the course are mothers, and all of them want to become nurses. They talk about the drawbacks of their current jobs (many work in care homes, where the pay is low and the prospects for advancement slim) and about how hard it is to work, study and look after children at the same time. They are a lively bunch, and it is a fun conversation. But the women become most animated when they talk about the men they know.

According to them, old assumptions about women being wholly responsible for running the household simply will not die in Teesside. 'You're very lucky these days to get a father who is supportive of anything the mother's doing,' complains one of the students. 'I'm in a relationship, but I struggle with him for childcare. He puts his job over my course.' Another, who also lives with her partner, describes a wildly unbalanced division of domestic labour: 'I have to think, Can I get the kids to school on time? When am I going to shop to get the tea in? All they have to think is, How am I getting to work and how am I getting home?' Some of the single mothers say that their former partners contributed little to the household when they were together, and contribute little or nothing now they are not. As one puts it, delicately: 'They might not *legally* have a job.' And those are among the students' more nuanced opinions of Teesside men. Others are withering. 'The men round here are not right in the head,' says one single mother. 'They're feral,' adds another.

This is only one side of the story. I have also met working-class men in Teesside who are doing their best to care for children. Some men who have separated from their partners tell painful stories about having to fight for months or even years to gain access to their offspring. But Teesside does seem to have an unusually hidebound culture when it comes to the division of labour. The valley has held on to antique ideas about male bread-winners and stay-at-home mothers even as deindustrialization has stripped it of steady, well-paid jobs for working-class men. No wonder women are cross and given to wondering why they need men in their lives at all.

To wait to have children until you are in a strong relationship with a responsible man who has a steady job might well be to pass up the opportunity for family life altogether. So women in Teesside's poorer neighbourhoods trust, and hope for the best. For many, it does not work out well. Their partnerships fracture and they are impoverished, together with their children. A group known as the North East Poverty Commission thinks it is partly because the region has so many single-parent families that house-hold poverty is far higher, and harder to bring down, than it is elsewhere in England. Single mothers in Teesside may well meet decent, steady men later in life, and the misty looks that come over some of them when they discuss these men suggest they have found happiness. But, in the meantime, their children have grown up poor.

The British government has made matters even worse for poor parents. Not only does the Treasury provide few financial incentives for couples to marry, as pro-marriage campaigners often complain, but for some poor couples it actually tips the scales in favour of separation. In 2017, the government stopped paying additional welfare benefits to parents who have more than two children. If a large household splits in two and each partner takes some children, though, some benefits can be regained. At a baby bank (like a food bank, but for baby stuff) in an evangelical church, I meet a woman who has separated from her husband. Three of her children live with her, and others with him. Although she does not claim that her family broke up specifically because of the two-child benefits rule, the policy seems to have nudged her that way. 'Because of universal credit, I can't have them all with me,' she says.

In America, hundreds of millions of dollars have been poured into programmes that promote marriage or try to strengthen relationships, particularly in poor areas. Pro-marriage advertisements have been created, parents who want to improve their relationships have been provided with advice, and couples who are thinking about divorce have been counselled. The results have been pretty feeble. An assessment of the programmes by Republicans in Congress found that some of them improve men's and women's behaviour, and help them to resolve disputes more graciously. But they seem not to encourage couples to marry, and they seem not to hold many relationships together. It looks very much as though people's economic circumstances matter more than their attitudes. Fixing marriage – or, as the women on the Access course would have it, fixing men – would probably be a lot easier if people were not so poor.

More evidence for that hunch comes from Asian families in Britain. Bangladeshi, Pakistani and Indian women all have low rates of childbirth outside marriage, and few children belonging to those ethnic groups grow up in single-parent households (by contrast, black African, mixed-heritage and black Caribbean women all have above-average rates of unmarried motherhood). Culture and religion are part of the explanation. Many British

Asian women have not shed the powerful stigma that attaches to lone parenthood in the Indian subcontinent. Still, Asian women living in the poorer parts of Britain behave differently from women in the richer parts. In Middlesbrough, 12 per cent of Asian children are growing up in single-parent families. In Wokingham, a wealthy commuter district west of London, 5 per cent are. Both of those proportions are low, but one is almost two and a half times as much as the other. Although culture matters a lot, it cannot overcome the effect of living in a poor place such as Middlesbrough. Single-parent families are even more common among Asians in Bradford, a poor city in Yorkshire, even though many of the Pakistani residents of that city (by far the largest Asian group) are culturally conservative, with a high rate of first-cousin marriage.

Some white working-class parents who cannot lean on their partners have a backup: they rely on their parents, or even on their grandparents. They may well be close at hand. In Britain as a whole, people without qualifications are about twice as likely to be able to reach their parents within fifteen minutes as people with degrees. But living close to your family does not guarantee that you will receive help, especially in a deprived place like Teesside. A surprising number of new mothers and fathers tell me that their own parents and extended families are nearby but cannot assist them much. A few have fallen out with their parents, or with their parents' new partners. But the most common problem is that their parents are ill. The awful health of many middle-aged and old people in Teesside does not only make their lives miserable, it also prevents them from helping their children. Some new parents explain that their mothers and fathers have their hands full dealing with other people's needs. One new mum says that her father is paralysed by anxiety, and her mother spends much of her time looking after him. Another explains that she had to wait until her grandmother died before she could ask her mother to help with childcare. Her mother had been too busy looking after her own mum.

White working-class families in Teesside have grown far more fragile than local people would like. A nasty loop has developed, in which poverty shatters people's relationships and broken relationships immiserate people. But there are a few hopeful signs of change. One is that teenage motherhood has become much rarer, in Teesside and in the country as a whole. In 2000, 16 per cent of births in Hartlepool and 15 per cent in Middlesbrough were to women under twenty. In 2021, those proportions stood at 5 per cent and 6 per cent – still higher than almost anywhere else in England and Wales, but a colossal improvement. And another reason for hope is that, in Teesside and elsewhere, attitudes to raising children are changing.

*

Unequal Childhoods, published in 2003, is one of the most influential sociology books of the past few decades. It deserves all of its success. Annette Lareau, a professor at the University of Pennsylvania, spent several years in the 1990s watching a dozen American families closely. She noted how children spoke to their parents and were spoken to, what activities they did, and how families dealt with schools and other institutions. Some of the families were comfortably middle class; others were solidly working class, with stable, decently well-paying jobs; others were poor and relied on welfare. Lareau expected to find a wide range of child-raising techniques. That isn't what she saw.

It turned out that the parents fell into two groups. The first lot, who were middle class, practised what Lareau called 'concerted cultivation'. They talked with their children a great deal and often responded to questions with questions of their own. Children were encouraged to argue politely. Their leisure time was so strictly scheduled that it wasn't really leisure time at all. The poor things were whisked from football practice to piano lessons, and given no time to muck around with their siblings or local children. Parents demanded a good deal from their children's coaches and teachers, and tended to get their way.

Working-class and poor parents, by contrast, went in for what Lareau dubbed 'the accomplishment of natural growth'. They kept their children safe, laid down sensible rules and helped them in many ways. But they spoke less to their offspring, and they acted as though children's development is something that happens naturally or in school. If the middle-class children were like bonsai trees, tortuously clipped and trained, the working-class and poor children were like rampant vines. Although all the parents wanted their little darlings to succeed, the working-class and poor ones were unable to bend schools or other institutions to their will.

Watching middle-class parents practise concerted cultivation on their children is, I submit, one of life's more teeth-grinding experiences. The endless chatter, the reasoning and the wheedling are exhausting and demeaning. But Lareau demonstrated that it works. The bonsai children grew into young adults who were highly capable of negotiating with institutions and authority figures. Middle-class parents had given their children something as valuable as money – the social tools for constructing a middle-class life. And the parents kept intervening in their children's lives even after they left university. Working-class and poorer parents, by contrast, tended to regard their children as 'grown' and independent by their late teens.

Around the same time, British academics described similar differences between middle-class and working-class child-raising styles. Diane Reay, a professor of education at Cambridge

University, wrote about how middle-class mothers prioritize reading with their children, or taking them to enriching activities, over humdrum household tasks. Many pay working-class women to handle duties such as cleaning while they concentrate on the brain-stretching stuff. Just like American middle-class parents, middle-class Britons demand a great deal of schools. Their many interventions in their children's lives, which might seem individually trivial, add up to huge social advantages. One of Reay's articles, published in 2005, is called 'Doing the dirty work of social class'. That's a perfect description.

There are a couple of ways of looking at this child-raising divide. One is to see it as inevitable and unbridgeable – yet more evidence of the class system at work. I don't think that is quite right. After all, middle-class parents did not always raise their children in a concerted way. Think of the privileged children in nineteenth-century novels, who were handed to governesses and packed off to boarding schools as quickly as possible. Even the most attentive fictional Victorian parents, such as Helen Huntingdon in Anne Brontë's novel *The Tenant of Wildfell Hall*, saw themselves as friends and protectors of their children rather than as architects of their minds. Just a few decades ago, middle-class children spent a good deal of time unsupervised. As a child in the 1970s, I spent many evenings playing football in the street, and I apologize to the car owners who lost wing mirrors as a consequence.

I think it is better to think about child-raising in terms of techniques and tools. Some child-raising methods work well, and middle-class parents were the first to adopt them, just as they were the first to acquire tools such as computers. But working-class parents are following. Time-use studies, which track what people do all day, show that middle-class and working-class parents alike spend far more time caring for their children than in the past. Fathers have gone from doing almost nothing in the early 1960s to quite a bit – though still much less than mothers. The bad news is that the gap between the classes, measured in minutes per day spent on childcare, has not disappeared. The good news is that working-class parents are catching up in relative terms. In a 2023 article, Giacomo Vagni showed that working-class mothers in Britain spent an average of 150 minutes a day on childcare in 2015, up from ninety-one minutes a day in 1960 (when mothers usually had more children to look after). Middle-class mothers put in twenty-one minutes a day more in both years. So working-class mums went from doing 81 per cent as much as the middle-class mums to 88 per cent as much. This dramatic change in working-class family life has been widely ignored by commentators, who almost always describe highly attentive parents as middle-class.

There is a growing pile of evidence that effective child-raising helps enormously. The good effects of doing things like reading to children regularly and having a warm relationship with them are so powerful that they can almost outweigh the dismal effects of poverty. In a 2011 paper, Kathleen Kiernan and Fiona Mensah looked at how children in a large cohort study fared in their first year of school. They found that 58 per cent of children in persistently poor homes who had good, attentive parents made good progress at school, according to teachers' assessments (parents were judged according to how much they read to their children, whether they put them to bed at regular times, whether they tended to praise them and so forth). By contrast, 42 per cent of children in non-poor homes who had less attentive parents made good progress. Not surprisingly, children who experienced no poverty *and* were well looked after fared best of all, and of course it is a lot easier to attend to a child's subtler needs if you can afford to pay a cleaner and don't have to work the night shift. The finding is encouraging all the same.

If highly effective child-raising is not simply an epiphenomenon of middle classness, but more like a series of tools and techniques, then it can be learned. And that is happening. Many local authorities now offer parenting classes, in person or via Zoom, or invite parents to join online courses. These seem to work well for the small numbers of people who take them. In Hartlepool, I meet one father who has taken several. His own childhood provided him with few clues about how to raise a child. He left home at fourteen, was raised (in a fashion) by young men in the neighbourhood, racked up a criminal record, had children and split from his partner. Now, after taking several courses, he has become so expert at talking to his teenage son about his moods and impulses that his son, with the gleeful provocativeness of youth, accuses him of being gay.

Across the neck of northern England, in Cumbria, I drop in on a group of parents who have just completed a ten-week parenting course run by Action for Children, a charity. Most of them have children in primary school. Among other things, the parents have been asked to think about how they were raised and what they learned from their own parents. They have concluded that they need to do much better than was done to them. One woman, who was frequently hit as a child, is determined not to fall into that habit. Another, who works in education, remembers being taught that children must do as they are told, and if they don't obey, they will suffer the consequences. She felt 'not particularly enjoyed' by her 'dismissive' mother. But, she says, 'I've got the intelligence to know what were the good bits, what were the bad bits, and I cherry-pick.'

Some of the parents in Cumbria are working class, whereas others are middle class. But all of them sense that expectations on parents and children have ratcheted up hugely over the years. When they were growing up, they might have been taken to an organized activity one evening a week, but they spent much of their time playing in the streets. Now, they say, parents are expected to expand their children's minds and take them to all sorts of after-school activities requiring time and money. It is exhausting. 'There is a lot of pressure on parents,' says an unemployed single mother in the group, rather desperately. 'Where did that begin? Who was it who set that off originally?' Another mother, who works as a cleaner, suggests an answer. In the past, she says, a boy from the area would probably have drifted straight from school into the army. These days, she says, 'There's too much choice when they leave school. There's fucking *hundreds* of things they could be.' She feels enormous pressure to prepare her children to thrive in this more complex, competitive world. It is hard and stressful. As she puts it, beautifully: 'You have to work like you don't have children, and be a parent like you don't work.'

People who have completed a parenting course are probably unusual: they would not have joined it if they did not believe they could become better parents. And too few courses exist for everyone to take one, even if they wanted to. But I think that their appearance reflects a broad change in society. All parents, but especially working-class ones, are more involved in their children's lives than they used to be. One study measured how closely parents monitor their children – for example, do they routinely ask them who they are with? It found that social-class differences were huge in the mid-1980s, but minor by the mid-2000s. It could be that everyone, middle class and working class alike, is coming around to the view that raising children is a skill that can be sharpened. That view is not only propagated by parenting courses. It can also be carried by word of mouth, by the mass media and by technology.

*

Among the many things that were said to me when I became a father, two quips have stuck in my mind. The first, said by a neighbour, is: 'well, the first eighteen years are the hardest'. The second, from a doctor, is: 'being a parent is fun!' Now that I have some experience, I know that both are right. Being a parent is exhausting, worrying and fun. One of the most fun things is working out how to do it, by selecting useful ideas and models and discarding other ones – cherry-picking, as the woman in Cumbria puts it. By doing this, you learn who you really are. You also shape the culture, in a small way. A new parent who is working out what she wants, who is testing and discarding fragments of the accepted wisdom, is a powerfully creative force. It can be a joy to witness, especially in people who have little control over other aspects of their lives.

In Devon, a teenage mother of two who works in a trampoline park is managing to drive everyone around her crazy. I meet her in a children's centre, where she goes occasionally to meet other young mums and their toddlers. When I ask her what she wants her children to be like when they are adults, she begins by saying they should be happy, healthy and well mannered. A few minutes later, she returns to my question and adds that she wants them to be successful. She practises what she calls 'gentle parenting', which she summarizes as 'trying to help them understand the world around them, instead of telling them off all the time'. She learned about gentle parenting by watching videos on social media, and she has struggled to convince her family that it is a valid approach to raising children: 'I explained it to my grandmother, and she said, "Where did you hear about that rubbish?"' The staff at the children's centre do not think much of it, either. They say that parents are forever coming in with child-raising notions that they have acquired from the internet. Still, the teenage mum is sticking to her guns. I think she is wonderful.

Another young mother in the same group, who worked as a technician in a school before her baby was born, turns out to be just as sceptical of the inherited wisdom about raising children. Her boyfriend, who works at night, is an active father. And his parents have given the couple a lot of child-raising advice. She has decided to ignore most of it in favour of more modern techniques. 'I get a lot of outdated advice,' she tells me. 'Put her in a pram and leave it at the bottom of the garden when she's crying, put whisky in her bottle, let her cry it out. Then I look at their children, and I think, hmm . . .' Her toddler, who will not sleep at night and looks thoroughly exhausted, babbles at her, and she babbles back.

White working-class Britons want the same things as everyone else. They want happy, fulfilling relationships that culminate in marriage. They want to raise well-adjusted children who are prepared to thrive in a more challenging world, and they want help with that. The differences lie in the range of options they have, the amount of stress they experience as a result of poverty, uncongenial jobs and dysfunctional surroundings, and the amount of help they receive. Politicians and charities that wish to help parents should work with the grain of people's desires and try to stabilize their economic lives. It will not be at all easy. But it will surely achieve more than complaining about the decline of old-fashioned family values.

Chapter Ten

The decline of class politics

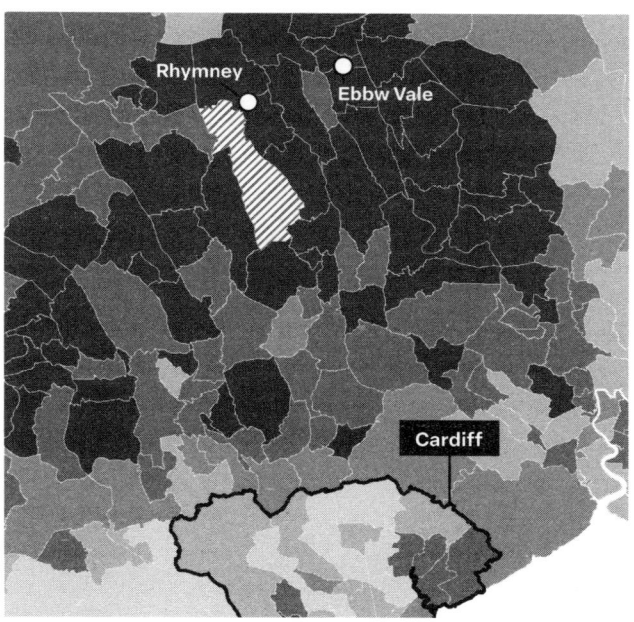

In his book *Family Britain, 1951–57*, the historian David Kynaston tells a marvellous story. Ronald Duncan, a poet and playwright, was in a railway station just after the 1951 general election, when Winston Churchill came to power at the head of a Conservative government. Duncan noticed a railway porter reading a newspaper that somebody had left on a train. The porter muttered that he was glad Churchill had won, so Duncan asked him whether he had voted Conservative. 'Of course not,' the porter replied. 'Being a working man I voted Labour, but all the same I 'oped old Winston would get in this time.'

Such people have almost vanished from Britain. I do not mean railway porters, although that is true. I mean people who vote strictly and self-consciously along social lines. Very few Britons would now say that the bonds of social class ought to be more important than a politician's record in government or the promises she makes, let alone that class should trump a voter's own desires. A person who admitted to voting deliberately along social lines today might be seen as an insufferable elitist if middle class, and a dinosaur if working class.

This chapter is about the decline of old-fashioned class politics. The change took place gradually, over many years, then suddenly. Two referendums – one in Scotland, the other in the whole of the United Kingdom – pushed it forward. Social class has not completely vanished from politics, any more than it has vanished from British society, but it has come to play a different role. Class no longer tells you how a person is likely to vote. Instead, it tells you whether they will vote at all.

White working-class Britons have led these changes. Although it is hard to be sure, because opinion polls usually reveal little about the preferences of ethnic groups, it seems that white working-class British people have come to behave differently from working-class people with ethnic-minority backgrounds. They are no longer especially likely to vote Labour, whereas working-class black and Asian people are. They are much more likely to vote for Reform UK, a right-wing populist party. More than other groups, white working-class Britons have pushed the country's politics in a new direction. If only the change were not so troubling.

In the middle decades of the twentieth century, if you wanted to predict somebody's political views, you would be well advised to find out what job they did. Most working-class people in what was then an overwhelmingly white country voted Labour, while almost all middle-class people voted Conservative. Labour activists were even advised to avoid canvassing middle-class suburbs. They would probably not convince anybody to support their party, and they might agitate the residents. 'Class is the basis of British party politics,' argued the political scientist Peter Pulzer in 1967. 'All else is embellishment and detail.'

The pubs and working men's clubs were not exactly fizzing with political talk. In 1952, Ferdynand Zweig reckoned that most working-class men were far more interested in sport than in politics. His fellow analyst of working-class life, Richard Hoggart, argued much the same. 'The great majority of working-class people have been unexpectant, politically as well as socially and financially,' he wrote. Working-class people voted Labour out of habit and instinct, because the party was in some sense 'for' them, not because they believed passionately in its policies.

And not all did. They couldn't have done. In the mid-twentieth century, the working class was so much bigger than the middle class that, if everybody had voted along class lines, the Conservative Party would not have won a single election. Some working-class people – such as middle-aged women, frequent churchgoers and those who saw their parents as middle class – were especially likely to vote Tory. Their reasons varied: a dislike of trade unions, a desire to see Britain play a more muscular role in the world, a deferential view of society. But they were exceptions to the rule.

The social divide among voters was mirrored in Parliament. Conservative MPs were overwhelmingly upper-middle-class. A study in 2024 by Erzsébet Bukodi and other academics at Oxford University found that, between 1945 and 1951, four fifths of Tory cabinet ministers and shadow cabinet ministers were the offspring of people who had worked in the highest reaches of management or the professions. Leading Labour MPs were more varied. Some of them came from upper-middle-class backgrounds, too, but one third were the children of manual workers, while one sixth were the offspring of self-employed people.

*

For a glimpse of the old world, in which politics revolved around social class, I strongly recommend a book called *Never a Yes Man*, published in 1991. The author was Eric Heffer, a left-wing Labour MP who represented a Liverpool constituency from 1964 until his death in the very year that his memoirs appeared. Heffer, who left school at fourteen to become a joiner, was a committed socialist from his earliest days: as a child, he was thrown out of a church choir after agitating for higher pay for singers. He served as a shadow minister and a minister, although his powerful convictions meant that he did not serve for long. An issue would crop up that triggered Heffer's socialist instincts; he would be told to toe the party line; he would refuse; he would be sacked.

Socialism was Heffer's ideological guiding star, but the thing that really drove him was the feeling of working-class solidarity. He believed that the point of socialism, and the point of the Labour Party, was to advance the interests of working-class people. Heffer described himself proudly as 'worker-oriented' and even 'workerist' – a term of abuse for some socialists, denoting a lack of sophistication. He justified almost all of his activities in class terms, no matter how leisurely they might seem. For a while, he made props for a Merseyside theatre. I suspect he found it fun. Po-faced, Heffer described his involvement in the theatre as 'a serious contribution to the working-class movement'.

According to him, the Labour Party members in his Liverpool constituency were overwhelmingly working class. Many were dockers, builders, seamen and boilermakers, with just a few white-collar workers and middle-class intellectuals. It is possible that some middle-class Liverpudlians voted for Heffer (defying the conventional advice, he campaigned in every street in his constituency), but he did not dwell on that. The important thing, he believed, was to win as many working-class votes as possible. He thought about other Labour MPs in the same way. At one point in *Never a Yes Man*, Heffer describes some MPs from Wales as 'the Welsh miners' MPs'. Those MPs also represented middle-class people such as estate agents and head teachers, but that was by the by. When Heffer retired, he declared that he was 'proud to have served the working class'.

To judge by his memoirs, Heffer did not believe that middle-class people were inherently malign or wrong-headed. His perspective was not 'working class good, middle class bad' but 'working class relevant to me, others not relevant to me'. If somebody or something was working class, then they were worth a look; otherwise, forget it. He thought the same way about culture. Whether the Beatles, and especially John Lennon, were working class is a complicated question. Heffer flatly asserted that they were, and loved them. He would occasionally break into 'From Me to You' in the middle of a speech.

I really like *Never a Yes Man*, and I probably would have liked its author. People who knew Heffer described him as decent and kind, even to his ideological opponents. Astonishingly, given his fervently socialist, pro-union views, Margaret Thatcher went to his funeral. I can also see why the Labour Party had less and less time for people like Heffer. If the party had allowed itself to be seen as a vehicle for advancing working-class people's interests, and only for that, it would have been cast into electoral oblivion.

By the time Heffer died in 1991, Labour was beginning to transform itself. Its leaders realized not only that the middle class had become large and politically powerful, but also that the working class was changing. Following Labour's defeat in the 1992 general election, the MP Giles Radice argued that the party must court upwardly mobile southern English voters who owned homes and cars. Some of those voters were working class, although they did not see themselves that way. As one Tory voter told Radice's researchers: 'Labour might be for the working class, but people don't think they're working class anymore.'

Labour Party leaders began to talk about social class in the past tense, as something that had no place in the bright modern Britain that they wanted to build. Tony Blair called the class system 'unequal and antiquated'. His mission, he explained in 1999, was to liberate Britain from 'old class divisions, old structures, old prejudices'. Ed Miliband, who led the Labour Party in the early 2010s, avoided the subject almost completely. In 2012, Miliband even had to deny that he had 'played the class card' after a conference speech in which he spoke about his education in a comprehensive school. Politicians concocted new terms to describe society, which nodded only vaguely to the old class categories. They claimed to speak for 'hard-working families', 'the just about managing' and 'the squeezed middle'.

Labour was not just speaking a different language; it had become a different party. By the 2010s, only one third of its leading lights came from working-class or self-employed backgrounds. Many Labour MPs were political careerists, who had moved into Parliament after working in think tanks or as advisers. The Conservative Party had changed, too. Between the 1940s and the 2010s, the proportion of its leading MPs who were the offspring of high-level managers and professionals fell, as the descendants of self-employed people gained ground. From being wildly unrepresentative, leading Tories had come to look more like the country – which had, of course, grown more middle class.

As MPs like Eric Heffer became rarer, the timbre of politics changed. In a 2019 article, Tom O'Grady, a political scientist at

University College London, showed that careerist Labour MPs behave differently from working-class ones (O'Grady classified MPs according to the jobs they did before becoming MPs, rather than looking at their parents' occupations). Political careerists tended to support welfare reforms, introduced by Blair, that tightened access to benefits. That might be because they were more ambitious and eager to please the party's leaders, or because they had scant experience of living and working alongside people who earned little and sometimes fell into poverty. Working-class Labour MPs were more likely to oppose the reforms. These were real personal differences, not the result of representing different constituencies.

The party changed in some ways that would have horrified Heffer. In the 1980s, the general-election manifestos produced by Labour and the Conservatives had been starkly different. In the late 1990s and 2000s, they converged. Both parties were for the responsible management of the economy, for free trade and free markets, albeit with the jagged edges sanded down. Both wanted to reform public services. Both were for law and order. Both, but especially Labour, might have found more to dislike in the previous manifestos of their own parties than in the ones produced by their opponents.

For the Labour Party, moving to the political centre and courting middle-class voters worked a treat. It won three general elections in a row – a record for the party. It even managed to prevent the Conservative Party from winning a majority in 2010 – a remarkable feat given the economic turmoil of the times. Amid the election-night celebrations, though, something was changing. Gradually, working-class people were becoming a smaller part of Labour's electoral coalition. In 1987, two thirds of Labour's vote came from the working class, but by 2010 only two fifths did. Working-class people were a shrinking proportion of the population, but that was not the only reason for the decline. More working-class people were voting Conservative, or for another party. A growing number were not voting at all.

The falling numbers of Labour MPs with working-class roots, like Heffer, may have been one reason for this change. Political scientists have tried to test voters' personal preferences by presenting them with hypothetical politicians from different social classes or with different levels of income, and asking what they think. The results are striking. One study by British and Austrian academics in 2020 found that an imaginary MP is viewed more kindly if his or her parents had been working class (it seemed to matter little if the imaginary MP had done a working-class job or a middle-class job before entering Parliament). The difference exists almost entirely because of working-class people, who strongly prefer politicians who are similar to them. Middle-class voters seem not to care about the class backgrounds of their politicians. Working-class voters really do.

Labour's policies may have driven working-class voters away, too. The party distanced itself from the trade unions. It grew relaxed about people migrating to Britain to work, although not about asylum-seekers, who it targeted with many draconian laws and policies. Some white working-class voters who detested mass immigration flirted with the far-right British National Party or with the more respectable UK Independence Party. There was little need, though. The Conservative Party wooed anti-immigration voters in 2005 with a thin manifesto that was heavy on promises to secure the borders. The party's slogan in that election was: 'Are you thinking what we're thinking?' Soon after the Tory manifesto appeared, I rang the BNP's press officer. 'They're thinking what we're thinking,' he said.

Until the financial crisis of 2007–8, Labour enjoyed such a strong reputation for economic management that the loss of some white working-class voters hardly mattered. Some people worried, all the same. Calls for more working-class MPs began to issue from the expected sources, such as trade unions and the hard left, but also from unexpected ones, such as Policy Exchange, a conservative think tank. In 2009, John Denham, a Labour cabinet minister, launched something called the 'connecting communities programme'. This offered money to local authorities, which they could use to arrange meetings in white working-class areas. The hope was that people would air their grievances about things like council-house allocation policies. The amount of money was small (just £12 million in total) and the language was vague, with lots of New Labourish verbiage about cohesion. But the aim, to spend money specifically on white working-class people, was novel and extraordinary.

In their 2020 book *Brexitland*, Maria Sobolewska and Robert Ford describe the gradual, almost imperceptible separation of white Britons into two groups. One group was mostly young, highly educated and socially liberal. The other was mostly older, less educated and socially conservative. These voters were stuck, not too happily, in a political system that was still organized along old social and economic lines. In 2016, a referendum would tear people out of their old camps and throw them into new ones. But first came an event that was just as shocking and disruptive in the country where it took place, in which white working-class people played a crucial role.

*

'It's almost like the Hindenburg,' says Paul Sweeney, gesturing towards the ruins of an enormous Victorian glasshouse in Springburn Park. It is a spectacular and tragic sight. For decades, the Winter Gardens transported Glaswegians from the grey skies of Scotland into a tropical jungle. But the building closed in 1983 after a storm, and it has been left to decay. All the palm trees and all the panes of glass have gone. The only things that remain are the brick base of the building, which is covered in graffiti, and the steel structure that once held the glass. If Sweeney, who is now a Labour Member of the Scottish Parliament, and other campaigners had not insisted that the steel be stabilized, the whole thing would have fallen down.

Springburn Park is one of Britain's finest bits of urban greenery. It has a solid Victorian bone structure of paths and ponds, and gives spectacular views over the city. It is also severely neglected. Its bowling greens closed during the worst of the Covid pandemic, and have not reopened. Parts of the park have been naturalized, 'which basically means left alone', according to a woman who has volunteered to mulch the rose garden – a task that would not be done if she did not do it. The cafe has been closed since 2022, when a burst pipe brought the ceiling down. Swans sometimes visit its ponds, but somebody kills the birds by throwing stones at them. Local rumour points to a child.

The park once symbolized Glasgow's industrial might. A statue in one corner commemorates James Reid, who owned a nearby locomotive works. He is posed in Victorian style: bushy beard, heavy coat, one leg stepping forward into the future. Locomotives and chemicals supplied many local people with jobs well into the mid-twentieth century. A retired man who helps out at Spirit of Springburn, a community group based in a shopping centre, remembers when thousands of workers poured out of the St Rollox engineering works at the end of each shift. The workers supported so many local shops that a trip into central Glasgow seemed unnecessary. Springburn's working-class inhabitants, most of whom rented their homes from the council, sneered at people who moved out of the area to buy houses in Glasgow's suburbs. They called one suburb 'Spam Valley', implying that its residents were spending so much of their income on mortgages that they could only afford to eat tinned meat.

Nobody sneers today. Since the 1960s, Springburn has lost almost all of its manufacturing jobs and many of its inhabitants. Although it is less than two miles from the centre of Glasgow, it feels cut off; between the two lies an expanse of derelict land contaminated with a hard-to-define substance known as galligu, a by-product of chemical manufacturing. Springburn has become one of the poorest, least healthy parts of a city that scores poorly on both counts. Springburn Park has turned into a symbol of decline. *To See Ourselves*, a film about Scotland's independence referendum in 2014, uses the park and the ruined Winter Gardens to illustrate the travails of urban Scotland.

That referendum sent a powerful jolt of political electricity through Springburn. Deciding your country's future is exciting, and referendums are wonderfully direct. Unlike a 'first past the post' parliamentary election, which gives more power to people living in marginal seats, every vote counts equally. In the constituency of Maryhill and Springburn, 73 per cent of eligible voters went to the polls – twice as many as had voted in elections to the Scottish Parliament three years earlier. In Springburn, and across Scotland, you could taste the excitement.

Scotland as a whole rejected independence by 55 per cent to 45 per cent. But in Maryhill and Springburn, the vote went the other way: 57 per cent for independence and 43 per cent against. That was the highest pro-independence vote recorded in Glasgow. It seems likely that working-class voters pushed up the Yes vote in Springburn. Polling before the referendum showed that working-class Scots were keener on independence than middle-class Scots, and the Yes vote was higher in more deprived areas. Sweeney, who campaigned for Scotland to remain in the United Kingdom, found a mixture of desperation and recklessness in the area: 'When I went round the doors, people said, "What have we got to lose? Look at the state of the place."'

It should not have been a surprise. Working-class Scots had gradually become disgruntled with the Labour Party and keen on nationalism. Two years before the referendum, Gerry Hassan and Eric Shaw's book *The Strange Death of Labour Scotland* described how the relationship had broken down. Between 1997 and 2001, the share of Scots who thought that Labour looked after working-class interests fell from 93 per cent to 61 per cent. The trade unionist Jimmy Reid, the hero of an industrial dispute in the Clydeside shipyards in the 1970s, joined the Scottish National Party in 2005, explaining that Labour had left him rather than the other way round. Sensing weakness in their rival, the SNP courted working-class voters in earnest.

The referendum prised many more working-class Scots away from Labour. It also catalysed a fierce emotional reaction, as pro-independence voters who had previously backed Labour came to believe that the party had betrayed them by supporting the union. East of Springburn lies a 'scheme', or what is known south of the border as a council estate, called Barmulloch. There, a man who has been a soldier and a carer tells me that he particularly resented the involvement of Gordon Brown, prime minister from 2007 to 2010: 'He was up here for the case against independence. He shouldn't have been doing that.' It was fine for a right-wing Englishman like David Cameron to oppose Scottish independence, he explains. For a left-wing Scot to do so was intolerable.

In the years after the referendum, the Scottish National Party assembled a mighty coalition of pro-independence voters, many of them working class, and demolished its political rivals. Although more Scots had rejected independence, unionist voters were divided among the Conservative, Labour and Liberal Democrat parties, leaving them weak. In the general election of

2015, the SNP jumped from six to fifty-six seats, while Labour collapsed from forty-one seats to one. Glasgow North East, which includes Springburn, went from safely Labour to firmly SNP. The following year, the SNP triumphed in elections to the Scottish Parliament. It did especially well in Springburn.

Scotland's turn against unionism and the Labour Party was seldom seen, in Scotland or anywhere else, as a specifically white working-class revolt. That could be because the independence campaign did not play on racial prejudices or xenophobia against people from outside the United Kingdom (the English were a rather different matter). And perhaps the whiteness of Scotland was taken as read. If so, it should not be. Between the censuses of 2011 and 2022, the proportion of people in Scotland who described themselves as white and Scottish or white and 'other British' fell from 92 per cent to 87 per cent. In the Scottish parliamentary constituency of Glasgow Maryhill and Springburn, which has many refugees, the share is 72 per cent.

If Scotland's political gyrations were not blamed on – or credited to – white working-class people, they were certainly associated with working-class people. The story of the 'Indyref', as told by nationalists, is a working-class uprising against a British government that had neglected them. I watched *To See Ourselves* in 2024, at an event in Glasgow organized by *The National*, a pro-independence newspaper. Afterwards, there was discussion of what one man called 'the Pilton paradox', after a poor part of Edinburgh. His premise was that the more working-class Scots suffer, the keener they are on independence.

*

Outside Scotland, Brexit is far more familiar than the Indyref. It affected many more people. And, whereas Scotland's referendum only promised to transform that country's constitution, Brexit

251

changed Britain's. The triumph of the Leave side in 2016, by a smaller margin than that enjoyed by unionists in Scotland, led to years of political disruption and then to Britain's departure from the European Union in 2020. In Scotland, a revolution was denied (or, in the nationalist telling of the story, delayed). In Britain, it went ahead.

The Brexit vote differed from Scotland's almost-revolution in important ways. It was primarily a revolt of older people, many of them socially conservative. In Scotland, by contrast, Yes voters were younger than No voters. The Leave campaign promised stronger national borders, and raised the spectre of uncontrolled immigration. 'TURKEY (population 76 million) IS JOINING THE EU' and 'BREAKING POINT' screamed its posters. The Scottish National Party did more or less the opposite, arguing that an independent Scotland might pursue a more liberal immigration policy. But, in other ways, Scotland reflected the rest of Britain.

In both, many white working-class voters had become disenchanted with the Labour Party. In both, some began to drift towards a nationalist alternative – the SNP in Scotland, the UK Independence Party in England and Wales. In both, an exciting referendum consolidated new political allegiances that had more to do with culture and views of the nation than social class. Britons were soon identifying more as Leavers or Remainers than as supporters of political parties.

The parallels continued after the votes. Following the Indyref and the Brexit referendum, one party (the SNP, the Conservatives) managed to monopolize the 'leave' vote. Rival parties scrapped over the other half of the population, and were routed. The Tories won a surprisingly large share of votes in heavily white working-class areas in the general election of 2017, and even more in 2019. Labour's 'red wall', a block of supposedly safe seats stretching across North Wales and northern England, crumbled.

The political turmoil of the 2010s in Scotland and the rest

of Britain shone a bright light on people and places that had previously been overlooked. Working-class voters, especially white working-class voters, had often been seen as an unexciting, shrinking group. Deborah Mattinson, who has spent much of her career advising Labour, wrote in her 2020 book *Beyond the Red Wall* that it had not even occurred to the party to convene a focus group in the largely working-class, Labour-voting bits of northern England. 'Their reliability was seen as a given,' she remembered.

Suddenly, white working-class people seemed more important than any other group. 'Traditionally disenfranchised voters, who largely come from white, working class communities, have headed to the polling booths en masse,' reported the *Daily Express* journalist Nick Gutteridge on the day of the EU referendum (Gutteridge predicted, correctly, that this was good news for the Leave side). 'It's the poor wot done it,' wrote Brendan O'Neill in *The Spectator* afterwards. 'A working-class revolt,' agreed John Harris, for *The Guardian*. A torrent of commentary about 'left behind' people and places followed. England turned out to be full of sorry-looking high streets and industrial ruins like the Winter Gardens in Springburn.

Not all working-class Scots left Labour or voted to leave the United Kingdom in 2014. Nor did all white working-class Britons vote to leave the EU in 2016, then embrace the Conservative Party. And those who switched ended up in political camps that also contained many middle-class people. Yet the shift was undeniable. Working-class Britons had long favoured the Labour Party over the Conservatives. By the 2017 election, that was barely true, and by 2019 the pattern had reversed. By some measures, the Conservative vote became slightly more working-class than the Labour vote. Admittedly, many of the Tories' new recruits were working-class pensioners. But still.

As this great political reshuffling occurred, many black and Asian Britons remained aloof. Unlike white Britons, they have continued to vote Labour, although this has become slightly less true of Asian Hindus and Asian Muslims (some of the second group showed their displeasure at Labour's equivocations over the war in Gaza by voting for independent candidates in the 2024 general election). Social class seems to have swayed them differently, in a rather old-fashioned way. The pollster James Kanagasooriam has shown that ethnic-minority people without degrees are more likely to vote Labour than ethnic-minority people with degrees. And ethnic-minority groups that are largely working class, such as Afro-Caribbeans and Pakistanis, are more likely to vote Labour than are more middle-class groups, such as Chinese and Indians.

Black and Asian Britons also seem to have responded to the Brexit referendum in a different way. Most obviously, they were less keen to leave: only about one third of people from minority ethnic backgrounds voted for Brexit. And it seems that most ethnic-minority Leave voters promptly went back to voting Labour. Brexit was for them a discrete issue, not a doorway to the political right, as it was for many white Britons. In short, the working-class desertion of the Labour Party seems to have been almost entirely a white British phenomenon.

*

The referendums of 2014 and 2016 had many awful consequences. Those on the losing sides, needless to say, were distraught. The Brexit vote seems to have affected the mental health of people living in Remain-voting areas. In one – thankfully extreme – case, a man who spent a good deal of time on social media after the referendum grew so paranoid about Leave voters that he came to believe that missiles were aimed at his house. By the time he arrived in hospital, he was in such a state that he attempted to escape from a room by digging through the floor with his hands.

In Scotland and in Britain, much time and energy were wasted on trying to secure a second referendum that might reverse the result of the first one. Even more energy was then expended on separating Britain from the EU. Politicians set about exploiting the new divisions in the electorate. Instead of governing their country as well as they could, Scottish nationalists fomented grievances against Westminster. South of the border, Conservative politicians scratched around, searching tirelessly for new cultural dividing lines that might allow them to keep hold of the socially conservative white working-class voters who had migrated to their camp after the Brexit vote. Would a row over statues of imperialists do the trick? How about hinting that immigrants could be sent to the back of the queue for social housing? How about a plan to send asylum seekers to Rwanda? None of it worked. Both the SNP and the Conservatives were crushed in the 2024 general election.

Yet the embarrassments of modern politics should not lead us to forget how dismal the old class-oriented politics could be. It certainly had its moments, as when Clement Attlee's post-war Labour government oversaw a construction boom that dramatic-ally improved the housing conditions of working-class Britons. But post-war Britain also suffered from terrible industrial rela-tions. And if the old class-based politics can be said to have built social housing in the 1940s, it could equally be said to have run down social housing in the 1980s. Besides, the conclusions that Labour reached in the 1990s are even more correct today. The party must be able to appeal to middle-class voters.

As I write, it is not entirely clear what happened in the general election of 2024, let alone what politics will look like in the future. The Conservatives appear to have been defeated because they lost voters to almost everyone – Labour, the Liberal Democrats, Reform UK, abstention and (because so many Conservative voters are old) the Grim Reaper. Both Labour and the Liberal Democrats benefited from a huge amount of anti-Tory tactical voting. Reform won 14 per cent of the vote, which is more than its predecessors, UKIP and the Brexit Party, had ever managed. In many northern English constituencies, Reform has become Labour's chief competitor. Post-election opinion polls suggest that social class made no difference when it came to Labour or Conservative voting: Labour won roughly a third of voters from every social class, whereas the Tories won roughly a quarter from every class. Reform has become more working-class than any other national political party. It seems to have picked up lots of support from people who are furious about immigration, who voted Conservative even before Brexit. Still, Nigel Farage's party won fewer votes from working-class people than Labour or the Conservatives did.

Although politics is unpredictable, my guess is that Britain will not return to the old pattern of voting along class lines. White working-class voters will continue to drift between political parties, to an extent that an observer could barely have imagined a few decades ago. The red wall will not be rebuilt. That once-solid Labour territory will become a political battleground, as will north-east England. Reform UK could pose a powerful threat to both Labour and the Conservatives. To do that, though, Reform will have to become a proper political party, rather than the Nigel Farage fan club it is at the moment; it will also have to decide whether it is a right-wing party or just right wing on immigration. In Scotland and Wales, the SNP and Plaid Cymru will scrap for working-class votes.

If I am right about the future, white working-class people might benefit. Politics can reward the fickle: groups with a reputation for drifting from one party to another are likely to attract attention and promises. After all, the Conservative Party did not just try to hold onto the white working-class voters it won in 2019 by drawing cultural dividing lines. It also attempted to 'level up' the towns where many of them lived. Those efforts achieved little, but they could be built on when the party returns to power. Labour has been prodded to talk more about class, and to tout the working-class backgrounds of its leaders. Sir Keir Starmer's speeches are thick with references to 'working people' – not quite the same as working-class people, but getting there.

*

Sad to say, I expect another pattern to persist. As social class has become less important in driving people to vote for Labour or the Conservatives, it has become more important in driving people towards or away from the polls. In 2022, the political scientists Ben Ansell and Jane Gingrich measured this change by dividing the population into five income groups. They showed that, although the poor have long been less likely to vote, the situation has got much worse. Before the year 2000, a person in the richest fifth of the population was up to ten percentage points more likely to vote than a person in the poorest fifth. Since 2010, the gap has been about twenty percentage points. Other fissures have opened, too. The old, the highly educated and homeowners have become much more likely to vote than the young, the less educated and those who do not own their homes.

It would be abhorrent to say that young working-class people who rent their homes do not matter. But, politically, they barely matter. Cut benefits for pensioners, and a noisy row will ensue, amplified by newspapers that have many elderly readers. Cut benefits for working-age people on low incomes, especially those with children, and you might hear a discontented murmur if you listen hard. Politicians might feel sorry for the struggling parents who I described in Chapter Nine, but they do not fear them, because they are unlikely to vote. The young working-class Eastern Europeans who I discussed in Chapter Six are even less politically important. Many of them are not British citizens, so they cannot vote in general elections.

In July 2024, the Labour Party won a huge parliamentary majority in an election that was notable for feeble turnout. Just under 60 per cent of eligible voters in Britain cast a ballot, the second-lowest figure for a century. Turnout in places with large working-class populations was especially pitiful: just 47 per cent in Glasgow North East; 43 per cent in Blaenau Gwent and Rhymney, in South Wales; and in Rusholme, an ethnically mixed constituency south of Manchester city centre, the figure was a mere 40 per cent.

People sometimes refrain from voting because they do not think much of the options on the ballot. In Blaenau Gwent and Rhymney, Reform UK's candidate withdrew from the race following reports that he had reposted conspiracy theories on social media. The Liberal Democrats did not field a candidate in Manchester Rusholme. It does not help when seats are barely contested. Nick Smith, the victorious Labour Party candidate in Blaenau Gwent and Rhymney, says that only Plaid Cymru, the Welsh nationalist party, put up much of a fight. As he points out, turnout was much higher in the nearby constituency of Monmouthshire, where Labour fought hard to snatch the seat from the Conservatives.

I went to Smith's constituency a few weeks after the general election, to ask people about voting. In Ebbw Vale, a modest town that once contained an enormous steelworks, I met a waitress who claimed that she would have voted if Reform UK had been on the ballot. I wondered whether that was a convenient excuse. In a Wetherspoon pub in Ebbw Vale, I got talking to half a dozen construction workers in their twenties and thirties, who had much franker attitudes. None of them had voted, not for any particular reason, but simply because it had not crossed their minds. 'Can't be bothered,' said one. 'All I know is work, pub, home,' said another. A third man maintained that he had not even known an election was taking place.

The following day, I drove to Rhymney, to meet nine people who were drinking tea and chatting after a service in St David's Church, known locally as 'top church'. They were a social mixture, but all were older than the construction workers in Ebbw Vale. Every one of them claimed to have voted. They were not enthusiastic about politics, and several were outright bitter, insisting that Labour never did anything for the town. They saw voting as a duty, all the same. A retired clerk told me that one of her own children had not voted. She had been furious, and the two had argued. These middle-aged and old people had voted not because they were keen on politics, but because voting was a habit. The young construction workers had not failed to vote because they loathed politics, but because voting was not a habit.

Down the Rhymney Valley, in Blackwood, Yvonne Murphy has created something in a shopping centre. I say 'something' because I am not sure how to categorize it. Certainly, it is known as the Talking Shop. When the shop is open – which depends on whether Murphy has managed to raise enough money to keep the heating and the lights on – it offers free tea, colouring pencils and a huge amount of information in English and Welsh about citizenship and democracy. People are encouraged to sit on sofas and chat about local issues, and to think about how the town and the country might be improved.

Murphy fears that the institutions that once got children and young people interested in politics and civic activity are weakening in South Wales, and in Britain as a whole. Miners' institutes, welfares and churches have emptied or closed. Parents used to take their children to polling stations: one Talking Shop regular, who now works as a housing officer, remembers her father peering over her shoulder the first time she voted, to check that she was putting a cross in the correct box. But as young working-class people fall out of the habit of voting, there might be nobody to drag the children along. The Talking Shop has its very own polling booth. Murphy installed it after realizing that many people had never seen one, and did not know how to behave in a polling station. Did they have to be silent, for example?

In places like Rhymney and Ebbw Vale, it is tempting to blame low turnout on a lack of political competition. South Wales is solidly Labour. In fact, Labour has dominated Welsh politics since 1922 – the longest spell of regional dominance by one party in a true democracy anywhere in the world, according to Richard Wyn Jones, an expert on Welsh politics at the University of Cardiff. When one party consistently wins by large margins, people seem to conclude that voting has no effect. But the sad truth is that fierce political competition can encourage a different kind of cynicism.

The people of Hartlepool, on the edge of Teesside, look at politicians much as cats look at birds – with a mixture of enthusiasm and murderous intent. In 2002, they elected as mayor Stuart Drummond, mascot of the local football team, who promised them free bananas. In 2012, they voted to abolish his job. They went on to vote for independent councillors. In 2021, they elected a Tory MP. Sacha Bedding, who runs a community group in the Dyke House neighbourhood, says that these swings have not increased people's confidence in politics. When I saw him a few weeks before the 2024 election, he summarized the prevailing view among the mostly white working-class people of Dyke House: 'Why would I bother voting? We tried Labour councillors, we tried independents, we tried Conservatives. None of it made any difference.' Sure enough, turnout was low in the general election, which saw Hartlepool return to Labour.

'We've got no faith in anybody,' confirms a Hartlepool resident who left school without taking any exams and has bounced from part-time job to part-time job. 'We're at the point where we don't care who's in charge.' This man, who says he is descended from shipbuilders, is deeply involved in the life of his neighbourhood. People often text him on a Friday, saying they are running short of food. He tries to rustle up something from his own cupboards and his family's cupboards. He just doesn't expect politicians to do much for him or the people he knows.

In some ways, voting is like prayer. People do it more because they feel an obligation than because they expect to see a return. It is a way of expressing membership of a community. Religious leaders tend to encourage it. As the man in Hartlepool suggests, participating in politics can seem like an act of faith. But faith can dissipate. You can wake up one morning to find it has gone.

Conclusion: No going back

When I go to a place I do not know, to meet people who may never have spoken to a journalist before, I often start by asking the same question: how has this area changed over the years? I have asked this in British community centres, in American diners and in Bangladeshi villages. It is a gentle, non-confrontational way of encouraging people to think about their neighbourhoods, and it establishes an important fact – that they know more than I do. People often tell me things I did not expect. I would not have guessed that residents of the spacious Coffee Hall housing estate in Milton Keynes (described in Chapter Five) have a rodent problem, which colours their view of the estate.

In Britain, people answer my question in all sorts of ways. Sometimes they talk about who has arrived and who has left, sometimes about the local council, crime, jobs, shops, or roads. But their answers tend to have a couple of things in common. One is that people often accentuate the negative. They are likely to talk more about businesses that have disappeared than about new businesses. I have been told a great many times that young people thereabouts no longer respect their elders, as they did in earlier decades (as a child of the 1970s and 1980s, I am not at all sure I believe this). Few people tell me that burglary has become rarer, or that the local school has improved.

Another thing I notice, especially in largely working-class areas, is that people tend not to think the changes they describe will ever be reversed. Once a shop or a pub has closed, local people rarely believe it will reopen – the question is about what happens to the building. The big firm that once employed many people from the area is regarded as gone for good. And nobody ever seems to think that immigrants and other newcomers will depart. People may be grumpy about the changes they see, but they nearly always look forwards. There is a sad truth in that, about people's severely limited power to control their surroundings and preserve the things they value. There is also a sensibleness, because many of the changes that have swept through Britain's streets are in fact irreversible.

Among these is the growing population of immigrants and ethnic minorities. The 2021 census showed that 17 per cent of the population of England and Wales was born outside Britain. Add Scotland and Northern Ireland, and the share falls only a little. That is a much higher share than at the turn of the century, and higher than elsewhere. In America, which trumpets itself as a nation of immigrants, less than 15 per cent of the population was born outside the country. Britain also has a higher share of foreign-born people than France, Italy, the Netherlands or Spain. It is behind only Germany, which threw open its doors to Syrian refugees in the mid-2010s.

Three out of every ten babies born in England and Wales these days have foreign-born mothers. And the babies who are carefully carried home from maternity wards are more varied than the adult population. Two thirds are white Britons, compared with more than three quarters of adults aged thirty or over. The others are a remarkable mixture. Parents, who were required to state their babies' ethnicity when filling in the 2021 census form, managed to stuff some of them into familiar categories, such as Indian, Pakistani and black African. But many other babies could not be classified so straightforwardly. Two and a half per cent of all children under one year were described as having a mixed white and Asian heritage; three and a half per cent were mixed white and black Caribbean or mixed white and black African. Many babies ended up in categories labelled 'other'. Britain's youngest inhabitants are so ethnically diverse that the old categories will not do.

If babies are increasingly hard to classify according to the old familiar labels, so are places. Britain has few ethnic-minority 'ghettos' – few intensely Afro-Caribbean or Bangladeshi or Polish areas – and most of the ones that do exist seem less like ghettos with every passing year. The conventional measure of segregation is the Index of Dissimilarity, which tells you what proportion of a given group would have to move in order to spread itself evenly across the country. By this measure, every ethnic-minority group in England and Wales became less segregated between the censuses of 2011 and 2021 (and, by the way, between the censuses of 2001 and 2011 too). With a few exceptions, places that contain few white Britons do not have an enormous population of one other ethnic group. They are just diverse. In the borough of Newham, in east London, no ethnic group accounts for more than one sixth of the population.

Sometimes, when visiting a largely white working-class village or town that I am unfamiliar with, I assume I will not see anybody who is not white. I am wrong about that every time. Immigrants and ethnic-minority people live in almost every corner of Britain, poor or rich. Hartlepool contains people who were born in St Lucia; Kingston upon Hull has people from the Gambia; Ceredigion has Hongkongers. Big cities remain the most diverse places in Britain, but everywhere else is moving more or less quickly along the same track. And Britain is bound to keep changing.

In 1968, the year when the Labour MP David Winnick accused Conservatives of cynically posing as the defenders of white working-class Britons against immigrants, 222,000 people arrived in the country for a lengthy stay. Some of them were British, some were not. An even larger number of people left Britain, often for Australia, and as a result net migration was minus 56,000. The net migration figure remained negative, or was only slightly positive, until the late 1990s, when it began to rise. In 2010, David Cameron, who would shortly become prime minister, pledged to keep net migration to the 'tens of thousands' per year – which was, as he pointed out, 'the sort of figure there was in the 1990s'. The two governments he led between 2010 and 2016 never managed to achieve this. Nor has any since, with one exception. Net migration did fall below 100,000 in 2020, when Covid raged and international travel became almost impossible. If a target can only be hit during a once-in-a-century pandemic, it is not much of a target.

Other countries have drastically cut immigration in the past – America did so in the first half of the twentieth century. But Britain is not at all like America a century ago. It is an ageing country with a low birth rate. It will need immigrants to pay into its pension system and to staff its hospitals and care homes, unless the government is prepared to tax people more heavily and spend the money on a big expansion of medical training and a big rise in pay, which it shows little sign of doing. And, sadly, there will probably be no shortage of chaos and oppression in the world, and therefore no lack of people traipsing towards Britain in search of refuge. Politicians can (and no doubt will) rail against uninvited asylum-seekers, but they will probably smile on other foreigners who provoke their sympathy. The Conservative governments led by Boris Johnson and Rishi Sunak passed law after law criminalizing asylum-seekers. At the same time, they welcomed hundreds of thousands of Hongkongers and Ukrainians fleeing authoritarianism and invasion.

It is perfectly reasonable to argue about the ideal levels of migration and net migration, and about the costs and benefits of widening or constricting the channels through which immigrants arrive in Britain. Indeed, a frank discussion would be good. But nobody should be under the impression that Britain can go back. There will be no return to a more homogeneous society, with small numbers of immigrants and ethnic minorities. And the growing diversity of Britain will be felt in all its corners, as people move out of big cities to small towns and villages. Britain can choose whether its population diversifies gradually or more quickly. To some extent, it can pick its immigrants, and speed or retard their integration into society – of which more in a moment. It cannot opt out of change.

Nor will the old jobs come back. Many observers of Britain have lamented the decline of industry over the past few decades, and I agree. The halving of manufacturing jobs since the early 1980s is a terrible shame, for working-class people and for the country as a whole. Britain ought to be far better at manufacturing than it is, and it would be good for society if it was, since manufacturing jobs tend to pay more than jobs in services.

But the drift from manufacturing to services employment appears to be inexorable in the rich world. It is happening even in countries like Germany and South Korea, which have done far more to support their industries than Britain has. And those who lament the lack of manufacturing jobs should explain what kind of jobs they are talking about and what skills the jobs will require. There are plenty of factory jobs around Boston in Lincolnshire, which can be done by people without qualifications. Those jobs are repetitive and ill paid, and few Britons want them (even the immigrants who actually have the jobs do not want them, as I showed in Chapter Six). Much better jobs can be found in advanced engineering firms. But those jobs are already technically complex and are likely to grow ever more so. They will require highly trained workers. When people talk about reviving manufacturing, I sometimes think they envisage high-paying, steady industrial jobs that can be done by people who have just left school with few qualifications. Those jobs have vanished.

Anybody who is concerned for white working-class Britons, or indeed concerned for the future of Britain in general, should start by accepting that the old world is gone. Politicians, journalists and other privileged Britons spend too much time and energy arguing about history and tradition. We love to argue about statues. We still call politicians 'Thatcherite' or 'Blairite', in reference to people whose political careers ended decades ago. Somehow, we even manage to turn arguments about new things into arguments about old things. Witness the long-running fight over the opening of a new coal mine in Cumbria. That row is less about the few hundred jobs a mine would provide than about how people feel about Britain's coal-mining past.

*

If the past is gone, the future is still up for grabs. Some things can be done to improve the lot of white working-class Britons. But not, I think, targeted things. Although it might sound odd in a book about them, I think it is a bad idea to aim policies at white working-class people specifically. It is morally wrong, since they are in many ways less deprived than working-class people from minority ethnic backgrounds. And I believe it is politically wrong. I think it highly unlikely that a policy explicitly favouring white working-class Britons would prove popular. If it was, the Conservative Party, which after the Brexit vote in 2016 came to believe that its fortunes rested largely on the group, would surely have enacted it during its time in government. I am not even convinced that a policy explicitly favouring white working-class people would be supported by a majority of white working-class people. Britons are big on fairness, and do not like to be pandered to.

Instead, I'm going to suggest four areas in which I think Britain could improve. Three of them do not target white working-class people explicitly, although they would benefit. The fourth is targeted in the opposite direction, at a different group.

Start with education. I explained in Chapter Two that children born into white working-class families tend to do badly in their GCSEs and are highly unlikely to go to university or to obtain the most coveted apprenticeships. These are irreducible facts, not statistical mirages, as the political left has sometimes argued. And the problem of educational underachievement is specifically a white working-class problem. White working-class children do not fare badly only because they are working class. Economic disadvantage has a particular effect on white British children, which is a little different from its effect on other ethnic groups. Those who deny these facts are not helping anybody.

What to do about it, though? It has sometimes been assumed that white working-class children require more funding and special help to catch up with their peers. Beginning in the mid-2010s, Conservative governments began to allocate special funds to schools in what were known as 'opportunity areas' and 'education investment areas'. These are not necessarily the poorest parts of Britain – which are often found in ethnically mixed inner cities – but the places where test results are worst. The list of educational investment areas includes many largely white working-class places, including the Isle of Wight. Strikingly, nowhere in London made the cut. The House of Commons education committee has even tried to persuade the Office for Students, which oversees universities' access efforts, to create targets for admitting more white working-class students. In 2023, the University of Bradford announced a scholarship scheme for a handful of white students from poor backgrounds.

Small schemes like that are fine. But the problem is not that universities are discriminating against white working-class teenagers at the moment, or that those teenagers are short of money relative to working-class students from minority ethnic backgrounds. The problem is that they fare poorly in their GCSEs and are less likely to apply to university than other students with similar grades. To some extent, as I have suggested, this may be because white teenagers know they will be favoured in the job market. But it may also be a cyclical process. Working-class white people do poorly at school, then send their children to the same schools. They expect, and get, much the same results from the education system.

Interrupting that cycle of low performance at school should be the priority. One way to do it is to offer free nursery places to children from poor families, so they get off to a better start. This is being done, at no small cost to the state, but in a confused way. Parents who are out of work are likely to have the neediest children, yet they do not receive as much financial assistance as working parents – a case of muddling the quite different goals of getting parents off welfare and helping poor kids. Another good idea, which is being pioneered in Brighton and Hove as a result of lobbying by a group called Class Divide, is to give children who receive free school meals priority in secondary-school admissions.

A further remedy, cheaper than the first and probably less controversial than the second, is for schools to work better with parents. I have been to too many places where the schools complain that parents are not involved in their children's learning, and the parents complain that schools are unbending and unsympathetic, and only contact them when their children get into trouble. Breaking this deadlock is hard, and different methods might work in different places: encouraging parents to volunteer in one school, texting them about homework in another, offering adult classes in a third. The essential thing is for schools to recognize that the problem is real and large, and that their teachers, who often had happy school lives and are now middle class, will have to work hard to understand people who are different from them.

The education system is designed for children who are academically able and want to go to university. It suits nobody else nearly so well. Worst off are those sometimes known as the 'forgotten fifth', who fail to obtain a grade 4 in either GCSE English or GCSE maths. They tend to be shunted into vocational courses, but are required to retake their GCSEs until they pass. That process is demoralizing, and many never succeed. They tend to miss out on higher education and good apprenticeships, look like failures to employers, and are liable to feel the same way about themselves. One good suggestion, made by the education expert Mary Curnock Cook, is to create a qualifications ladder for English and maths outside the GCSE system, which would allow young people to show what they can do. It would be similar to the music grading system. A teenager who passes a new grade 1 maths test would be demonstrating only a very rudimentary knowledge of the subject, but that is better than nothing, and he or she could move on to grade 2. Such a person ought not to be thought a failure, any more than a person who has passed grade 1 violin is thought a failure at the violin. More able students could carry on showing GCSE examiners how well they can solve quadratic equations, as they do at the moment.

My second suggestion concerns a subject where the temptation to gaze enviously at the past is especially strong: housing. Some people, particularly on the political left, have argued that Britain ought to recover its post-war zeal for building social housing. Sir Sadiq Khan, the mayor of London, boasted when his city created more council homes than everywhere else in England put together. Others, usually on the right, contend that social housing should be reserved for people who have lived in a particular place, or in Britain, for many years. Both policies would seem to benefit white working-class Britons, the second more brazenly. I'm afraid I think neither one is a goer.

Some of the large housing estates that were built around the middle of the twentieth century were wonderful. A great many others were not. Their colossal social problems stemmed not just from their design and construction – the crappy windows, the crumbling concrete, the naive 'streets in the sky' – but from the fact that they ended up being populated by severely disadvantaged people and almost nobody else. New estates would probably develop the same problems if homes were allocated the same way. It makes more sense to mix new social housing with private housing, as is usually done now, even though less social housing will be created as a result.

As for the demand that local people should be given priority for social housing and recent immigrants kept out, that happens already. Local authorities tend to insist that potential renters live nearby for several years or have a family connection to somebody who has. These local criteria are blended with measures of need, so the strongest candidates for housing are extremely needy people who have lived in the area for some time. This seems a reasonable balance. Tilting the balance more firmly towards local connections or long-term residence in Britain would immiserate some extremely needy people, many of whom are children. It might not even be popular. Conservative commentators who gripe that 'long-standing British nationals' should not be expected to queue behind people 'who simply were not in Britain twenty or thirty years ago' are pushing an extreme view of the welfare state, in which certain rights are only acquired through birth or long residence. Only about one in ten British people share this view.

Britain does not need lots more social housing or a radical change in how it is allocated. It just needs more housing. England and Wales are severely under-supplied with homes compared with other countries, as can be seen from the tiny proportion of vacant properties. The resulting squeeze, which is tightest in the south-east, keeps prices and rents high. That obviously costs people, but it also costs the government, which must spend an inordinate amount of money on housing benefits. The high price of housing is probably affecting people's behaviour and their relationships. People in their twenties are much more likely to be living with their parents than in the past, which may be suppressing the birth rate.

Politicians and officials have come up with many clever ways to help people into Britain's overpriced homes, from Help to Buy equity loans, to discounted rents, to shared-ownership schemes. Special pathways to home ownership have been created for people with long-term disabilities and people over the age of sixty-five. None of these remedies would be necessary if housing were cheaper. And the way to make housing cheaper is almost certainly to build more of it. Although house prices are strongly influenced by interest rates and lending conditions, it seems unlikely that the property market is wholly immune to the forces of supply and demand. It probably does not matter greatly what kind of housing is built. Even if Britain were to build huge numbers of large houses and luxury flats and nothing else, demand for smaller, cheaper properties ought to fall as people trade up. Pressure on

273

social housing would lift. Many white working-class people would benefit, although they would hardly be the only ones.

The problem, of course, is getting homes built. Local authorities can block new housing, and frequently do. People feel, often rightly, that allowing new construction near them will make their lives worse, and they express these opinions to councillors. We have ended up in a bizarre situation, in which the government has handed local politicians huge powers to block development but also puts huge pressure on them to build. The best way out, I think, is to give them more skin in the game. If Britain had a proper system of local property taxes, and if councils were able to keep more of the proceeds from new home sales, rather than the money flowing to the Treasury as it does at the moment, local people might begin to see the advantages of building near their backyards.

*

A third way of improving the lives of white working-class Britons is to boost economic growth outside southern England. As I showed in Chapter One, white working-class people tend to live some way from the country's most dynamic cities, especially London. You would expect that: the capital's highly productive, knowledge-oriented economy creates many middle-class jobs and attracts large numbers of immigrants. Planning reforms would help a bit. If it were easier to build homes in and around London and other thriving cities, more white working-class people would be able to find a toehold in Britain's most successful corners. Still, not everybody would move, even if it were easy. Britain must also find ways of boosting economic growth far from the capital.

It is a giant task. London and south-east England – and, to an extent, Scotland – have been wealthier than everywhere else for a very long time. The gap is sometimes wider, sometimes narrower, but it has never seemed likely to disappear. By international standards, parts of Britain have become truly badly off. The regions of North East England and Yorkshire and the Humber are poorer than the American states of Alabama and Mississippi, or Brandenburg in the former East Germany. The scale of the problem is enormous. When Germany reunified in 1990, fewer than one fifth of its inhabitants lived in the communist German Democratic Republic. The United Kingdom is divided into twelve regions, of which six have a gross domestic product per head that is at least 15 per cent below the national average. More than a third of the country's inhabitants, some 24 million people, live in those regions.

If there was a straightforward, cheap way of gingering up the far-from-London economy, it would have been done already. Politicians have lamented the poverty of northern England and complained about London's strength for decades. A huge number of initiatives have been launched to do something about it, from the Special Areas Scheme in the 1930s to the recent 'levelling up'. The country often seems to be going round in circles. Governments forget about (or actually abolish) their predecessors' efforts to deal with the problem, create entirely new solutions, then hand the reins to a new government, which forgets what they did.

It would help to describe the problem correctly. The great economic divide in Britain is not between big cities and small towns, as it is in countries such as America, and as British politicians sometimes imply. The divide is between one huge area centred on London (and a smaller area centred on Edinburgh) and everywhere else. Large British cities such as Birmingham, Cardiff, Leeds and Manchester are simply not all that successful. They are a lot poorer than London, and also poorer than similar-sized cities in other rich countries. Their weak performance impoverishes the small towns around them, just as London's success enriches the small towns around it. The regions will rise on the backs of cities like Birmingham and Manchester, or they will not rise at all.

One likely reason for Britain's extreme regional inequality is its extreme political centralization, which is far greater than that of most other countries of its size. British politicians outside Westminster have much less power, particularly over the raising and spending of money, than regional politicians in other large, well-off countries. A few years ago, I met the head of the municipal council in Gothenburg, a port city in Sweden. He described various difficulties with transport, schools and crime, so I asked him a simple question: 'Do you have enough power to solve your city's problems?' He answered immediately: 'In general, yes.' I struggle to imagine a local politician in Britain giving the same answer.

It can seem as though Britain's regions outside London and south-east England do well out of centralization, because they get more money from the Treasury than they contribute to it. The catch is that they do not control their destiny. Cities and local authorities are perpetual supplicants, begging for whatever Westminster happens to be handing out that day. The result is sometimes comic. In 2023, the central government invited councils to bid for money to install outdoor chess tables. 'High footfall areas that attract diverse demographics would be ideal locations for the chess tables,' it added, as though that might not have occurred to local officials. Cities cannot make decisions about priorities – about whether it is more important to spend scarce resources on health, education, chess tables, job training or public transport. They just try to grab what the central government is offering. Only Scotland and, increasingly, Wales have anything resembling a steering wheel.

Any policy that pulls against centralization would be good for places far from London and for the white working-class people who tend to live in those places. It would also be good for Britain as a whole: the country cannot be benefiting from its enormous poor hinterland. Local and metropolitan governments ought to be able to raise more of their own money, and spend it more as they wish. The country would have to tread carefully; it would, for example, still need a system for redistributing some cash, otherwise places like Teesside would be utterly impoverished. And it is the work of decades, not years. British politicians will have to push not just against the civil service, which hates relinquishing power, but also against a London-centred media. They will have to push against their own instincts.

My final suggestion, which would appear to have nothing at all to do with white working-class Britons, is to work harder at folding immigrants into society. The country made a good start under the Labour government led by Tony Blair, creating citizenship tests and charming naturalization ceremonies. Then it slid back. The price of citizenship soared as the Home Office used immigrants to subsidize its other activities. When it comes to integrating asylum-seekers, Britain has gone from bad to worse. They are often shipped to the poorest parts of the country, and are prevented from working while the Home Office considers their claims because of the belief – which is probably false – that allowing asylum-seekers to work would draw more of them to our shores. What skills they possess quietly atrophy.

Many are not even taught English. Asylum-seekers are often not offered free classes until they have been in the country for six months, and their stipends are far too stingy to pay for classes in the meantime. Those who have been around for longer may be unable to find courses. Funding for English teaching has been slashed over the years – it fell by more than half after the Conservative–Liberal Democrat coalition government came to power in 2010. Whenever they are asked about teaching English to refugees and other immigrants, ministers intone that it is an excellent idea. They ought to pay for it. Depriving people of English lessons is a spectacularly false economy, given its importance in the labour market. The government should want people to be more productive.

Opinion polls show overwhelming support for helping refugees learn English – and, incidentally, for allowing asylum-seekers to work if they have waited more than six months for a decision. And the British government already finances English lessons for Hongkongers – who, in addition, receive a warm welcome to Britain and various other kinds of assistance. Why them and not others? Hongkongers are not unusually needy, as migrants go. They do have a distinctive legal status as British nationals, but they are still subject to immigration controls. If the answer is that the British government wishes to express support for democracy in Hong Kong, why not also favour the people who have fled awful regimes in Afghanistan and elsewhere?

Helping immigrants integrate into British society would not help white working-class people directly. But it might lessen the resentment that some feel, and confirm the truth of an opinion that most hold already. White working-class Britons, and indeed Britons in general, tend to believe that immigrants are here to stay and that they will eventually become British. Most think that immigrants should be treated the same as everybody else. These healthy views are stronger in Britain than they are in many other countries, as international opinion polls have shown. In 2022, a large poll known as the World Values Survey revealed that 30 per cent of Britons believe that, when jobs are scarce, employers should give priority to natives. That might sound like a lot, but it is the third-lowest proportion out of twenty-four countries polled. Only Germany and Sweden were more liberal. It would be a good idea to sustain people's faith by giving them daily examples of immigrants working to become more like them.

I apologize if these suggestions seem dull and technocratic. Surely there must be a big, radical policy that could dramatically boost white working-class Britons' fortunes? Can't we just revive heavy industry, or start believing in vocational training? I'm afraid it isn't that simple. Rich democracies like Britain seldom improve through sudden lurches; they tend to proceed step by cautious step. The important thing is that the steps are in the right direction. Radicalism is for the opinion pages of newspapers, not for real life. If you want to see what a really dramatic, roll-the-dice policy looks like, and how much it has benefited the country, I refer you to Brexit.

If white working-class Britons were a group apart, or few in number, or highly concentrated in a particular place or a particular industry, or in an exceptionally desperate condition, it might be a good idea to single them out for special treatment. None of those things are true. As I said in the Introduction, the white working class is Britain. Its problems are Britain's problems. White working-class Britons will fare well if the entire country manages to pull in a sensible direction. If not, they won't.

Notes and References

PREFACE

2 **result in Hartlepool:** Paul Waugh, 'Six Reasons Why Labour Lost The Hartlepool By-Election', HuffPost UK (website), 7 May 2021, https:// www.huffingtonpost.co.uk/entry/six-reasons-labour-lost-hartlepool-byelection_uk_6094fdd9e4b0b37f89476272; Khalid Mahmood, 'Hartlepool is a Wake-Up Call for my Party', Policy Exchange (think tank), 21 May 2021, https://policyexchange.org.uk/blogs/hartlepool-is-a-wake-up-call-for-my-party/.

3 **'besieged' by asylum-seekers:** Hansard, HC Debate, Vol. 738, Col. 321, 18 October 2023.

3 **hypothetical voter called 'Workington Man':** Will Tanner and James O'Shaughnessy, 'The Politics of Belonging', Onward (think tank), 3 October 2019, https://www.ukonward.com/wp-content/ uploads/2021/08/Politics-of-Belonging-FINAL.pdf.

INTRODUCTION

5 **bird, known as Maggie:** 'Bomb Hoax Clears Schools', *Liverpool Echo*, 13 November 1968; Paul Connew, 'Baby Talk for Two Famous Mothers', *Daily Mirror*, 14 November 1968; George McCarthy, 'Trade Deficit Doubles as Imports Rise and Exports Drop', *The Scotsman*, 14 November 1968; Douglas Slight, 'Maggie the Magpie Swears His Way Out of a Job', *Daily Mirror*, 14 November 1968.

6 **champions of the white person:** Hansard, HC Debate, Vol. 773, Col. 461, 13 November 1968.

6 **not entirely white:** Enda Delaney, *The Irish in Post-War Britain* (Oxford: Oxford University Press, 2007).

7 **'our voters':** The Lockdown Files Team et al., 'Ministers feared "racist" label if they spoke about Covid spread', *The Telegraph*, 9 March 2023, https://www.telegraph.co.uk/news/2023/03/09/ministers-feared-racist-label-covid-spread-message/.

8 **appalled by the riots:** 'Are Britain's rioters representative of views on immigration?', *The Economist*, 8 August 2024, https://www.economist.com/britain/2024/08/08/are-britains-rioters-representative-of-views-on-immigration; Dylan Difford and Matthew Smith, 'The public reaction to the 2024 riots', YouGov (website), 6 August 2024, https://yougov.co.uk/politics/articles/50257-the-public-reaction-to-the-2024-riots.

8 **'deaths of despair':** Chris Marshall, 'Sir Angus Deaton: "A lot of people feel they're not in control of their lives anymore"', Holyrood (website), 25 April 2022, https://www.holyrood.com/inside-politics/view,sir-angus-deaton-a-lot-of-people-feel-theyre-not-in-control-of-their-lives-anymore.

9 **They don't adapt:** The most important studies of the British white working class (not all of which share this view) are: Justin Gest, *The New Minority: White Working Class Politics in an Age of Immigration and Inequality* (New York, NY: Oxford University Press, 2016); Michael Collins, *The Likes of Us: A Biography of the White Working Class* (London: Granta, 2004); Open Society Foundations, *White Working Class Communities in Manchester* (New York, NY: Open Society Foundations, 2014), available at https://www.opensociety-foundations.org/publications/white-working-class-communities-manchester; Kjartan Páll Sveinsson (ed.), *Who Cares about the White Working Class?* (London: Runnymede, 2009), available at https://www.runnymedetrust.org//publications/who-cares-about-the-white-working-class; Harris Beider, *White Working Class Voices: Multiculturalism, Community-Building and Change* (Bristol: Policy Press, 2015).

9 **The commentary was frequently venomous:** Suzanne Moore, 'Debating the word "chav" is irrelevant to the working-class experience', *The Guardian*, 4 June 2011, https://www.theguardian.com/commentisfree/2011/jun/04/suzanne-moore-chavs-working-class; Dominic Ponsford, 'The Rod Liddle article which threatened

Stephen Lawrence trial as it had barely begun', Press Gazette (website), 4 January 2012, https://pressgazette.co.uk/comment-analysis/the-rod-liddle-article-which-threatened-stephen-lawrence-trial-as-it-had-barely-begun-51305/; James Delingpole, 'A conspiracy against chavs? Count me in', *The Times*, 13 April 2006, https://www.thetimes.co.uk/article/a-conspiracy-against-chavs-count-me-in-j76sbkpk877; Andrew Gimson, 'Immigrants Pay Britain the Greatest Compliment', *The Daily Telegraph*, 27 November 2002. For many other examples see: Owen Jones, *Chavs: The Demonization of the Working Class*, updated ed. (London: Verso, 2012).

11 'a sort of informal alliance': Matthew Goodwin, *Values, Voice and Virtue* (London: Penguin, 2023); David Goodhart, *The Road to Somewhere: The Populist Revolt and the Future of Politics* (London: Hurst & Company, 2017); David Skelton, *The New Snobbery: Taking On Modern Elitism and Empowering the Working Class* (London: Biteback Publishing, 2021); Michael Lind, *The New Class War: Saving Democracy from the Metropolitan Elite* (London: Atlantic Books, 2020); Nick Timothy, *Remaking One Nation: The Future of Conservatism* (Cambridge: Polity, 2020); Paul Embery, *Despised: Why the Modern Left Loathes the Working Class* (Cambridge: Polity, 2021); '"If you look white-working class, they think you're breaching peace": Are the police bias?', GBNews, 2023, available at https://www.youtube.com/watch?v=SURV-O_LJNA; Matthew Goodwin, 'So why does nobody talk about THESE children?', Mail Online, 2 April 2021, https://www.dailymail.co.uk/debate/article-9431489/PROFESSOR-MATT-GOODWIN-says-findings-white-working-class-race-report-shamefully-ignored.html.

11 shadowy liberal elite: J. D. Vance, *Hillbilly Elegy: A Memoir of a Family and Culture in Crisis* (London: William Collins, 2016); J. D. Vance, 'How Donald Trump seduced America's white working class', *The Observer*, 10 September 2016, https://www.theguardian.com/commentisfree/2016/sep/10/jd-vance-hillbilly-elegy-donald-trump-us-white-poor-working-class.

13 Left-wingers often try to change the subject: David Goodhart, 'Tony's world', *Prospect*, 19 August 2002, accessed 23 March 2024, https://www.prospectmagazine.co.uk/essays/59588/tonys-world; Claire Ainsley, *The New Working Class: How to Win Hearts, Minds and Votes* (Bristol: Policy Press, 2018); Jeremy W. Bohonos, 'Critical race

theory and working-class White men: Exploring race privilege and lower-class work-life', *Gender, Work & Organization* 28, no. 1 (2021), pp. 54–66, https://doi.org/10.1111/gwao.12512; Faiza Shaheen and Ellie Mae O'Hagan, 'How Not to Think About Class', in Omar Khan and Faiza Shaheen (eds.), *Minority Report: Race and Class in post-Brexit Britain* (London: Runnymede, 2017), available at https://www.runnymedetrust.org/publications/minority-report-race-and-class-in-post-brexit-britain; David Gillborn, 'The White Working Class, Racism and Respectability: Victims, Degenerates and Interest-Convergence', *British Journal of Educational Studies* 58, no. 1 (18 February 2010), pp. 3–25, https://doi.org/10.1080/00071000903516361.

14 **Parliament tried to investigate:** Education Committee, 'The Forgotten: How white working-class pupils have been let down, and how to change it', House of Commons, 2021, accessed 23 March 2024, https://publications.parliament.uk/pa/cm5802/cmselect/cmeduc/85/8502.htm. For the Labour MPs' response, see the formal minutes.

16 **households without enough bedrooms:** Calculated from Office for National Statistics, Census 2021.

18 **move from one ethnic group to another:** Ludi Simpson, Stephen Jivraj and James Warren, 'The Stability of Ethnic Identity in England and Wales 2001–2011', *Journal of the Royal Statistical Society Series A: Statistics in Society* 179, no. 4 (1 October 2016), pp. 1025–49, https://doi.org/10.1111/rssa.12175. For a personal account, see Sunder Katwala, *How to Be a Patriot: Why Love of Country Can End Our Very British Culture War* (Manchester: HarperNorth, 2023), chapter 8.

19 **eight-part classification:** Office for National Statistics, 'The National Statistics Socio-economic classification (NS-SEC)', accessed 23 July 2024, https://www.ons.gov.uk/methodology/classificationsandstandards/otherclassifications/thenationalstatisticssocioeconomicclassificationnssecrebasedonsoc2010; John H. Goldthorpe, *Social Mobility and Class Structure in Modern Britain*, 2nd ed. (Oxford: Clarendon, 1987).

19 **admirably rigorous and precise:** Robert Erikson and John Goldthorpe, *The Constant Flux: A Study of Class Mobility in Industrial Societies* (Oxford: Clarendon, 1992); Michael Savage, *Social Class in the 21st Century* (London: Pelican, 2015).

20 **not just the underclass:** Robert Macdonald, Tracy Shildrick and Andy Furlong, 'In search of "intergenerational cultures of workless-ness": Hunting the Yeti and shooting zombies', *Critical Social Policy* 34, no. 2 (1 May 2014), pp. 199–220, https://doi.org/10.1177/0261018313501825.

22 **block immigrants from getting council homes:** Oliver Wright, 'Tories consider giving UK citizens priority for social housing', *The Times*, 23 March 2024, https://www.thetimes.co.uk/article/tories-consider-giving-uk-citizens-priority-for-social-housing-cg55z3r8d; Department For Levelling Up, Housing and Communities, 'Consultation on reforms to social housing allocations', 30 January 2024, https://www.gov.uk/government/consultations/consultation-on-reforms-to-social-housing-allocations/consultation-on-reforms-to-social-housing-allocations.

22 *The Uses of Literacy*: Richard Hoggart, *The Uses of Literacy: Aspects of Working-Class Life, with Special Reference to Publications and Entertainments* (London: Chatto and Windus, 1957); Richard Hoggart, *A Local Habitation* (London: Chatto & Windus, 1988); Lynsey Hanley, *Respectable: The Experience of Class* (London: Allen Lane, 2016); Collins, *The Likes of Us*. For a feminist criticism of Hoggart, see: Carolyn Steedman, *Landscape for a Good Woman: A Story of Two Lives* (London: Virago, 1986).

23 **'average worker does not exist':** Ferdynand Zweig, *The British Worker* (London: Penguin Books, 1952); Ferdynand Zweig, *Women's Life and Labour* (London: Gollancz, 1952); Joseph Shister, 'The British Worker. Ferdynand Zweig', *American Journal of Sociology* 59, no. 2 (September 1953), pp. 176–7, https://doi.org/10.1086/221303.

CHAPTER ONE

29 **coal was cheap:** G. W. Wade and J. H. Wade, *Monmouthshire*, Little Guides (London: Methuen, 1909); Thomas Jones, *Rhymney Memories* (Newtown: Welsh Outlook Press, 1938).

29 **eighth most deprived area:** 'Welsh Index of Multiple Deprivation 2019', Welsh Government (website), https://wimd.gov.wales/.

31 **local teacher, D. T. Williams:** David Thomas Williams and George Askey, *My People's Ways: An Anthology of the Works of D. T. Williams* (Rhymney Valley District Council, 1978).

33 'red wall voter': James Kanagasooriam and Elizabeth Simon, 'Red Wall: The Definitive Description', *Political Insight* 12, no. 3 (1 September 2021), pp. 8–11, https://doi.org/10.1177/20419058211045127.

34 strong vein of opposition to racism: Paul Golding, 'An In-Depth Analysis of the Local Elections 2022', Britain First (website), accessed 1 June 2024, https://www.patriot-organisation.com/an_in_depth_analysis_of_the_local_elections_2022_by_paul_golding. Wales's response to the statues controversy that was stimulated by the Black Lives Matter movement was swifter, more comprehensive and more impressive than anything seen in England or Scotland. See: Task and Finish Group, 'The Slave Trade and the British Empire: an audit of commemoration in Wales', Welsh Government (website), 8 December 2021, https://www.gov.wales/slave-trade-and-british-empire-audit-commemoration-wales.

36 deep poverty in a pleasant setting: 'Indices of Deprivation 2000', Department for Communities and Local Government, accessed 1 June 2024, https://webarchive.nationalarchives.gov.uk/ukgwa/20100407204456/http://www.communities.gov.uk/archived/general-content/communities/indicesofdeprivation/indicesofdeprivation/.

36 slum behaviour: Derick Deakin, *Wythenshawe: The Story of a Garden City* (Chichester: Phillimore, 1989); Ann Hughes and Karen Hunt, 'A Culture Transformed? Women's Lives in Wythenshawe in the 1930s', in Andrew Davies and Steven Fielding (eds.), *Workers' Worlds: Cultures and Communities in Manchester and Salford, 1880–1939* (Manchester: Manchester University Press, 1992), pp. 74–101. The quote is on page 86. The association between neighbourly tea-drinking and slums is also noted in (Allan) James Tucker, *Honourable Estates* (London: Victor Gollancz, 1966), pp. 27–31.

37 'very offensive': 'Hoodie pic "proves Cameron point"', BBC News (website), 23 February 2007, http://news.bbc.co.uk/1/hi/uk_politics/6389277.stm; Matthew Davis, 'Heald Green residents rail against "offensive" station sign', *Manchester Evening News*, 29 March 2012, https://www.manchestereveningnews.co.uk/news/greater-manchester-news/heald-green-residents-rail-against-685472.

38 Keralan girl: 'Team win "Oscar" for protecting nurses', *Manchester Evening News*, 14 August 2007, https://www.manchestereveningnews.co.uk/news/local-news/team-win-oscar-for-protecting-nurses-1052811. For another account of racial harassment, see Lorena Liliana

Valencia Galvez, 'Mothering Practices in Wythenshawe, South Manchester' (PhD thesis, University of Manchester, 2013), p. 167, available at https://pure.manchester.ac.uk/ws/portalfiles/portal/54533677/FULL_TEXT.PDF.

39 **almost one in five votes:** 'Wythenshawe by-election interview: John Bickley', BBC News (website), 7 February 2014, https://www.bbc.co.uk/news/av/uk-politics-26064305; 'Wythenshawe Community Leaders Say Tommy Robinson's "Far-Right" Political Views Not Welcome', LBC News (website), 25 April 2019, https://www.lbc.co.uk/news/tommy-robinson-not-welcome-bbq-whythenshawe/.

40 **a passing shock:** Eric Kaufmann, 'Levels or changes? Ethnic context, immigration and the UK Independence Party vote', *Electoral Studies* 48 (1 August 2017), pp. 57–69, https://doi.org/10.1016/j.electstud.2017.05.002; Christopher Claassen and Lauren McLaren, 'Does Immigration Produce a Public Backlash or Public Acceptance? Time-Series, Cross-Sectional Evidence from Thirty European Democracies', *British Journal of Political Science* 52, no. 3 (July 2022), pp. 1013–31, https://doi.org/10.1017/S0007123421000260.

40 **racist comment to a player:** 'Wythenshawe Town manager suspended over "racism" walk-off', BBC News (website), 10 April 2019, https://www.bbc.co.uk/news/uk-england-manchester-47381830.

42 **'First of London's overspills':** *Thetford and Watton Times*, 5 June 1953.

43 **exceptionally audacious:** 'Big Expansion Plan at Thetford', *Thetford and Watton Times*, 24 April 1953; Mark Clapson, *Invincible Green Suburbs, Brave New Towns: Social Change and Urban Dispersal in Post-War England* (Manchester: Manchester University Press, 1998).

43 **only way to revive the town:** D. J. Osborne, *Thetford: A Century Remembered: From 1900 to the Present Day* (Thetford: D. Osborne, 1996); Alan Crosby, *A History of Thetford* (Chichester: Phillimore, 1986).

44 **made themselves poorer:** Malcolm J. Moseley, 'Some Problems of Small Expanding Towns', *The Town Planning Review* 44, no. 3 (1973), pp. 263–78; Osborne, *Thetford*, volume 2, pp. 132–3.

45 **Multicultural London English:** Jenny Cheshire et al., 'Contact, the feature pool and the speech community: The emergence of Multicultural London English', *Journal of Sociolinguistics* 15, no. 2 (2011), pp. 151–96, https://doi.org/10.1111/j.1467-9841.2011.00478.x.

46 **two fifths of the employees were women:** *Thetford and Watton Times*, 10 April 1959, 25 November 1960. Women were more likely to work in London than elsewhere. See: Barra Roantree and Kartik Vira, *The rise and rise of women's employment in the UK* (London: IFS, 27 April 2018), available at https://doi.org/10.1920/BN.IFS.2019. BN0234.

48 **the same tiny area of south London:** Christina Beatty, Steve Fothergill and Ryan Powell, 'The Caravan Communities of the Lincolnshire Coast', Sheffield Hallam University, for East Lindsey District Council, 1 July 2011, accessed 8 June 2024, https://www.shu. ac.uk/centre-regional-economic-social-research/publications/the-caravan-communities-of-the-lincolnshire-coast.

49 **a Labour redoubt:** Colin Rallings and Michael Thrasher, 'Breckland District Council Election Results 1973–2011', Elections Centre, Plymouth University, https://www.electionscentre.co.uk/wp-content/uploads/2015/06/Breckland-1973-2011.pdf.

CHAPTER TWO

55 **frankly, even gleefully:** Carole Dennett, 'Education officers dismiss official exam result figures', *Isle of Wight Observer News*, 6 September 2022, https://iwobserver.co.uk/education-officers-dismiss-official-exam-result-figures/; Lucy Morgan, 'Isle of Wight's GCSE results for 2022 and why context is crucial', *Isle of Wight County Press*, 27 October 2022, https://www.countypress.co.uk/news/23079982.isle-wights-gcse-results-2022-context-crucial/.

56 **the prevailing view:** 'CRE Chair Trevor Phillips argues tough new strategy needed to help black boys do better at school', BBC Press Release, 7 March 2005, https://www.bbc.co.uk/pressoffice/pressreleases/stories/2005/03_march/07/phillips.shtml; 'Bad Attitudes', *The Economist*, 10 March 2005, https://www.economist.com/britain/2005/03/10/bad-attitudes; Trevor Phillips, 'Running faster into the same brick wall', *The Guardian*, 31 May 2005, https://www.theguardian.com/politics/2005/may/31/schools.social exclusion.

57 **committee had another crack:** House of Commons Education Committee, 'Underachievement in Education by White Working Class Children', House of Commons, 11 June 2014, https://

publications.parliament.uk/pa/cm201415/cmselect/cmeduc/142/142.
pdf; House of Commons Education Committee, 'The forgotten: how
White working-class pupils have been let down, and how to change
it', House of Commons, 16 June 2021, https://committees.parliament.
uk/publications/6364/documents/70802/default/.

57 **quibble with them:** David Gillborn, 'How white working-class underachievement has been used to demonise antiracism', *The Guardian*,
23 June 2021, https://www.theguardian.com/commentisfree/2021/
jun/23/how-white-working-class-underachievement-has-been-used-
to-demonise-antiracism; Claire E. Crawford, 'The one-in-ten:
quantitative Critical Race Theory and the education of the "new
(white) oppressed"', *Journal of Education Policy* 34, no. 3 (4 May
2019), pp. 423–44, https://doi.org/10.1080/02680939.2018.1531314.

57 **very badly in their GCSEs:** Lindsey Bowes et al., 'Understanding
progression into higher education for disadvantaged and under-
represented groups', Department for Business, Innovation & Skills,
November 2015, https://dera.ioe.ac.uk/id/eprint/24682/1/BIS-15-462-
understanding-progression-into-higher-education-final.pdf; Lee
Elliot Major and Sam Parsons, 'The forgotten fifth: Examining the
early education trajectories of teenagers who fall below the expected
standards in GCSE English language and maths examinations at age
16' (London: UCL Centre for Longitudinal Studies, 2022).

58 **offspring of better-off Indian parents:** Steve Strand, 'Ethnicity,
gender, social class and achievement gaps at age 16: intersectionality
and "getting it" for the white working class', *Research Papers in
Education* 29, no. 2 (15 March 2014), pp. 131–71, https://doi.org/10.108
0/02671522.2013.767370.

60 **whisked off to Bangladesh:** *Education for All: The Report of the
Committee of Inquiry into the Education of Children from Ethnic
Minority Groups* (London: Her Majesty's Stationery Office, 1985),
Cmnd. 9453.

60 **Bangladeshi girls do even better than boys:** Steve Strand, 'Ethnicity,
deprivation and educational achievement at age 16 in England:
trends over time', Department for Education, June 2015, https://
assets.publishing.service.gov.uk/government/uploads/system/
uploads/attachment_data/file/439867/RR439B-Ethnic_minorities_
and_attainment_the_effects_of_poverty_annex.pdf.pdf; 'Department
for Education, KS4 Education Statistics', accessed 15 May 2024,

https://explore-education-statistics.service.gov.uk/data-tables/
key-stage-4-performance-revised.

60 **Some universities have changed quickly:** 'Entry rates into higher
education', UK Government (website), 21 November 2023, https://
www.ethnicity-facts-figures.service.gov.uk/education-skills-and-
training/higher-education/entry-rates-into-higher-education/latest/;
'UCAS Undergraduate End of Cycle Data Resources 2023', UCAS
(website), 28 November 2023, https://www.ucas.com/data-and-
analysis/undergraduate-statistics-and-reports/ucas-undergraduate-
end-cycle-data-resources-2023.

60 **less selective 'recruiting' universities:** 'Students starting at higher
education providers with high, medium and low entry tariffs', UK
Government (website), 6 December 2023, https://www.ethnicity-
facts-figures.service.gov.uk/education-skills-and-training/higher-
education/entrants-at-higher-education-providers-with-high-
medium-and-low-entry-tariffs/latest/; 'UCAS Undergraduate End
of Cycle Data Resources 2023'.

61 **immigrants' children do better:** *PISA 2022 Results (Volume I): The
State of Learning and Equity in Education* (Paris: Organisation for
Economic Co-operation and Development, 2023), https://www.oecd-
ilibrary.org/education/pisa-2022-results-volume-i_53f23881-en;
Carlotta Balestra and Lara Fleischer, 'How Do OECD Countries
Collect Data on Ethnic, Racial and Indigenous Identity?',
Organisation for Economic Co-operation and Development,
8 November 2018, https://one.oecd.org/document/SDD/DOC(2018)9/
En/pdf.

64 **policy paper on teaching:** Department for Education, 'The
Importance of Teaching: The Schools White Paper 2010' (London:
Her Majesty's Stationery Office, 2010), https://assets.publishing.
service.gov.uk/media/5a7b4029ed915d3ed9063285/CM-7980.pdf.

65 **Will Baker and others:** Will Baker et al., 'Aspirations, education and
inequality in England: insights from the Effective Provision of
Pre-school, Primary and Secondary Education Project', *Oxford
Review of Education* 40, no. 5 (3 September 2014), pp. 525–42,
https://doi.org/10.1080/03054985.2014.953921.

65 **high aspirations and high expectations:** Nabil Khattab, 'Students'
aspirations, expectations and school achievement: what really
matters?', *British Educational Research Journal* 41, no. 5 (2015),

pp. 731–48, https://doi.org/10.1002/berj.3171; Bowes et al., 'Understanding progression into higher education'; Francis Green et al., 'Dreaming Big: Self-Evaluations, Aspirations, High-Valued Social Networks, and the Private-School Earnings Premium', *Cambridge Journal of Economics* 42, no. 3 (May 2018), pp. 757–78, https://doi.org/10.1093/cje/bex023.

67 **build a bridge:** Simon Squibb, 'The Wight We Want: "Island Conversation" Survey Results 2017', Isle of Wight Council, 23 May 2018, https://www.iow.gov.uk/azservices/documents/2981-Wight-We-Want-Survey-Report-v3-FINAL-2-v1.pdf.

68 **When distance is added:** 'The Influence of Place: Geographical Isolation and Progression to Higher Education', Bridge Group, February 2019, https://www.dannydorling.org/wp-content/files/dannydorling_publication_id7134.pdf.

68 **high-level vocational qualifications:** Héctor Espinoza et al., 'Post-18 Education: Who is Taking Different Routes and How Much do they Earn?', Centre for Vocational Education Research, September 2020, https://cver.lse.ac.uk/textonly/cver/pubs/cverbrf013.pdf.

68 **The benefits of university-going remain:** Christine Farquharson, Sandra McNally and Imran Tahir, 'Education Inequalities', IFS Deaton Review of Inequality, 16 August 2022, https://ifs.org.uk/inequality/education-inequalities/; Ben Waltmann et al., 'The impact of undergraduate degrees on lifetime earnings', The IFS, 29 February 2020, https://doi.org/10.1920/re.ifs.2020.0167. For a more sceptical view of the returns to higher education, see Anna Stansbury, Dan Turner and Ed Balls, 'Tackling the UK's regional economic inequality: Binding constraints and avenues for policy intervention', Mossavar-Rahmani Center for Business and Government, Harvard Kennedy School, March 2023, https://www.hks.harvard.edu/sites/default/files/centers/mrcbg/files/198_AWP_final.pdf.

69 **their own children tend to go down that route:** Common Sense Group, 'Common Sense: Conservative Thinking For a Post-Liberal Age', Common Sense Group, 2021, https://www.marcolonghi.org.uk/sites/www.marcolonghi.org.uk/files/2021-05/Common-Sense.pdf.

69 **perpetually cash-strapped:** Luke Sibieta and Imran Tahir, 'What has happened to college teacher pay in England?', The IFS, 30 March 2023, https://doi.org/10.1920/re.ifs.2023.0254.

69 **31 per cent of newly enrolled university students:** Nicole Gicheva

and Kathryn Petrie, *Vocation, Vocation, Vocation: The role of vocational routes into higher education* (London: Social Market Foundation, 2018), https://www.smf.co.uk/wp-content/uploads/2018/01/SMF-Vocation-Vocation-Vocation.pdf.

70 **dropout rate:** 'Damian Hinds technical education speech', Department for Education, 6 December 2018, https://www.gov.uk/government/speeches/damian-hinds-technical-education-speech; Billy Camden and Shane Chowen, 'National apprenticeship achievement rate rises to 54%', *FE Week*, 21 March 2024, https://feweek.co.uk/national-apprenticeship-achievement-rate-rises-to-54/; Tom Richmond and Eleanor Regan, 'No train, no gain: An investigation into the quality of apprenticeships in England', EDSK (think tank), 2022, https://www.edsk.org/wp-content/uploads/2022/11/EDSK-No-Train-No-Gain.pdf.

71 **the most demanding apprenticeships:** Chiara Cavaglia, Sandra McNally and Guglielmo Ventura, 'The Recent Evolution of Apprenticeships: Apprenticeship pathways and participation since 2015', Sutton Trust, December 2022, https://www.suttontrust.com/wp-content/uploads/2022/12/The-recent-evolution-of-apprenticeships.pdf.

71 **doctor's child:** Sam Friedman and Daniel Laurison, 'The class pay gap: why it pays to be privileged', *The Guardian*, 7 February 2019, https://www.theguardian.com/society/2019/feb/07/the-class-pay-gap-why-it-pays-to-be-privileged.

72 **they do not see the point:** Sammy Wright, 'Bad Kids', *Tank Magazine*, n.d., https://magazine.tank.tv/issue-94/features/sammy-wright; Sammy Wright, *Exam Nation: Why Our Obsession With Grades Fails Everyone* (London: Penguin, 2024).

72 **miners' libraries of South Wales:** Jonathan Rose, *The Intellectual Life of the British Working Classes* (New Haven, CT: Yale University Press, 2001), chapter 7.

73 **bridging social capital:** Robert MacDonald et al., 'Growing Up in Poor Neighbourhoods: The Significance of Class and Place in the Extended Transitions of "Socially Excluded" Young Adults', *Sociology* 39, no. 5 (1 December 2005), pp. 873–91, https://doi.org/10.1177/0038038505058370; Sue Heath, Alison Fuller and Brenda Johnston, 'Young people, social capital and network-based educational decision-making', *British Journal of Sociology of Education* 31, no. 4 (1 July 2010), pp. 395–411, https://doi.org/10.1080/01425692.2010.484918.

74 **higher education seems like a smaller step:** Matt Grogan, 'Who exactly is this white working class?', Wonkhe (website), 19 October 2020, http://wonkhe.com/blogs/who-exactly-is-this-white-working-class/.

75 **the 'London advantage':** Bowes et al., 'Understanding progression into higher education'; Simon Burgess, 'Understanding the success of London's schools', The Centre for Market and Public Organisation, October 2014, https://ideas.repec.org//p/bri/cmpowp/14-333.html; Andy Ross et al., 'Examining the London advantage in attainment: evidence from LSYPE', Department for Education, November 2020; Tariq Modood, 'Capitals, ethnic identity and educational qualifications', *Cultural Trends* 13, no. 2 (1 June 2004), pp. 87–105, https://doi.org/10.1080/0954896042000267170.

75 **Asian- or African-sounding names:** Simon Burgess and Ellen Greaves, 'Test Scores, Subjective Assessment, and Stereotyping of Ethnic Minorities', *Journal of Labor Economics* 31, no. 3 (2013), pp. 535–76, https://doi.org/10.1086/669340; Tammy Campbell, 'Stereotyped at Seven? Biases in Teacher Judgement of Pupils' Ability and Attainment', *Journal of Social Policy* 44, no. 3 (July 2015), pp. 517–47, https://doi.org/10.1017/S0047279415000227; Wouter Zwysen, Valentina Di Stasio and Anthony Heath, 'Ethnic Penalties and Hiring Discrimination: Comparing Results from Observational Studies with Field Experiments in the UK', *Sociology* 55, no. 2 (1 April 2021), pp. 263–82, https://doi.org/10.1177/0038038520966947.

76 **black African men with degrees earn less:** Lorraine Dearden, Jack Britton and Ben Waltmann, 'The returns to undergraduate degrees by socio-economic group and ethnicity', The IFS, 26 March 2021, https://doi.org/10.1920/re.ifs.2021.0186.

CHAPTER THREE

80 **uncertain but rather disappointing conclusions:** Roger Matthews and Julie Trickey, *The New Parks Crime Reduction Project* (Leicester: University of Leicester, Centre for the Study of Public Order, 1994).

82 **16 per cent live in 'social rented housing':** 'English Housing Survey 2022 to 2023: Headline Report', Department for Levelling Up, Housing and Communities, 14 December 2023, https://www.gov.uk/government/collections/english-housing-survey-2022-to-2023-headline-report; '50 Years of the English Housing Survey',

Department for Communities and Local Government, 2017, https://assets.publishing.service.gov.uk/media/5a81fa8ced915d74e623521f/EHS_50th_Anniversary_Report.pdf.

84 **'fascist popularity came from housing'**: E. J. B. Rose et al., *Colour and Citizenship: A Report on British Race Relations* (London: published for the Institute of Race Relations by Oxford University Press, 1969); Fred Lindop, 'Racism and the Working Class: Strikes in Support of Enoch Powell in 1968', *Labour History Review* 66, no. 1 (April 2001), pp. 79–100, https://doi.org/10.3828/lhr.66.1.79.

85 **Politicians and journalists have frequently indulged this view:** Margaret Hodge, 'A Message to My Fellow Immigrants', *The Observer*, 20 May 2007, https://www.theguardian.com/commentisfree/2007/may/20/comment.politics; Neil O'Brien, 'It's Reasonable to Give British People Greater Priority for Social Housing', Neil's Substack (blog), 30 January 2024, https://www.neilobrien.co.uk/p/its-reasonable-to-give-british-people; Matthew Goodwin, 'How mass immigration is worsening the housing crisis', *The Spectator*, 8 December 2023, https://www.spectator.co.uk/article/how-mass-immigration-is-worsening-the-housing-crisis/.

85 **the least desirable properties:** O'Brien, 'It's Reasonable'; Mariña Fernández-Reino and Carlos Vargas-Silva, 'Migrants and Housing in the UK', Migration Observatory, University of Oxford, 2 September 2022, https://migrationobservatory.ox.ac.uk/resources/briefings/migrants-and-housing-in-the-uk/; 'Social Housing Quality Programme: Residents Survey Report', Department for Levelling Up, Housing and Communities, December 2022, https://assets.publishing.service.gov.uk/media/639c8fbde90e075877b30b88/SHQP_Residents_Survey_Report.pdf.

86 **A perfect little world:** Stanley Gale, *Modern Housing Estates: A Practical Guide to Their Planning, Design and Development for the Use of Town Planners, Etc.* (London: B. T. Batsford, 1949).

87 **resemble old-fashioned villages:** John Boughton, *Municipal Dreams: The Rise and Fall of Council Housing* (London: Verso, 2018), pp. 96–7.

88 *Honourable Estates*: (Allan) James Tucker, *Honourable Estates* (London: Victor Gollancz, 1966); Mark Clapson, *Invincible Green Suburbs, Brave New Towns: Social Change and Urban Dispersal in Post-War England* (Manchester: Manchester University Press, 1998).

89 **no electric lights:** New Parks Tenants' Association, *The New Parks 'Voice': Official Organ of the New Parks Tenants' Association* (Leicester: 1948).

90 **'a black mark in regard to this serious problem':** *New Parks 'Voice'*, issue 10: 7.

90 **The tenants' association became less active:** W. Lycett, 'New Parks Souvenir', undated booklet, available in New Parks library, Leicester; Norman Dennis, 'Changes in Function and Leadership Renewal: A Study of the Community Association Movement and Problems of Voluntary Small Groups in the Urban Locality', *The Sociological Review* 9, no. 1 (1 March 1961), pp. 55–84, https://doi.org/10.1111/j.1467-954X.1961.tb01085.x.

90 **Suburban ones were being ignored:** Hansard, HC Debate, Vol. 122, Col. 1038, 17 November 1987.

91 **panic buttons in the vicarage:** Heather Stephen, 'Is Nothing Sacred? Life for Today's Inner-City Clergymen', *Leicester Mercury*, 26 August 1996; Paul Grinnell, 'Elderly Claim Council Ignores Estate Crime', *Leicester Mercury*, 20 March 1995.

91 **only half of residents felt safe:** Rachel Tuffin, Julia Morris and Alexis Poole, *An Evaluation of the Impact of the National Reassurance Policing Programme* (London: Home Office Research, Development and Statistics Directorate, January 2006), https://doc.ukdataservice. ac.uk/doc/7450/mrdoc/pdf/7450_hors296.pdf; 'Woman linked to baby mauled by dogs is killed', Mail Online, 25 May 2024, https://www. dailymail.co.uk/news/article-406739/Woman-linked-baby-mauled-dogs-killed.html; 'Man jailed for life for stabbing', BBC News (website), 2 July 2007, http://news.bbc.co.uk/1/hi/england/leicester-shire/6261986.stm.

93 **a detailed report on social housing:** John Hills, 'Ends and Means: The Future Roles of Social Housing in England', Centre for Analysis of Social Exclusion, 2007, https://thinkhouse.org.uk/site/assets/files/1869/hills.pdf.

94 **gone downhill:** Interview with Geraldine Woodland, British Library sound archive, C900/09015.

96 **keeping suburban estates white:** Jennifer Maureen Lowe, 'Social Justice and Localities: The Allocation of Council Housing in Tower Hamlets' (PhD thesis, Queen Mary College, University of London, 2004), https://core.ac.uk/download/pdf/30695843.pdf; Séan Carey

and Abdus Shukur, 'A profile of the Bangladeshi community in East London', *New Community* 12, no. 3 (1 December 1985), pp. 405–17, https://doi.org/10.1080/1369183X.1985.9975918.

96 **high bar for what constituted harassment:** 'Youth Did Not Want "Pakis" – Set Fire to House', *Leicester Mercury*, 5 October 1972; Marian Fitzgerald, [Untitled report on racial harassment in Leicester council estates], *c.* 1987.

96 **young men from the estate:** 'Gang of youths kicked chef unconscious in "bestial attack"', *Leicester Mercury*, 31 December 1977; 'Asians were "viciously" abused as mob ran wild outside cinema', *Leicester Mercury*, 13 October 1978; Hilary Grant, 'Asian man hit by brick', *Leicester Mercury*, 5 August 1988; 'Bid to tempt more Asians on to estates', *Leicester Mercury*, 5 February 1985.

97 **desist from housing Asian families:** *Living in Terror: A Report on Racial Violence & Harassment in Housing* (London: Commission for Racial Equality, 1987).

98 **only grew uglier:** Steve Garner et al., 'Sources of Resentment, and Perceptions of Ethnic Minorities among Poor White People in England', Department for Communities and Local Government, January 2009; Harold Carter, 'Building the Divided City: Race, Class and Social Housing in Southwark, 1945–1995', *The London Journal* 33, no. 2 (1 July 2008), pp. 155–85, https://doi.org/10.1179/174963208X307343; Les Back, *New Ethnicities and Urban Culture: Racisms and Multiculture in Young Lives*, Race and Representation 2 (London: UCL Press, 1996).

98 **segregated by elevation:** Danny Dorling, Ben Wheeler, Mary Shaw and Richard Mitchell, 'Counting the 21st Century Children of Britain: the extent of advantage and disadvantage', *Twenty-First Century Society* 2, no. 2 (1 June 2007), pp. 173–89, https://doi.org/10.1080/17450140701325873.

98 **a peculiar sort of victory:** Lindsay Judge, 'Social Renting: A Working Hypothesis', Resolution Foundation, 10 April 2019, https://www.resolutionfoundation.org/comment/social-renting-a-working-hypothesis/; Wendy Sigle-Rushton, 'Intergenerational and Life-Course Transmission of Social Exclusion in the 1970 British Cohort Study', Centre for Analysis of Social Exclusion, LSE, 1 February 2004, https://sticerd.lse.ac.uk/CASE/_new/publications/abstract/?-index=2041; Harminder Battu, Ada Ma and Euan Phimister, 'Housing Tenure, Job Mobility and Unemployment in the UK', *The*

Economic Journal 118, no. 527 (1 March 2008), pp. 311–28, https://doi. org/10.1111/j.1468-0297.2007.02122.x.

99 **only about 30,000 a year:** 'Live Tables on Housing Supply: Indicators of New Supply', UK Government (website), 28 March 2024, https://www.gov.uk/government/statistical-data-sets/live-tables-on-house-building. Table 244.

102 **allocations policies have changed:** Wendy Wilson and Cassie Barton, 'Allocating Social Housing (England)', House of Commons Library, 17 February 2022, https://commonslibrary.parliament.uk/ research-briefings/sn06397/.

CHAPTER FOUR

108 **Football was too important:** Matthew Taylor, 'The People's Game and the People's War: Football, Class and Nation in Wartime Britain, 1939–1945', *Historical Social Research / Historische Sozialforschung* 40, no. 4 (154) (2015), pp. 270–97.

108 **English Premier League fans:** 'Premier League Football: Research into viewing trends, stadium attendance, fans' preferences and behaviour, and the commercial market', Ofcom / Human Capital, *c.* 2005, https://ec.europa.eu/competition/antitrust/cases/dec_docs/ 38173/38173_104_7.pdf; Geoff Wicken, 'Football Watchers Have Become a Better Reflection of Society', AMSR (website), 27 June 2021, https://www.amsr.org.uk/football-watchers-have-become-a-better-reflection-of-society/.

108 **skilled manual workers or clerical workers:** For a similar finding see: Andrew Bengry-Howell and Christine Griffin, 'Self-made Motormen: The Material Construction of Working-class Masculine Identities through Car Modification', *Journal of Youth Studies* 10, no. 4 (1 September 2007), pp. 439–58, https://doi.org/10.1080/ 1367626070136o683.

111 **visited by car cruisers:** Dan Bevis, 'A Brief History of Car Modifying', *Fast Car* (website), 29 August 2023, https://www.fastcar.co.uk/tuning-tech-guides/a-brief-history-of-car-modifying/; 'Car Cruisers: A Partnership Bridging the Gap Between "Car Cruisers" and the Authorities', Avon and Somerset Constabulary, 2002, https://popcenter. asu.edu/sites/default/files/library/awards/tilley/2002/02-02(W-p).pdf.

111 ***Max Power* was poorly written:** *Max Power*, no. 46 (March 1997).

Notes and References

113 **they would drive a hundred miles:** Zannagh Hatton, 'The Tarmac Cowboys: An Ethnographic Study of the Cultural World of Boy Racers' (PhD thesis, University of Plymouth, 2007); Clifty [possibly Andy Clift], Report on cruise in Crewe, *Redline* 30 (October 2000), pp. 46–7.

114 **'between Traffic and Disorder':** 'Car Cruisers: A Partnership Bridging the Gap between "Car Cruisers" and the Authorities', 2002.

114 **thirty-nine official warnings:** Syreeta Lund, 'Fast and Furious', *Jane's Police Review*, 26 September 2003, pp. 18–19; Karen Lumsden, 'Policing the roads: traffic cops, "Boy Racers" and anti-social behaviour', *Policing and Society* 23, no. 2 (1 June 2013), pp. 204–21, https://doi.org/10.1080/10439463.2012.696642.

115 **more respectable car modifiers:** 'We're all being tarred with the same brush', *North Wales Live*, 10 September 2004, https://www.daily-post.co.uk/news/north-wales-news/were-being-tarred-same-brush-2923229; Karen Lumsden, *Boy Racer Culture: Youth, Masculinity and Deviance* (Abingdon: Routledge, 2013).

115 **'Bouley bashers':** Lumsden, 'Policing the roads'; Karen Lumsden, 'Anti-Social Behaviour Legislation and the Policing of Boy Racers: Dispersal Orders and Seizure of Vehicles', *Policing: A Journal of Policy and Practice* 8, no. 2 (1 June 2014), pp. 135–43, https://doi.org/10.1093/police/pau005.

116 **'rave on wheels':** Melanie Greenwood, 'Bumper Cars', *Weston & Worle News*, 2 September 1999.

120 **'excessive noise' and 'revving engines':** Great Yarmouth Borough Council, 'Public Spaces Protection Order No 2 – vehicle-related anti-social behaviour', 2017, https://www.great-yarmouth.gov.uk/pspo2-vehicle#prohibited%20activities; Stevenage Injunction Order, GOOLU797, 1 February 2023, https://www.stevenage.gov.uk/documents/news-and-events/car-cruising-2023/goolu797-stevenage-bc-v-persons-unknown-injunction-order-1-2-23.pdf.

121 **'you don't see many girls':** *Max Power*, August 1997; Karen Lumsden, 'Gendered Performances in a Male-Dominated Subculture: "Girl Racers", Car Modification and the Quest for Masculinity', *Sociological Research Online* 15, no. 3 (1 August 2010), pp. 75–85, https://doi.org/10.5153/sro.2123.

124 **'parallel lives':** 'Community Cohesion: A Report of the Independent Review Team Chaired by Ted Cantle', Home Office, 2001, available at: https://tedcantle.co.uk/pdf/communitycohesion%20cantlereport.pdf.

Notes and References

CHAPTER FIVE

128 **very important indeed:** Alexander Kustov, 'Do Anti-Immigration Voters Care More? Documenting the Issue Importance Asymmetry of Immigration Attitudes', *British Journal of Political Science* 53, no. 2 (April 2023), pp. 796–805, https://doi.org/10.1017/ S0007123422000369.

132 **hostility, reflection and sympathy:** Donald R. Kinder, *Us against Them: Ethnocentric Foundations of American Opinion*, Chicago Studies in American Politics (Chicago, IL: University of Chicago Press, 2009); Harris Beider, *White-Working Class Voices: Multiculturalism, Community-Building and Change* (Bristol: Policy Press, 2015); 'White Working Class Communities in Manchester', Open Society Foundations, June 2014, https://www.opensociety foundations.org/publications/white-working-class-communities-manchester. For a particularly good example, see 'Interview with Terry Burford', British Library sound archive, C900/09023.

136 **the streets have grown quiet:** Yago Zayed and Grahame Allen, 'Hate Crime Statistics', House of Commons Library, 15 January 2024, https://researchbriefings.files.parliament.uk/documents/CBP-8537/ CBP-8537.pdf.

136 **not all were young:** Pamela Duncan et al., 'Local. Left Behind. Prey to Populist Politics? What the Data Tells Us About the 2024 UK Rioters', *The Guardian*, 25 September 2024; 'Statistical Bulletin On the Public Disorder of 6th to 9th August 2011 – September 2012 Update', Ministry of Justice Statistics Bulletin, 13 September 2012, https://assets.publishing.service.gov.uk/media/5a7cc4e04of0b6629523 bb38/august-public-disorder-stats-bulletin-130912.pdf.

137 **people who complain most loudly:** Jane Green and Roosmarijn de Geus, 'Red Wall, Red Herring? Economic Insecurity and Voting Intention in Britain', Nuffield Politics Research Centre, University of Oxford, 24 May 2022, https://politicscentre.nuffield.ox.ac.uk/ media/5142/nprc-econ-insecurity-report_bridges_final.pdf.

138 **'heaping up its own funeral pyre':** J. Enoch Powell, *Freedom and Reality* (London: Batsford, 1969), pp. 213–19.

139 **'a little careless':** Hansard, HoC Debate, Vol. 763, Col. 75, 23 April 1968.

139 **the strikes and the demonstrations:** 'Docks, Factories Stop Work To

Support Powell', *Birmingham Daily Post*, 24 April 1968; Douglas Haig, 'Callaghan Suspends Immigration Man For Backing Powell', *Birmingham Daily Post*, 25 April 1968.

139 **reducing property values:** Powell, *Freedom and Reality*, p. 223.

140 **an enormous congregation:** 'In Defence of Powell', *The Scotsman*, 23 April 1968; Douglas E. Schoen, *Enoch Powell and the Powellites* (London: Macmillan, 1977).

141 **'pathetically misguided minority':** Fred Lindop, 'Racism and the working class: strikes in support of Enoch Powell in 1968', *Labour History Review* 66, no. 1 (April 2001), pp. 79–100, https://doi.org/10.3828/lhr.66.1.79; C. C. Aronsfeld, 'British dockers and coloured immigrants', *Patterns of Prejudice* 2, no. 4 (1 July 1968), pp. 8–12, https://doi.org/10.1080/0031322X.1968.9968760; Liz Fekete, 'Dockers Against Racism: an interview with Micky Fenn', *Race & Class* 58, no. 1 (1 July 2016), pp. 55–60, https://doi.org/10.1177/0306396816643004.

141 **working-class admirers:** Amy Whipple, 'Revisiting the "Rivers of Blood" Controversy: Letters to Enoch Powell', *Journal of British Studies* 48, no. 3 (2009), pp. 717–35.

142 **'sparingly-educated urban community':** Godfrey Elton, *The Unarmed Invasion: A Survey of Afro-Asian Immigration* (London: Geoffrey Bles, 1965).

142 **she said 'swamped' twice:** 'TV Interview for Granada *World in Action*', Margaret Thatcher Foundation, 27 January 1978, accessed 15 June 2024, https://www.margaretthatcher.org/document/103485; R. W. Apple, 'Mrs. Thatcher Touches a Nerve and British Racial Tension Is Suddenly a Political Issue', *The New York Times*, 22 February 1978, https://www.nytimes.com/1978/02/22/archives/mrs-thatcher-touches-a-nerve-and-british-racial-tension-is-suddenly.html; Margaret Thatcher, *The Path To Power* (London: Harper Press, 2011), pp. 406–9.

142 **Politicians who agree on little else:** Richard Ford, 'Middle Classes Benefit from Immigration, Says John Denham', *The Times*, 2 December 2009, https://www.thetimes.com/article/middle-classes-benefit-from-immigration-says-john-denham-z3whq3k85sz; James Brokenshire, 'Speech to Demos', Demos (think tank), 6 March 2014, https://demos.co.uk/wp-content/uploads/files/JamesBrokenshire SpeechtoDemos.pdf; Theresa May, 'Britain after Brexit. A vision of

a Global Britain. May's Conference speech: full text', Conservative Home (website), 2 October 2016, https://conservativehome. mystagingwebsite.com/2016/10/02/britain-after-brexit-a-vision-of-a-global-britain-theresa-mays-conservative-conference-speech-full-text/.

143 **any effect is small:** Michael A. Clemens and Jennifer Hunt, 'The Labor Market Effects of Refugee Waves: Reconciling Conflicting Results', National Bureau of Economic Research, Working Paper 23433, https:// www.nber.org/system/files/working_papers/w23433/w23433.pdf; Marco Manacorda, Alan Manning and Jonathan Wadsworth, 'The Impact of Immigration on the Structure of Wages: Theory and Evidence from Britain', *Journal of the European Economic Association* 10, no. 1 (2012), pp. 120–51, https://doi.org/10.1111/j.1542-4774.2011.01049.x; Francesco Campo, Giuseppe Forte and Jonathan Portes, 'The Impact of Migration on Productivity and Native-Born Workers' Training', IZA Discussion Paper No. 11833, *SSRN Electronic Journal*, 2018, https://doi.org/10.2139/ssrn.3261692; Florence Jaumotte, Ksenia Koloskova and Sweta Saxena, 'Impact of Migration on Income Levels in Advanced Economies', Spillover Notes No. 2016/008, IMF, 24 October 2016, https://www.imf.org/en/Publications/Spillover-Notes/ Issues/2016/12/31/Impact-of-Migration-on-Income-Levels-in-Advanced-Economies-44343.

145 **minority ethnic in-law:** Elizabeth Simon, 'Demystifying the link between higher education and liberal values: A within-sibship analysis of British individuals' attitudes from 1994–2020', *The British Journal of Sociology* 73, no. 5 (2022), pp. 967–84, https://doi.org/ 10.1111/1468-4446.12972; Ralph Scott, 'Does university make you more liberal? Estimating the within-individual effects of higher education on political values', *Electoral Studies* 77 (1 June 2022), https://doi.org/10.1016/j.electstud.2022.102471; Maria Sobolewska and Robert Ford, *Brexitland: Identity, Diversity and the Reshaping of British Politics* (Cambridge: Cambridge University Press, 2020), p. 66.

145 **4 per cent of people had been born abroad:** Lord Andrew Green, 'A summary history of immigration to Britain', Migration Watch UK, 12 May 2014, accessed 15 June 2024, https://www.migrationwatchuk. com/briefing-paper/document/48.

146 **the teenage years are especially important:** Lauren McLaren, Anja Neundorf and Ian Paterson, 'Diversity and Perceptions of Immigration: How the Past Influences the Present', *Political Studies*

69, no. 3 (1 August 2021), pp. 725–47, https://doi.org/10.1177/0032321720922774.

146 **Plymouth Argyle player Jack Leslie:** 'Jack Leslie Statue Unveiled at Plymouth Argyle', BBC News (website), 7 October 2022, https://www.bbc.co.uk/news/uk-england-devon-63158563.

147 **modernist architectural showcase:** Mark Clapson, *A Social History of Milton Keynes: Middle England/Edge City* (London: Frank Cass, 2004).

149 **spitting in the street:** 'White Working Class Communities in Manchester'; Beider, *White-Working Class Voices*, p. 154; Steve Garner, 'The entitled nation: how people make themselves white in contemporary England', Sens Public (web journal), 2010, https://sens-public.org/static/git-articles/SP729/SP729.pdf.

150 **might lose their places:** Steve Garner et al., 'Sources of Resentment, and Perceptions of Ethnic Minorities among Poor White People in England', Department for Communities and Local Government, January 2009.

CHAPTER SIX

155 **'chaffing and bawdy songs':** Karl Marx, *Capital*, Volume 1, Chapter 25. For an up-to-date account, see: Jennifer Frances, 'The role of gangmasters and gang labour in the UK food chain network: past and present', House of Commons – Environment, Food and Rural Affairs, accessed 14 July 2024, https://publications.parliament.uk/pa/cm200203/cmselect/cmenvfru/691/3060402.htm.

157 **more people born in Ireland:** Bronwen Walter, 'Time–Space Patterns of Second-Wave Irish Immigration into British Towns', *Transactions of the Institute of British Geographers* 5, no. 3 (1980), pp. 297–317, https://doi.org/10.2307/621844; 'Irish In Britain: Preliminary Findings from the 2021 Census of England and Wales', 6 April 2023, https://www.irishinbritain.org/assets/files/Irish-in-Britain-summary-report---April-2023.pdf; 'Historical Census Tables', London Datastore, accessed 14 July 2024, https://data.london.gov.uk/dataset/historical-census-tables.

157 **They were often looked down upon:** Enda Delaney, *Demography, State and Society: Irish Migration to Britain, 1921–1971* (Liverpool: Liverpool University Press, 2000); Enda Delaney, *The Irish in*

Post-War Britain (Oxford: Oxford University Press, 2007); Gavin Schaffer and Saima Nasar, 'The white essential subject: race, ethnicity, and the Irish in post-war Britain', *Contemporary British History* 32, no. 2 (3 April 2018), pp. 209–30, https://doi.org/10.1080/13619462.2018.1455031.

158 **Exactly how many varies:** 'One in four Britons claim Irish roots', BBC News (website), 16 March 2001, http://news.bbc.co.uk/1/hi/uk/1224611.stm; Simon Maybin, 'How many Britons are entitled to an Irish passport?', BBC News (website), 2 September 2016, https://www.bbc.com/news/magazine-37246769.

159 **Nor is assimilation a predictable, one-way process:** Mary Lennon, Marie McAdam and Joanne O'Brien, *Across the Water: Irish Women's Lives in Britain* (London: Virago Press, 1988), p. 101; Ludi Simpson, Stephen Jivraj and James Warren, 'The Stability of Ethnic Identity in England and Wales 2001–2011', *Journal of the Royal Statistical Society Series A: Statistics in Society* 179, no. 4 (1 October 2016), pp. 1025–49, https://doi.org/10.1111/rssa.12175; David O'Dornan, 'Noel Gallagher Reckons Oasis Only Existed Because They Came from Irish Stock', *The Irish Sun*, 5 January 2022, https://www.thesun.ie/tvandshowbiz/music/8161125/noel-gallagher-oasis-hugely-emotional-reason-supersonic-irish-roots/; Miranda Sawyer, 'Liam Gallagher: "Rock'n'roll Saved My Life"', *The Guardian*, 4 June 2017, https://www.theguardian.com/music/2017/jun/04/liam-gallagher-interview-rock-n-roll-saved-my-life-oasis-beady-eye.

161 **average incomes:** 'Income estimates for small areas, England and Wales: financial year ending 2020', Office for National Statistics (website), accessed 14 July 2024, https://www.ons.gov.uk/peoplepopulationandcommunity/personalandhouseholdfinances/incomeandwealth/bulletins/smallareamodelbasedincomeestimates/financialyearending2020.

165 **Women born in Eastern Europe:** 'Migrants in the UK Labour Market: An Overview', Migration Observatory (website), accessed 14 July 2024, https://migrationobservatory.ox.ac.uk/resources/briefings/migrants-in-the-uk-labour-market-an-overview/.

166 **fathers from Africa:** 'Parents' Country of Birth', Office for National Statistics (website), accessed 14 July 2024, https://www.ons.gov.uk/peoplepopulationandcommunity/birthsdeathsandmarriages/livebirths/datasets/parentscountryofbirth.

170 **pressing need for more workers:** 'Full text: Blair's migration speech', *The Guardian*, 27 April 2004, https://www.theguardian.com/politics/2004/apr/27/immigrationpolicy.speeches.

170 **women from both Pakistan and Romania:** 'Parents' Country of Birth', Office for National Statistics (website), accessed 14 July 2024, https://www.ons.gov.uk/peoplepopulationandcommunity/births-deathsandmarriages/livebirths/datasets/parentscountryofbirth.

171 **Indians received 323,000 visas:** 'Immigration system statistics data tables', UK Government (website), accessed 13 June 2024, https://www.gov.uk/government/statistical-data-sets/immigration-system-statistics-data-tables. See table Vis_D02.

173 **Jakub Krupa:** Jakub Krupa, 'Redefining "Home" – the UK's Polish Diaspora', in *Crossing Points: UK–Poland* (British Council, 2018), pp. 76–82, https://www.britishcouncil.org/sites/default/files/3593_bc_uk-poland_essay_series_aw_for_screen_use_0.pdf; S. Young, 'Experiences of Polish-Born Adolescents in Britain in the Run-up to Brexit', in M. Fleming, (ed.), *Brexit and Polonia: Challenges facing the Polish Community during the process of Britain leaving the European Union* (London: PUNO Press, 2018), pp. 63–82. The Brexit referendum upset many young people: Charlotte Hervy et al., 'Diverging Mental Health after Brexit: Evidence from a Longitudinal Survey', *Social Science & Medicine* 302 (1 June 2022): 114993, https://doi.org/10.1016/j.socscimed.2022.114993.

173 **a 'populist paradox':** Heather Rolfe, Sunder Katwala and Steve Ballinger, 'Shifting Views: Tracking attitudes to immigration in 2022', Ipsos / British Future, October 2022, https://www.britishfuture.org/wp-content/uploads/2022/10/Shifting-Views-Report-Oct-2022-FINAL.pdf; Cassilde Schwartz et al., 'A Populist Paradox? How Brexit Softened Anti-Immigrant Attitudes', *British Journal of Political Science* 51, no. 3 (July 2021), pp. 1160–80, https://doi.org/10.1017/S0007123419000656.

173 **allow Europeans to stay:** Steve Ballinger, '"Let EU migrants stay" say the British public, plus voices from business and politics', British Future (website), 3 July 2016, https://www.britishfuture.org/15131/.

174 **adopted prejudiced views:** Magda Mogilnicka, 'Conditional citizenship in the UK: Polish migrants' experiences of diversity', *Ethnicities* 22, no. 6 (1 December 2022), pp. 838–56, https://doi.org/10.1177/14687968221089926. Prejudice is not entirely one-directional: Nicole

S. Martin and Maria Sobolewska, 'The End of the Ethnic Bloc Vote? Ethnic Minority Leavers After the Brexit Referendum', *PS: Political Science & Politics* 56, no. 4 (October 2023), pp. 566–71, https://doi. org/10.1017/S1049096523000288.

CHAPTER SEVEN

176 **it made him cry:** 'Profile: John Prescott', BBC News (website), 27 August 2007, http://news.bbc.co.uk/1/hi/uk_politics/6636565.stm; Louise Sassoon, 'How John Prescott wooed his lady with sausages', *Daily Express*, 6 September 2012, https://www.express.co.uk/celebrity-news/344357/How-John-Prescott-wooed-his-lady-with-sausages.

177 **leave their home in South Wales:** 'Levelling Up the United Kingdom', Department for Levelling Up, Housing and Communities, 2 February 2022, https://assets.publishing.service.gov.uk/media/ 61fd3c71d3bf7f78df30b3c2/Levelling_Up_WP_HRES.pdf; Rachel Reeves, 'A New Business Model For Britain', Labour Together, May 2023, https://static1.squarespace.com/static/64f707cf512076037f612f60/ t/6502d760c087cb1853b8f5c4/1694685033194/A+NEW+BUSINESS+ MODEL+FOR+BRITAIN_0.pdf; Rachel Reeves, 'Securonomics', Peterson Institute, Washington DC, 24 May 2023, https://labour.org. uk/updates/press-releases/rachel-reeves-securonomics/.

177 **British opinion has divided in a peculiar way:** 'Levelling Up Poll', Public First, 2021, https://www.publicfirst.co.uk/wp-content/ uploads/2021/11/Levelling_Up_Poll.pdf.

178 **slowdown has continued:** Ian Shuttleworth, Thomas Cooke and Tony Champion, 'Why did fewer people change address in England and Wales in the 2000s than in the 1970s? Evidence from an analysis of the ONS Longitudinal Study', *Population, Space and Place*, no. 25.2 (2019), https://doi.org/10.1002/psp.2167; 'People in England and Wales with a different address in the UK a year before the census: Census 2021', Office for National Statistics, accessed 8 July 2024, https://www.ons.gov.uk/peoplepopulationandcommunity/ populationandmigration/migrationwithintheuk/bulletins/ peoplewithadifferentaddressinmarch2020tocensusday2021 englandandwales/census2021.

178 **a 'brain drain':** 'Geographical mobility of young people in English towns and cities', Office for National Statistics, 15 March 2024,

https://www.ons.gov.uk/peoplepopulationandcommunity/
educationandchildcare/datasets/geographicalmobilityofyoung
peopleinenglishtownsandcities; Anna Stansbury, Dan Turner and Ed
Balls, 'Tackling the UK's regional economic inequality: Binding
constraints and avenues for policy intervention', Mossavar-Rahmani
Center for Business and Government, Harvard Kennedy School,
March 2023, https://www.hks.harvard.edu/sites/default/files/centers/
mrcbg/files/198_AWP_final.pdf.

179 **Out-migration from Scotland:** 'Migration Flows', National Records
of Scotland, 9 July 2024, https://www.nrscotland.gov.uk/statistics-
and-data/statistics/statistics-by-theme/migration/migration-statistics/
migration-flows. The Tennent's advert is often known as 'Caledonia'.

179 **praise the people who stick around:** David Goodhart, *The Road to
Somewhere: The Populist Revolt and the Future of Politics* (London:
Hurst & Company, 2017).

179 **also occurred in other rich countries:** Maximiliano Alvarez, Aude
Bernard and Scott N. Lieske, 'Understanding internal migration
trends in OECD countries', *Population, Space and Place*, 2021, https://
doi.org/10.1002/psp.2451.

180 **women are a little more footloose:** Frances Darlington-Pollock, Nik
Lomax and Paul Norman, 'Ethnic internal migration: The import-
ance of age and migrant status', *The Geographical Journal* 185, no. 1
(2019), pp. 68–81, https://doi.org/10.1111/geoj.12286; Nissa Finney and
Ludi Simpson, 'Internal migration and ethnic groups: evidence for
Britain from the 2001 Census', *Population, Space and Place* 14, no. 2
(2008), pp. 63–83, https://doi.org/10.1002/psp.481; Jack Britton et al.,
'London Calling? Higher Education, Geographical Mobility and
Early-Career Earnings', Institute for Fiscal Studies, September 2021,
https://ifs.org.uk/sites/default/files/output_url_files/Higher-
education-geographical-mobility-and-early-career-earnings.
pdf.

180 **places where jobs are plentiful:** Ran Abramitzky and Leah Boustan,
Streets of Gold: America's Untold Story of Immigrant Success (London:
Hachette UK, 2022).

181 **Staveley Coal and Iron Company:** Dave Fordham, *Yorkshire Main
Colliery & New Edlington: Early Development*, First edition (Norton,
Doncaster, South Yorkshire: Fedj-el-Adoum Publishing, 2014); Peter
Tuffrey, *Edlington, Maltby & Warmsworth*, New pocket ed., Pocket

Images (Stroud: Nonsuch, 2007); Barry Jackson, *When I Worra Lad: Growing up in a South Yorkshire Pit Village in the 1940s and 1950s* (Sheffield: Sheaf Publishing, 2002).

182 **community of strangers:** Fred Kitchen, *Brother to the Ox: The Autobiography of a Farm Labourer*, Penguin Country Library (Harmondsworth: Penguin, 1983).

184 **National Coal Board did much the same:** Peter Scott, 'The state, internal migration, and the growth of new industrial communities in inter-war Britain', *The English Historical Review* 115, no. 461 (2000), pp. 329–53, https://doi.org/10.1093/ehr/115.461.329; Rex Taylor, 'Migration and the Residual Community', *The Sociological Review* 27, no. 3 (1 August 1979), pp. 475–89, https://doi.org/10.1111/j.1467-954X.1979.tb00346.x.

184 **a plan to move you:** Mark Clapson, *Invincible Green Suburbs. Brave New Towns: Social Change and Urban Dispersal in Post-War England* (Manchester: Manchester University Press, 1998); *An Enquiry into People's Homes; a Report Prepared by Mass-Observation* (London: Advertising Service Guild, 1943).

184 **'immigrants' and 'assimilated':** Margaret M. Attlee, *Mobility of Labour. A Consideration of the Question of Industrial Transference, Etc.* (Oxford: Catholic Social Guild, 1944). See also Brian Staines, 'The Movement of Population from South Wales', in Colin Barber and L. J. Williams, *Modern South Wales: Essays in Economic History* (Cardiff: University of Wales Press, 1986), pp. 237–50.

185 **a remarkably large number of awful headlines:** 'Four Hurt In Petrol Bomb Car Attack', *Huddersfield Daily Examiner*, 2 September 1995; Undated Article from the *Doncaster Star* about the closure of Georgina Mullis's shop, marked '27593', could be 27 May 1993, cutting available in Edlington Library; Report on Teenagers Arrested on Vandalism Charges, *Doncaster Star*, 1 May 1998, cutting available in Edlington Library; Lord Carlile, 'The Edlington Case: A Review', 2012, https://assets.publishing.service.gov.uk/media/5a7b0481ed915d3ed906187c/The_Edlington_case.pdf.

185 **surrounded by water:** 'Internal migration in England and Wales', Office for National Statistics, year ending June 2023, https://www.ons.gov.uk/peoplepopulationandcommunity/populationandmigration/populationestimates/datasets/internalmigrationinenglandandwales.

185 **Coal miners moved less in the 1980s:** Emma Hollywood, 'Mining,

Migration and Immobility: Towards an Understanding of the Relationship between Migration and Occupation in the Context of the UK Mining Industry', *International Journal of Population Geography* 8, no. 4 (2002), pp. 297–314, https://doi.org/10.1002/ijpg.264.

186 **husbands' slimmer pay packets:** Christina Beatty, Stephen Fothergill and Ryan Powell, 'Twenty Years on: Has the Economy of the UK Coalfields Recovered?', *Environment and Planning A: Economy and Space* 39, no. 7 (1 July 2007), pp. 1654–75, https://doi.org/10.1068/a38216.

188 **a core–periphery divide:** Philip McCann, *The UK Regional-National Economic Problem: Geography, Globalisation and Governance* (Abingdon: Routledge, 2016); Philip McCann, 'Perceptions of regional inequality and the geography of discontent: insights from the UK', *Regional Studies* 54, no. 2 (1 February 2020), pp. 256–67, https://doi.org/10.1080/00343404.2019.1619928.

189 **a small city at rush hour:** John Burn-Murdoch, 'The Nimby tax on Britain and America', *Financial Times*, 25 August 2023, https://www.ft.com/content/9aa0fcc0-31fb-44be-b5a0-57ceb7fb7a52; Tom Forth, 'Birmingham Is a Small City', Tom Forth (blog), 14 January 2019, https://www.tomforth.co.uk/birminghamisasmallcity/; 'British cities have far too little power, and it's holding them back', *The Economist*, 6 October 2022, https://www.economist.com/britain/2022/10/06/british-cities-have-far-too-little-power-and-its-holding-them-back.

190 **share in their success:** 'Levelling Up the United Kingdom', 2 February 2022; Henry Overman, '"Levelling up": the government's plans aren't enough to promote economic growth and tackle inequality', LSE British Politics and Policy (blog), 2 February 2022, https://blogs.lse.ac.uk/politicsandpolicy/levelling-up-the-governments-plans-arent-enough-to-promote-economic-growth-and-tackle-inequality/.

191 **goodness do they use it:** Felicia Rankl, Cassie Barton and Helena Carthew, 'Green Belt', House of Commons Library, 15 December 2023, https://researchbriefings.files.parliament.uk/documents/SN00934/SN00934.pdf; 'Edlington Town Neighbourhood Plan 2016–2032', Edlington Town Council, July 2018, https://dmbcwebstolive01.blob.core.windows.net/media/Default/Planning/Documents/Neighbourhood%20Plans/Edlington%20NP/

Edlington%20Town%20Neighbourhood%20Plan%20-%20
Adopted%20Version.pdf.

191 **'decisions about land for housing'**: R. V. C. Grainger, article in
Edlingtonian: the Edlington Town Magazine, April 1978, available in
Edlington Library.

193 **from cold spots to hot spots**: 'State of the Nation 2017: Social
Mobility in Great Britain', Social Mobility Commission, November
2017, https://assets.publishing.service.gov.uk/government/uploads/
system/uploads/attachment_data/file/662744/State_of_the_Nation_
2017_-_Social_Mobility_in_Great_Britain.pdf.

193 **Some people are more discouraged than others**: Henry Overman
and Xiaowei Xu, 'Spatial Disparities Across Labour Markets', Institute
for Fiscal Studies, 2 February 2022; Britton et al., 'London Calling?
Higher Education, Geographical Mobility and Early-Career
Earnings', September 2021; 'Moving out to move on: Understanding
the link between migration, disadvantage and social mobility', Social
Mobility Commission, July 2020, https://www.employment
studies.co.uk/system/files/resources/files/Moving_out_to_move_
on%20%281%29.pdf.

194 **'blessedly little risk'**: Don Paterson, *Toy Fights: A Boyhood* (London:
Faber & Faber, 2023), p. 360.

CHAPTER EIGHT

197 **1,395 armed robberies**: Neil Darbyshire, *The Flying Squad* (London:
Headline, 1993), p. 236, p. 280.

197 **sent back to prison with an increased sentence**: 'Fugitive "Skull
Cracker" Jailed for Life', BBC News (website), 29 May 2014, https://
www.bbc.com/news/uk-england-27623436.

197 **Wes Streeting**: Wes Streeting, *One Boy, Two Bills and a Fry Up: A
Memoir of Growing Up and Getting On* (London: Hodder &
Stoughton, 2023).

198 **Crime boosted their fortunes only briefly**: Before the Second World
War, however, Arthur Harding moved between armed robbery and
skilled trades such as cabinetmaking. He even ran shops. Raphael
Samuel, *East End Underworld: Chapters in the Life of Arthur Harding*,
History Workshop Series (London: Routlege & Kegan Paul,
1981).

Notes and References

199 **More of a craftsman:** Bruce Reynolds, *The Autobiography of a Thief*, updated ed. (London: Virgin, 2005).

199 **money that was more vulnerable:** Mary McIntosh, *The Organisation of Crime*, Studies in Sociology (London: Macmillan, 1975).

200 **divided the money:** Razor Smith, *A Few Kind Words and a Loaded Gun: The Autobiography of a Career Criminal* (London: Penguin, 2005), p. 267.

200 **The people who did this were not particularly varied:** Roger Matthews, *Armed Robbery*, Crime and Society Series (Cullompton: Willan, 2002), p. 21; Shona Morrison and Ian O'Donnell, *Armed Robbery: A Study in London* (Oxford: University of Oxford, Centre for Criminological Research, 1994).

201 **at least one Londoner:** Darbyshire, *The Flying Squad*, p. 297.

201 **'go out and get big money':** Freddie Foreman, *Respect: Autobiography of Freddie Foreman* (London: Arrow, 1997), p. 89.

201 **an uncomfortable niche:** Enda Delaney, *The Irish in Post-War Britain* (Oxford: Oxford University Press, 2007); Dick Hobbs, *Doing the Business: Entrepreneurship, the Working Class and Detectives in the East End of London* (Oxford: Oxford University Press, 1989).

203 **the robbers loved to swagger:** Reynolds, *The Autobiography of a Thief*, Chapter 15; Noel 'Razor' Smith, *The Dirty Dozen: The Rise and Fall of London's Most Feared Armed Robbery Gang* (London: John Blake, 2020), Chapter 4.

203 **David Bailey:** David Bailey, *Look Again: The Autobiography* (London: Macmillan, 2020), Chapter 4.

203 **Raphael Samuel, a left-wing intellectual:** Billy Bragg, *Roots, Radicals and Rockers: How Skiffle Changed the World* (London: Faber & Faber, 2017); David Kynaston, *A Northern Wind: Britain, 1962–65* (London: Bloomsbury, 2023), p. 463.

205 **threatening an off-duty police officer:** Paul Smith, 'Bindon Is Jailed For Knife Threat', *Daily Mirror*, 19 September 1984.

205 **they describe themselves as workers:** Dick Hobbs, *Bad Business: Professional Crime in Modern Britain* (Oxford: Oxford University Press, 1995); 'Jack Ord Interviewed by Neil Gander', British Library Sound Archive, C900/01608.

205 **wave upon wave of change:** 'Tony Benson – an Overview of Unique

Taggant Technology', Banknote Watch UK, 2014, https://www.youtube.com/watch?v=Ihdk_SGGEfQ.

206 **the riverine environment:** Dick Hobbs, 'The Firm: Organizational Logic and Criminal Culture on a Shifting Terrain', *The British Journal of Criminology* 41, no. 4 (2001), pp. 549–60.

206 **the cashier, a South Asian:** Matthews, *Armed Robbery*, p. 43.

207 **'you swear far too much':** Smith, *A Few Kind Words and a Loaded Gun*, p. 96.

208 **two men were sufficient:** Terry Smith, *The Art of Armed Robbery* (London: John Blake, 2003).

209 **six out of ten robberies were solo:** Barry Reilly, Neil Rickman and Robert Witt, 'Robbing Banks: Crime Does Pay – But Not Very Much', *Significance* 9, no. 3 (2012), pp. 17–21, https://doi.org/10.1111/j.1740-9713.2012.00570.x.

209 **7 per cent were self-employed:** 'Long-Term Trends in UK Employment: 1861 to 2018', Office for National Statistics, accessed 15 August 2024, https://www.ons.gov.uk/economy/nationalaccounts/uksectoraccounts/compendium/economicreview/april2019/longtermtrendsinukemployment1861to2018.

211 **a group of elderly British men:** Duncan Campbell, Alexandra Topping and Vikram Dodd, 'Cops and ex-robbers on Hatton Garden heist: "This is no bunch of mugs"', *The Guardian*, 10 April 2015, https://www.theguardian.com/uk-news/2015/apr/10/hatton-garden-jewel-heist-cops-robbers-clients.

211 **less risky money:** Smith, *The Art of Armed Robbery*, p. 296.

CHAPTER NINE

214 **154 essays:** Dawn Lyon, Bethany Morgan Brett and Graham Crow, 'Working with material from the Sheppey archive', *International Journal of Social Research Methodology* 15, no. 4 (1 July 2012), pp. 301–9, https://doi.org/10.1080/13645579.2012.688314; Dawn Lyon and Graham Crow, 'The Challenges and Opportunities of Re-Studying Community on Sheppey: Young People's Imagined Futures', *The Sociological Review* 60, no. 3 (1 August 2012), pp. 498–517, https://doi.org/10.1111/j.1467-954X.2012.02096.x; 'School Leavers Study, 1978', UK Data Service, accessed 9 July 2024, https://beta.ukdataservice.ac.

uk/datacatalogue/studies/study?id=4867&type=Data%20catalogue#!/
access-data. A puzzle I have not been able to solve is why the
archive contains 154 essays, whereas Pahl mentioned collecting
142. The 'extra' ones all appear to have been written by 17-year-old
girls.

216 **one out of every ten babies:** 'Births in England and Wales: summary
tables', Office for National Statistics, accessed 9 July 2024, https://
www.ons.gov.uk/peoplepopulationandcommunity/births
deathsandmarriages/livebirths/datasets/birthsummarytables;
'Divorces in England and Wales', Office for National Statistics,
accessed 9 July 2024, https://www.ons.gov.uk/peoplepopulationand
community/birthsdeathsandmarriages/divorce/datasets/divorce
sinenglandandwales.

216 **born to women aged forty or older:** 'Marriages in England and
Wales', Office for National Statistics, accessed 9 July 2024, https://
www.ons.gov.uk/peoplepopulationandcommunity/birthsdeathsand
marriages/marriagecohabitationandcivilpartnerships/datasets/
marriagesinenglandandwales2013; 'Marriage statistics, cohabitation
and cohort analyses', Office for National Statistics, accessed 9 July
2024, https://www.ons.gov.uk/peoplepopulationandcommunity/
birthsdeathsandmarriages/marriagecohabitationandcivilpartner
ships/datasets/marriagestatisticscohabitationandcohortanalyses;
'Births in England and Wales: summary tables', Office for National
Statistics; 'Births by parents' characteristics', Office for National
Statistics, accessed 9 July 2024, https://www.ons.gov.uk/people
populationandcommunity/birthsdeathsandmarriages/livebirths/
datasets/birthsbyparentscharacteristics.

217 **children living in single-parent households:** 'Mean age of mother at
birth of first child, by highest achieved educational qualification,
1996 to 2016, England and Wales', Office for National Statistics,
accessed 9 July 2024, https://www.ons.gov.uk/peoplepopulationand
community/birthsdeathsandmarriages/conceptionandfertilityrates/
adhocs/008981meanageofmotheratbirthoffirstchildbyhighestachieved
educationalqualification1996to2016englandandwales; 'Society At a
Glance 2019', OECD, n.d.; 'Births by parents' characteristics', Office
for National Statistics.

217 **hotspot for unmarried motherhood:** 'Live births by postcode sector,
England and Wales: select years from 1999 to 2018', Office for National

Statistics, accessed 9 July 2024, https://www.ons.gov.uk/peoplepopulation andcommunity/birthsdeathsandmarriages/livebirths/adhocs/11309 livebirthsbypostcodesectorenglandandwalesselectyears from1999to2018.

217 **ethnically diverse inner-city areas:** Ian Gordon, 'Family Structure, Educational Achievement and the Inner City', *Urban Studies* 33, no. 3 (1 April 1996), pp. 407–23, https://doi.org/10.1080/0042098965011834.

218 **extra nine years of good health:** 'Suicides in England and Wales by local authority', Office for National Statistics, accessed 9 July 2024, https://www.ons.gov.uk/peoplepopulationandcommunity/births deathsandmarriages/deaths/datasets/suicidesbylocalauthority; 'Health state life expectancies, UK: 2018 to 2020', Office for National Statistics, accessed 9 July 2024, https://www.ons.gov.uk/people populationandcommunity/healthandsocialcare/healthandlife expectancies/bulletins/healthstatelifeexpectanciesuk/2018to2020# glossary.

218 **'a larger slice of the cake':** Ben Houchen, 'Full speech: A record of delivery, a promise of more', Ben Houchen (website), 11 May 2018, https://www.benhouchen.com/news/full-speech-record-delivery-promise-more.

221 **You might expect that divorce has become less harmful:** Fabrizio Bernardi and Diederik Boertien, 'Understanding Heterogeneity in the Effects of Parental Separation on Educational Attainment in Britain: Do Children from Lower Educational Backgrounds Have Less to Lose?', *European Sociological Review* 32, no. 6 (1 December 2016), pp. 807–19, https://doi.org/10.1093/esr/jcw036; Kandyce Larson and Neal Halfon, 'Parental divorce and adult longevity', *International Journal of Public Health* 58, no. 1 (1 February 2013), pp. 89–97, https://doi.org/10.1007/s00038-012-0373-x; Wendy Sigle-Rushton, John Hobcraft and Kathleen Kiernan, 'Parental divorce and subsequent disadvantage: A cross-cohort comparison', *Demography* 42, no. 3 (August 2005), pp. 427–46, https://doi.org/ 10.1353/dem.2005.0026.

221 **it impoverishes them:** Hayley Fisher and Hamish Low, 'Recovery From Divorce: Comparing High and Low Income Couples', *International Journal of Law, Policy and the Family* 30, no. 3 (1 December 2016), pp. 338–71, https://doi.org/10.1093/lawfam/ ebw011; Mike Brewer and Alita Nandi, 'Partnership dissolution: how

does it affect income, employment and well-being?', ISER working paper series (September 2014), https://www.iser.essex.ac.uk/wp-content/uploads/files/working-papers/iser/2014-30.pdf.

221 **2022 report for the Institute of Fiscal Studies:** Kathleen Kiernan, Sam Crossman and Angus Phimister, 'Families and Inequalities', Institute for Fiscal Studies Deaton Review of Inequalities, 23 June 2022, https://ifs.org.uk/inequality/families-and-inequalities/.

222 **subsidize marriage:** 'Family Structure Still Matters', Centre for Social Justice, August 2020, https://www.centreforsocialjustice.org.uk/wp-content/uploads/2020/10/CSJJ8372-Family-structure-Report-200807.pdf; 'It Is Time To Back Marriage', Centre for Social Justice, February 2012, https://www.centreforsocialjustice.org.uk/wp-content/uploads/2018/03/Itistimetobackmarriage.pdf.

224 **marriage has become less important to teenagers:** Lyon and Crow, 'The Challenges and Opportunities of Re-Studying Community on Sheppey'.

224 **the doorway to family life:** 'YouGov Survey Results: Marriage', field-work conducted 2 March – 23 April 2022, YouGov, n.d., https://d3nkl3psvxxpe9.cloudfront.net/documents/YouGov_Results_-_Marriage.pdf; Elizabeth Clery, 'A Liberalisation In Attitudes?', British Social Attitudes 40, National Centre For Social Research, September 2023, https://natcen.ac.uk/sites/default/files/2023-09/BSA%2040%20Moral%20issues.pdf; Stephanie Coontz, *Marriage, a History: From Obedience to Intimacy, or How Love Conquered Marriage* (New York, NY: Viking, 2005).

225 **committed to each other, if not married:** This is often described as a local peculiarity, but there is some evidence that people develop more conservative views on gender if they grow up amid high unemployment. Andrew McNeil, Davide Luca and Neil Lee, 'The long shadow of local decline: Birthplace economic adversity and long-term individual outcomes in the UK', *Journal of Urban Economics* 136 (1 July 2023): 103571, https://doi.org/10.1016/j.jue.2023.103571.

227 **North East Poverty Commission:** 'Getting the building blocks wrong: Early childhood poverty in the North East', North East Child Poverty Commission, September 2022, https://nechildpoverty.org.uk/content/images/uploads/Getting_the_building_blocks_wrong_Early_childhood_poverty_in_the_North_East.pdf.

228 **results have been pretty feeble:** 'Building a Happy Home: Marriage Education as a Tool to Strengthen Families', SCP report no. 1-22, March 2022, https://www.jec.senate.gov/public/_cache/files/3d102525-6f0d-48ed-92f4-d71edd468ad6/building-a-happy-home.pdf.

229 **high rate of first-cousin marriage:** Rosemary R. C. McEachan et al., 'Cohort Profile Update: Born in Bradford', *International Journal of Epidemiology* 53, no. 2 (1 April 2024): dyae037, https://doi.org/10.1093/ije/dyae037.

229 **reach their parents within fifteen minutes:** Tak Wing Chan and John Ermisch, 'Residential proximity of parents and their adult offspring in the United Kingdom, 2009–10', *Population Studies* 69, no. 3 (2 September 2015), pp. 355–72, https://doi.org/10.1080/0032472 8.2015.1107126.

230 **the parents fell into two groups:** Annette Lareau, *Unequal Childhoods: Class, Race, and Family Life*, 2nd ed., with an update a decade later (Berkeley, CA: University of California Press, 2011).

232 **'Doing the dirty work of social class':** Diane Reay, 'Doing the Dirty Work of Social Class? Mothers' Work in Support of their Children's Schooling', *The Sociological Review* 53, no. 2_suppl (1 December 2005), pp. 104–15, https://doi.org/10.1111/j.1467-954X.2005.00575.x.

233 **highly attentive parents:** Giacomo Vagni, 'Bringing It All Back Home: Social Class and Educational Stratification of Childcare in Britain, 1961–2015', *Journal of Time Use Research* 18, no. 1 (n.d.), pp. 37–57.

233 **The finding is encouraging:** Kathleen E. Kiernan and Fiona K. Mensah, 'Poverty, family resources and children's early educational attainment: The mediating role of parenting', *British Educational Research Journal* 37, no. 2 (1 April 2011), pp. 317–36, https://doi.org/10.1080/01411921003596911; Matthias Doepke and Fabrizio Zilibotti, 'The role of parenting in child development', IFS Deaton Review of Inequality, 2022.

235 **how closely parents monitor their children:** Ann Hagell, 'Time Trends in Parenting and Outcomes for Young People', Nuffield Foundation, 2009, https://www.nuffieldfoundation.org/wp-content/uploads/2019/12/Time-trends-in-parenting-and-outcomes-for-young-people-vFINAL.pdf.

CHAPTER TEN

239 **marvellous story:** David Kynaston, *Family Britain, 1951–57* (London: Bloomsbury, 2010), pp. 41–2.

241 **embellishment and detail:** David Butler and Donald Stokes, *Political Change in Britain: College Edition* (London: Palgrave Macmillan UK, 1971), pp. 47–70, https://doi.org/10.1007/978-1-349-00140-8_4.

241 **not exactly fizzing:** Ferdynand Zweig, *The British Worker, Etc.* (Harmondsworth: Penguin Books, 1952), chapter 19; Richard Hoggart, *A Local Habitation* (London: Chatto & Windus, 1988), p. 47.

241 **exceptions to the rule:** Robert Mackenzie and Allan Silver, *Angels in Marble: Working Class Conservatives in Urban England* (London: Heinemann Educational Books, 1968).

241 **highest reaches of management:** Erzsébet Bukodi et al., 'The Changing Class and Educational Composition of the UK Political Elite since 1945: Implications for Representation', *British Politics*, 27 March 2024, https://doi.org/10.1057/s41293-024-00253-6.

242 *Never a Yes Man*: Eric S. Heffer, *Never a Yes Man: The Life and Politics of an Adopted Liverpudlian* (London: Verso, 1991).

244 **upwardly mobile southern English voters:** Giles Radice, *Southern Discomfort* (Fabian Society, 1992).

244 **new terms to describe society:** Geoffrey Evans and James Tilley, *The New Politics of Class: The Political Exclusion of the British Working Class* (Oxford: Oxford University Press, 2017); Hélène Mulholland, 'Ed Miliband Denies Playing Class Card in One Nation Speech', *The Guardian*, 3 October 2012, https://www.theguardian.com/politics/2012/oct/03/ed-miliband-class-card-one-nation.

244 **careerist Labour MPs:** Tom O'Grady, 'Careerists Versus Coal-Miners: Welfare Reforms and the Substantive Representation of Social Groups in the British Labour Party', *Comparative Political Studies*, 16 July 2018, https://doi.org/10.1177/0010414018784065.

245 **In the late 1990s and 2000s they converged:** Nicholas Allen and Judith Bara, 'Clear Blue Water? The 2019 Party Manifestos', *Political Quarterly* 92, no. 3 (22 May 2021), pp. 531–40.

245 **smaller part of Labour's electoral coalition:** Jamie Furlong and Will Jennings, *The Changing Electoral Map of England and Wales* (Oxford: Oxford University Press, 2024); Anthony Heath, Roger

Jowell and John Curtice, *The Rise of New Labour: Party Policies and Voter Choices* (Oxford: Oxford University Press, 2001); Evans and Tilley, *The New Politics of Class*.

246 **class backgrounds of their politicians:** Nick Vivyan et al., 'Do Humble Beginnings Help? How Politician Class Roots Shape Voter Evaluations', *Electoral Studies* 63 (1 February 2020), https://doi. org/10.1016/j.electstud.2019.102093; Rosie Campbell and Philip Cowley, 'Rich Man, Poor Man, Politician Man: Wealth Effects in a Candidate Biography Survey Experiment', *The British Journal of Politics and International Relations* 16, no. 1 (1 February 2014), pp. 56–74, https://doi.org/10.1111/1467-856X.12002.

246 **flirted with the far-right:** Robert Ford and Matthew Goodwin, *Revolt on the Right: Explaining Support for the Radical Right in Britain* (Abingdon, Oxon: Routledge, 2014).

247 **New Labourish verbiage:** John Denham, 'Connecting Communities', *Cohesion & Society: Journal of Community Cohesion*, no. 1 (July 2010), pp. 17–20, https://tedcantle.co.uk/pdf/June%2010%20 iCoCo%20Cohesion%20and%20Society%20journalv3.pdf.

247 **two groups:** Maria Sobolewska and Robert Ford, *Brexitland: Identity, Diversity and the Reshaping of British Politics* (Cambridge: Cambridge University Press, 2020).

249 **higher in more deprived areas:** John Curtice, 'How Scotland Voted: Economic Perceptions in the Scottish Independence Referendum', *University of Strathclyde International Public Policy Institute*, 2015, https://strathprints.strath.ac.uk/53562/1/CurticeJ_IPPI_2015_How_ Scotland_voted_economic_perceptions_in_the_Scottish_ independence_referendum.pdf.

250 *The Strange Death of Labour Scotland*: Gerry Hassan and Eric Shaw, *The Strange Death of Labour Scotland* (Edinburgh: Edinburgh University Press, 2012).

251 **the English were a rather different matter:** Guy Adams, 'The Savage Racism Turning Scotland into a No-Go Zone for the English', Mail Online, 5 September 2014, https://www.dailymail.co.uk/news/article-2745565/Savage-racism-turning-Scotland-no-zone-English.html; Julia Rampen, 'Extreme Scottish Nationalists: Hunting Lapdogs and Traitors', *New Statesman* (blog), 11 April 2017, https://www. newstatesman.com/politics/2017/04/extreme-scottish-nationalists-hunting-lapdogs-and-traitors. For the strength of ethnocentrism and

anti-English feeling among the Scottish electorate, see Sobolewska and Ford, *Brexitland*, chapter 9.

252 **identifying more as Leavers or Remainers:** John Curtice, 'The Emotional Legacy Of Brexit: How Britain Has Become A Country Of "Remainers" And "Leavers"', NatCen Social Research, October 2018, https://www.whatukthinks.org/eu/wp-content/uploads/2018/10/WUKT-EU-Briefing-Paper-15-Oct-18-Emotional-legacy-paper-final.pdf; Sara B. Hobolt, Thomas J. Leeper and James Tilley, 'Divided by the Vote: Affective Polarization in the Wake of the Brexit Referendum', *British Journal of Political Science* 51, no. 4 (October 2021), pp. 1476–93, https://doi.org/10.1017/S0007123420000125.

253 **reliability was seen as a given:** Deborah Mattinson, *Beyond the Red Wall: Why Labour Lost, How the Conservatives Won and What Will Happen Next?* (London: Biteback Publishing, 2020).

253 **'left behind' people:** Nick Gutteridge, 'Reports of HUGE EU Referendum Turnout Which "would Favour Leave"', Express.co.uk, 24 June 2016, https://www.express.co.uk/news/politics/682890/EU-referendum-Reports-huge-EU-referendum-turnout-favour-Leave-Brexit; John Harris, 'Britain Is in the Midst of a Working-Class Revolt', *The Guardian*, 17 June 2016, sec. Opinion, https://www.theguardian.com/commentisfree/2016/jun/17/britain-working-class-revolt-eu-referendum; Brendan O'Neill, 'Not Thick or Racist: Just Poor', *The Spectator*, 2 July 2016, https://www.spectator.co.uk/article/not-thick-or-racist-just-poor/.

253 **Conservative vote became slightly more working-class:** 'The Re-Shaping Of Class Voting By Geoffrey Evans and Jonathan Mellon', The British Election Study, 6 March 2020, https://www.british electionstudy.com/bes-findings/the-re-shaping-of-class-voting-in-the-2019-election-by-geoffrey-evans-and-jonathan-mellon/; 'The State of Public Opinion: 2023', UK In a Changing Europe, December 2023, https://media.ukandeu.ac.uk/wp-content/uploads/2023/12/UKICE-The-State-of-Public-Opinion-2023-2-.pdf; Robert Ford, Tim Bale, William Jennings and Paula Surridge, *The British General Election of 2019* (Basingstoke: Palgrave Macmillan, 2021).

254 **pollster James Kanagasooriam:** 'Minorities Report: The Attitudes of Britain's Ethnic Minority Population', UK In a Changing Europe, 8 October 2024, https://media.ukandeu.ac.uk/wp-content/

uploads/2024/10/UKICE-FOCALDATA-MINORITIES-REPORT-
081024-FINAL.pdf.

254 **discrete issue:** Nicole S. Martin and Maria Sobolewska, 'The End of
the Ethnic Bloc Vote? Ethnic Minority Leavers After the Brexit
Referendum', *PS: Political Science & Politics* 56, no. 4 (October 2023),
pp. 566–71, https://doi.org/10.1017/S1049096523000288.

255 **digging through the floor:** Charlotte Hervy et al., 'Diverging Mental
Health after Brexit: Evidence from a Longitudinal Survey', *Social
Science & Medicine* 302 (1 June 2022), 114993, https://doi.
org/10.1016/j.socscimed.2022.114993; Christopher W. N. Saville,
'Mental Health Consequences of Minority Political Positions: The
Case of Brexit', *Social Science & Medicine* 258 (1 August 2020),
113016, https://doi.org/10.1016/j.socscimed.2020.113016; Mohammad
Zia Ul Haq Katshu, 'Acute Transient Psychotic Disorder Precipitated
by Brexit Vote', *BMJ Case Reports* 12, no. 10 (1 October 2019),
e232363, https://doi.org/10.1136/bcr-2019-232363.

257 **twenty percentage points:** Ben Ansell and Jane Gingrich, 'Political
Inequality', Deaton Review of Inequalities (Institute for Fiscal
Studies, 2 December 2022), https://ifs.org.uk/publications/politi-
cal-inequality; Oliver Heath, 'Policy Alienation, Social Alienation
and Working-Class Abstention in Britain, 1964–2010', *British Journal
of Political Science* 48, no. 4 (October 2018), pp. 1053–73, https://doi.
org/10.1017/S0007123416000272.

258 **a mere 40 per cent:** Georgina Sturge, '2024 General Election:
Turnout', House of Commons Library, 5 September 2024, https://
commonslibrary.parliament.uk/general-election-2024-turnout/;
Richard Cracknell and Carl Baker, 'General Election 2024: Results
and Analysis', Research Briefing, House of Commons Library,
24 September 2024, https://researchbriefings.files.parliament.uk/
documents/CBP-10009/CBP-10009.pdf.

260 **a lack of political competition:** Richard Wyn Jones, 'Understanding
a Century of Labour Dominance: Social Science and the Puzzle of
Voting Behaviour in Wales', *Transactions: Honourable Society of
Cymmrodorion* 28 (2022), pp. 25–45, https://orca.cardiff.ac.uk/id/
eprint/155446/3/Darlith%20Cymmrodorion%20THSC%2023.5.2022.
pdf; Jack Vowles, Gabriel Katz, and Daniel P. Stevens, 'Electoral
Competitiveness and Turnout in British Elections, 1964–2010', 10
March 2015, https://ore.exeter.ac.uk/repository/handle/10871/18580.

Notes and References

CONCLUSION

265 **the old categories will not do:** 'Births by parents' country of birth, England and Wales: 2022', Office for National Statistics', accessed 3 August 2024, https://www.ons.gov.uk/peoplepopulationand community/birthsdeathsandmarriages/livebirths/bulletins/ parentscountryofbirthenglandandwales/2022. The ethnicity of babies can be calculated by using the Office for National Statistics' 'Create a custom dataset' tool.

265 **They are just diverse:** Gemma Catney et al., 'Ethnic diversification and neighbourhood mixing: A rapid response analysis of the 2021 Census of England and Wales', *The Geographical Journal* 189, no. 1 (2023), pp. 63–77, https://doi.org/10.1111/geoj.12507; Richard Harris, 'A tale of four cities: Neighbourhood diversification and residential desegregation in and around England's "no majority" cities', *The Geographical Journal* 190, no. 2 (2024): e12561, https://doi.org/10.1111/ geoj.12561.

266 **not much of a target:** 'Explore 50 years of international migration to and from the UK', Office for National Statistics, 1 December 2016, https://www.ons.gov.uk/peoplepopulationandcommunity/ populationandmigration/internationalmigration/articles/explore 50yearsofinternationalmigrationtoandfromtheuk/2016-12-01; 'Long-term international migration, provisional: year ending December 2023', Office for National Statistics, 23 May 2024, https://www.ons. gov.uk/peoplepopulationandcommunity/populationandmigration/ internationalmigration/bulletins/longterminternationalmigration provisional/yearendingdecember2023.

267 **the drift from manufacturing to services:** Chris Rhodes, 'Manufacturing: international comparisons', Briefing Paper no. 05809, House of Commons Library, 5 January 2018, https://research-briefings.files.parliament.uk/documents/SN05809/SN05809.pdf; Chris Rhodes, 'Manufacturing: statistics and policy', Briefing Paper no. 01942, House of Commons Library, 10 January 2020, https:// researchbriefings.files.parliament.uk/documents/SN01942/SN01942. pdf; 'Employment by activity', OECD, accessed 3 August 2024, https://www.oecd.org/en/data/indicators/employment-by-activity.html.

268 **Britain's coal-mining past:** 'Why "red wall" Tories want to open a

320

coal mine', *The Economist*, 27 February 2021, https://www.economist.com/britain/2021/02/27/why-red-wall-tories-want-to-open-a-coal-mine.

270 **white students from poor backgrounds:** 'Education Investment Areas: selection methodology', Department for Education, February 2022, https://assets.publishing.service.gov.uk/media/64352e807de82b001231380d/Education_Investment_Areas_-_selection_methodology.pdf; 'Foundation's new scholarship offers help to students', University of Bradford (website), 20 December 2023, https://www.bradford.ac.uk/news/archive/2023/foundations-new-scholarship-offers-help-to-students.php.

271 **Breaking this deadlock is hard:** 'Parental Engagement: Technical Appendix', EEF (website), accessed 3 August 2024, https://educationendowmentfoundation.org.uk/education-evidence/teaching-learning-toolkit/parental-engagement/technical-appendix; Clare Campbell, 'How to involve hard-to-reach parents: encouraging meaningful parental involvement with schools', National College For School Leadership, autumn 2011, https://assets.publishing.service.gov.uk/media/5a7d5d0440f0b60aaa293fa6/how-to-involve-hard-to-reach-parents-full-report.pdf.

271 **known as the 'forgotten fifth':** Lee Elliot Major and Sam Parsons, 'The forgotten fifth: Examining the early education trajectories of teenagers who fall below the expected standards in GCSE English language and maths examinations at age 16' (London: UCL Centre for Longitudinal Studies, 2022); Mary Curnock Cook, 'Tertiary Education for the 21st Century: the who, the what and the how', HEPI (think tank), 14 December 2023, https://www.hepi.ac.uk/2023/12/14/tertiary-education-for-the-21st-century-the-who-the-what-and-the-how/.

272 **the mayor of London:** Sir Sadiq Khan, 'From Walthamstow to Wandsworth, and from Barking to Barnet, London councils are building again', LBC (website), 5 January 2024, accessed 3 August 2024, https://www.lbc.co.uk/opinion/views/london-councils-are-building-houses-again/.

273 **an extreme view of the welfare state:** Matthew Goodwin, 'How mass immigration is worsening the housing crisis', *The Spectator*, 8 December 2023, https://www.spectator.co.uk/article/how-mass-immigration-is-worsening-the-housing-crisis/; 'Migration to the UK after Brexit: policy, politics and public opinion', UK in a Changing

Europe, 10 June 2024, https://media.ukandeu.ac.uk/wp-content/uploads/2024/04/UKICE-migration-report.pdf.

273 **It just needs more housing:** Alex Morton and Elizabeth Dunkley, 'The Case for Housebuilding', Centre for Policy Studies, January 2023, https://cps.org.uk/wp-content/uploads/2023/01/CPS_THE_CASE_FOR_HOUSEBUILDING2.pdf.

273 **clever ways to help people into Britain's overpriced homes:** 'UK Affordable Housing Schemes: A Complete Overview', Build to Rent (website), 6 January 2022, https://blog.buildtorent.io/blog/article/uk-affordable-housing-schemes-a-complete-overview.

275 **24 million people:** International comparisons have been calculated using the OECD Data Explorer: Gross domestic product – regions, PPP adjusted, https://data-explorer.oecd.org/; '"Two million fewer Germans in former East"', DW (website), 29 September 2015, accessed 3 August 2024, https://www.dw.com/en/two-million-fewer-people-in-former-east-since-german-reunification/a-18749892; 'Regional economic activity by gross domestic product, UK: 1998 to 2021', Office for National Statistics, accessed 3 August 2024, https://www.ons.gov.uk/economy/grossdomesticproductgdp/bulletins/regionaleconomicactivitybygrossdomesticproductuk/1998to2021.

276 **'ideal locations for the chess tables':** 'Installing chess tables in parks and public spaces: prospectus', UK Government (website), 1 September 2023, https://www.gov.uk/government/publications/installing-chess-tables-in-parks-and-public-spaces-prospectus/installing-chess-tables-in-parks-and-public-spaces-prospectus.

277 **draw more of them to our shores:** Timothy Hatton, 'Refugees and Asylum Seekers, the Crisis in Europe and the Future of Policy', Economic Policy / European University Institute, October 2016, https://www.economic-policy.org/wp-content/uploads/2016/10/992_Refugees-and-Asylum-Seekers.pdf.

278 **teaching English to refugees:** Sue Hubble et al., 'Investment in the Provision of English for Speakers of Other Languages', Debate Pack, House of Commons Library, 1 July 2019; David Foster and Paul Bolton, 'Adult ESOL in England', Briefing Paper, House of Commons Library, 25 April 2018.

278 **allowing asylum-seekers to work:** 'YouGov / Refugee Action Survey Results', fieldwork conducted 30 April – 1 May 2019, YouGov, https://d25d2506sfb94s.cloudfront.net/cumulus_uploads/document/

w3dpyaotd7/RefugeeAction_190501_RefugeeResults_W.pdf; 'YouGov / Refugee Action Survey Results', fieldwork conducted 8–9 March 2022, YouGov, https://docs.cdn.yougov.com/ihe1pmjsxm/YouGov%20 Refugee%20Action%20-%20Working%20during%20asylum%20claim. pdf.

278 **Only Germany and Sweden were more liberal:** 'UK attitudes to immigration: how the public became more positive', Kings College London / Behavioural Insights Team, February 2023, https://www. kcl.ac.uk/policy-institute/assets/uk-attitudes-to-immigration-1018742pub01-115.pdf.

Acknowledgements

My thanks, first of all, to three current and former editors at *The Economist*: John Micklethwait, Zanny Minton-Beddoes and Andrew Palmer. All of them kindly allowed me to take time off from my job at the magazine. Given my complete inability to do two things at once, this book would not have existed without their generosity.

My agent at Wylie, Emma Smith, helped me with a great many things, as did my former agent, Alba Ziegler-Bailey. Georgina Morley and Andrea Henry at Picador have been superb, patient editors. I am grateful to Connor Hutchinson for spotting some embarrassing things in my copy. James Fransham and Sarah Teague kindly wrangled some tricky data, and Helen Atkinson turned some of that data into maps.

I would like to thank everybody who has spoken to me over the years about the themes in this book, and everybody I interviewed specifically for it. Some of them are named in the text, but many are anonymous or are not mentioned at all. Almost all of my interviewees were kind and patient, as British people usually are. I don't know how I would react if somebody walked up to me and said: 'I am writing a book. Could you tell me about your neighbourhood?' Probably not as well as my interviewees did.

In particular I would like to thank the following people, who are experts on their patches or their communities. They introduced me around, shared their deep knowledge of the places where they live and work, and fed me many cups of tea. In no particular order: Katie Schad in Lancaster; the staff at Stanleys Community Centre in Morecambe; Emilie de Brujin and Sacha Bedding in Hartlepool; Claire Camp in Stockton; Joanne Randall, John Blackmore, Shaun Hunt and Judith Wray in Leicester; Ruta Dalton in Peterborough; Jurate Matulioniene in Boston; Sam Siddall in New Edlington; Michal Siewniak in Welwyn Garden City; Ros Parker, Rachel Thomson and Julian Wadsworth in the Isle of Wight; David Llewellyn and Kevyn Price in Rhymney; the Spirit of Springburn community group and Nicola Thomas in Glasgow; Kirsty Taylor and Sarah Woolley in Manchester; Andreea Dumitrache of The 3 Million; Tara Beaumont and Nathanael Mosley in Rotherham; Stuart Wright in Thetford; and all the staff at Action for Children, but especially Emma Marshall.

Finally, thanks and apologies are due to my family. Maria, Sam and Olly put up with the frequent disappearances of me and the car, which tended to occur with little notice. They let me wrestle with paragraphs when I should have been attending to them. Writing is a solitary activity, but its annoyances are shared.

Joel Budd has written for *The Economist* magazine since 2003. He has covered topics as wide-ranging as crime, California, international development and demography, as well as writing many articles and leaders about Britain. Before joining *The Economist* he studied and taught European history at New York University. He is a photographer, a baritone singer and an enthusiastic hiker, who is sadly not as young as he was. *Underdogs* is his first book.